Mulattas
and
Mestizas

Mulattas and Mestizas

REPRESENTING MIXED IDENTITIES IN THE AMERICAS, 1850–2000

Suzanne Bost

THE UNIVERSITY

OF GEORGIA PRESS

ATHENS AND LONDON

© 2003 by the University of Georgia Press
Athens, Georgia 30602
All rights reserved
Designed by Betty Palmer McDaniel
Set in 11/13 Weiss by Bookcomp, Inc.
Printed and bound by Thomson-Shore
The paper in this book meets the guidelines for
permanence and durability of the Committee on
Production Guidelines for Book Longevity of the
Council on Library Resources.

Printed in the United States of America
02 03 04 05 06 C 5 4 3 2 1
Library of Congress Cataloging-in-Publication Data

Bost, Suzanne.
Mulattas and mestizas : representing mixed identities in the
Americas, 1850–2000 / Suzanne Bost.
p.   cm.
Includes bibliographical references (p.) and index.
ISBN 0-8203-2325-X (hardcover : alk. paper)
1. American literature—Minority authors—History and
criticism.   2. Racially mixed people in literature.
3. Latin American literature—Women
authors—History and criticism.   4. American
literature—Women authors—History and
criticism.   5. Women and literature—United
States—History.   6. Women and literature—Latin
America—History.   7. Identity (Psychology) in
literature.   8. Human skin color in literature.
9. Group identity in literature.   10. Miscegenation
in literature.   11. Race in literature.   I. Title.
PS153.M56 B67 2003
810.9'920693—dc21   2002007444

British Library Cataloging-in-Publication Data available

This is the future.
America is becoming a mestizo nation.

Rubén Martínez

According to the racial zodiac,
2000 is the official Year of the Mulatto.

Danzy Senna

Contents

Acknowledgments

The things I learned first about American literature would surprise many critics. As a high school student in New Mexico, I read Rudolfo Anaya alongside Nathaniel Hawthorne. As an undergraduate at the University of Texas at Austin, I read as much Latin American, Chicana/o, and African-American literature as canonical white texts. For this I am grateful. When I later managed to "catch up" and to study in-depth the works of Melville, Wharton, Hemingway, and Faulkner, I read them in reference to the other works that I had known first. I was finding Anaya in Faulkner, rather than the reverse. In this way, I experienced American literature as derivative of those Others it had pushed to the margins. I could not separate the white from the nonwhite. During my first years of graduate school, when I began reading postmodern theory, I found European models of what I had long considered characteristic practices of bilingual Chicana/os and migrant writers. Reading contemporary feminism, I found echoes of Sor Juana Inés de la Cruz, the radical seventeenth-century Mexican nun who dared to criticize the patriarchal system. I am indebted to my teachers in New Mexico and at the University of Texas for providing me with this unique perspective.

I wrote *Mulattas and Mestizas* to emphasize this other, marginalized, culturally grounded, and politically responsive foundation for contemporary theories of race, sex/gender, and identity. I began my work for this project at Vanderbilt University, with the assistance of a Mellon Fellowship and a Vanderbilt University Dissertation Enhancement Grant, which enabled me to travel to Texas and New Mexico to consult archival materials at the University of New Mexico, the University of Houston, and the University of Texas at Austin. I would especially like to thank Jay Clayton, who guided my research, my writing, and my publication efforts. I could not have done this work without his insightful readings and critical suggestions as well as those of Myriam J. A. Chancy, Thadious Davis, Jane Landers, William Luis, and Cecelia Tichi. I would also like to thank James Madison University and the University of Florida for supporting me during the final stages of my writing.

Encouragement from my family—Stuart Wick, Jonathan Bost, Mary Anne Bost, and Kathleen Bost—has provided the foundation on which I work. Discussion with friends—including Beth Breau, Lucy Corin, June Ellis, Rebecca Feind, Frances Leyba, Risa Nystrom, Kristen Peterson, Gary Richards, Karyn Sproles, and Nicole Villegas—has helped me to keep my textual discoveries framed by the bigger picture. I also thank the readers, editors, and copyeditors at the University of Georgia Press for their invaluable assistance.

Early versions of portions of this research have been published previously as articles: "Fluidity without Postmodernism: Michelle Cliff and the Tragic Mulatta Tradition," *African American Review* 32 (winter 1998): 673–89; "Transgressing Borders: Puerto Rican and Latina *Mestizaje*," *MELUS* 25 (summer 2000): 187–211.

This book is dedicated to my grandmothers, Beatrice Bost (1917–83) and Marian Cassidy (1910–93), who encouraged my reading and writing from the start.

Mulattas
and
Mestizas

Introduction

In its provocative fall 1993 special issue, "The New Face of America," *Time* magazine sensationally represents hybridity as a dramatic development that is forcing a "new" look on America. The issue highlights how racial mixture is redefining American identity, heralding the future, when whites will be "just another minority" (Henry, "Politics" 73). Many of the issue's articles investigate how mixture literally changes the face of America and discuss the visual implications of this change. The magazine's cover, the new face of America, is a light-skinned woman who is supposed to represent the fusion of the different races in the United States, the racial average calculated by computer technology. The managing editor of the special issue, James R. Gaines, represents this mixture as a major shift in American racialization, challenging the ways in which we attach racial qualifiers to individuals. Gaines uses the word *dramatic* twice in one paragraph to describe the "morphing," the "striking alteration," "the symbol of the future" that this artificial "new Eve" embodies (2). In a recent essay, "The Face of America and the State of Emergency," Lauren Berlant says of this image, "the wish of the dream cover is that American racial categories will have to be reinvented as tending toward whiteness or lightness" (420). With its 1990s technical capabilities, *Time* eases the white majority's potential fears by replacing the "ugly" reality of actual mixture with an artificially constructed (and thus sterile) "new" face—one that repeats conventions of white beauty from fashion magazines, assimilates differences into one light-skinned whole, and promises that the new hybrid U.S. race will still look white.

Why is the "new face" a woman? She charms—the employees at *Time* reportedly fall in love with her—and yet she is taboo, bloodless, impure.[1]

Her pleasing image draws in Americans to the idea of mixed-race identity as an alluring new physical standard, an aesthetic ideal that mitigates the threat to race as we know it, which her image supposedly signifies. Her near-white beauty attracts readers coaxed by popular rhetoric to fear the demise of whiteness, as her apparently "white" femininity makes her seem innocent and nonthreatening. This image appeals to racist sentiment at the same time that it masks the racial subversion its mixture represents. Gaines describes the woman as "beguiling if mysterious" (2). Her image is a 1990s revision of the nineteenth-century tragic mulatta narratives I study, in which women are portrayed as the sexually magnetic vessels through which mixture is produced. Even in the case of computer-generated reproduction—"cybergenesis," Gaines calls it (2)—a woman is targeted as the source and the face of mixture. Throughout popular culture and literature, debates about the nature of mixed-race identity are mapped out on the body of a woman because thinking about racial mixture inevitably leads to questions of sex and reproduction.

Jill Smolowe's article, "Intermarried . . . with Children," in the same issue of *Time*, features pictures of interracial couples, side by side, with pictures of their mixed-race children underneath. Visually, the children's photos unsettle the black-white distinction of the parents' photos. The subjects, photographed from the shoulders up, are all bare skinned, provocatively drawing attention to the body and to skin color. The article argues that interracial reproduction is the ultimate assimilator, emphasizing the transformations of American culture on the level of the body (64). Smolowe's tone is almost apocalyptic, as she mixes signifiers of shock with those of reproduction: "ever increasing numbers of couples *crash* through racial, ethnic and religious barriers"; "Americans are being *forced* to rethink and redefine themselves"; "the number of couples *breaching* once *impregnable* barriers of color, ethnicity and faith is *startling*" (64, emphasis added). One gets the sense of a sexual, moral, and racial violation being committed. Smolowe concludes with the image of the jumble—"muddled masses," as she earlier says—that mixture produces: compound identities like the "Native American–black–white–Hungarian–French–Catholic–Jewish–American children" for whom the hyphen "divides even as it compounds" (65). The awkwardness of this hyphenated label reflects the attitude that life was simpler back when America was "an unhyphenated whole" (65), a fictitious, mythic monoculturalism that exists only in ethnocentric imagination.

The article that follows Smolowe's, "Rebirth of a Nation, Computer-

Style," invokes the racist film *Birth of a Nation* in a dystopian vision of computerized interracial reproduction. Both *Birth of a Nation* and "Rebirth of a Nation" encode the feared demise of white purity posed by nonwhite Others' threats to miscegenate. The editors of the *Time* article employ a software package called Morph 2.0—significantly, an "offspring" of the same Hollywood special-effects equipment that produced "the evil robot that wreaks havoc in *Terminator 2*"—to enact a computerized "genetic engineering" (66). The program combines the images of seven men and seven women of different racial backgrounds to imagine the offspring of different interracial couplings. The article features a chart, much like a multiplication table, with forty-nine different "cybernetic offspring" of racial mixture.[2]

Since each "offspring" is created by superimposing the features of the two parents, most of the images are sexually ambiguous, female-looking men and male-looking women. Morph 2.0 thus mixes sex as it mixes race. The editors even admit, "One of our tentative unions produced a distinctly feminine face—sitting atop a muscular neck and hairy chest. Back to the mouse on that one" (66). This crossbreed presents the article's final image—and its final threat: mixture not only blurs distinctions of color but also produces sexual aberrations. The editors' emphasis on the bisexed morph's hairy chest is significant, since the photos in the magazine show nothing below the shoulders. Either the editors are looking at more body than the readers see, or the hairy chest is fictionalized to create shock value, to render grotesque this computerized subversion of sexual nature. The challenge to sexual identity is assumed to be a threat, something that can (and should) be erased with computer technology ("back to the mouse"). Linking actual racial mixture in America with this Frankensteinian computer hybrid inflects interracial mixing with a sense of deviancy. The article's futuristic and alarmist rhetoric implies that reproduction in the 1990s has "fallen" from the biological reproduction of pure races to disorderly fusions of black and white, male and female, computer and human. Berlant concludes that this biologizing imagery obscures public conflict with an emphasis on bodies and reproduction: "The American future has nothing to do with vital national world-making activities, nor public life: just technologies of reproduction that are, like all eugenic programs, destructive in their aim. . . . Of course you wouldn't discover this violent desire in the tone of the special issue, which demonstrates an overarching optimism about the culturally enriching effects of all kinds of reproduction" (421). The editors' goal may have been to create a celebratory account of U.S. racial diversity, and Berlant certainly reads this optimism into the special issue, but I find the tone to be more disturbing, almost Orwellian in its description of computer-age reproduction and hybridity. The entire issue of *Time* creates a sort of panic about the changing nature of race, overloading readers with an excess of faces and colors, statistics about the soaring incidence of interracial mixture, immigration, and promiscuous relations among seven men, seven women, and a computer. In this sense, *Time* repeats history in its resemblance to eugenics, "muleology," and racist fears of miscegenation. As with the elaborate racial hierarchies of the nineteenth century, precise measurements of degrees of mixture reflect anxieties about challenges to racial purity.[3]

Mixture is deployed today in popular culture as a sign of millennial shifts in American identity. Newsmagazines sell the idea of "new" American faces at the same time that mixed-race musicians, actors, and sports heroes are promoted as icons of a "new" America. But this trend is not new. As mixed identities become more prominent in the media, it is important to keep in mind America's long history of representing racial mixture and to be on guard against segregationist reactions like those that culminated in antimiscegenation laws and Jim Crow. A primary impulse behind this book is a desire to counter apocalyptic end-of-the-millennium writings with analyses of the ways in which mixture has already shaped delineations of American identity. As in earlier periods, the subversion of familiar racial categories creates anxieties. Today, these anxieties include those of whites who resist the notion that they might become a minority as well as the fears of racialized peoples who want to hold onto categories—such as "black," "Hispanic," and "Puerto Rican"—on which social movements have been founded and through which these peoples have gained political leverage. Racial mixture has been targeted, perhaps scapegoated, as American media feed panic about the dissolution of essential identity categories.

Since these futuristic representations often repeat earlier conceptions of identity, it is important to consider why they have now become an issue. Why again? Is it just another symptom of Y2K panic? While this "new" mixed aesthetic might appear to be liberal and welcoming of difference, it might also satisfy a racist, nostalgic desire to return to white supremacy after decades of civil rights movement and affirmative action. Romesh Ratnesar writes in *The New Republic*, "all at once, multiracialism has become an American fashion, commercially chic. . . . We are all Tiger Woods now" (43). This embracing of mixture does not necessarily indicate any decline in racism. Ratnesar suggests that the "old rigid classifications of black and white give way to 'many shades of beige'" (43). Using "beige" as the standard suggests that people of color are becoming less colored. As nineteenth-century literature preferred mulatta heroines whose "white blood" would draw sympathy from the dominant population, prominent faces of color are today getting whiter. Danzy Senna, a novelist of mixed African- and Euro-American descent, writes about the "mulatto millennium" on the horizon of popular culture: "Strange to wake up and realize you're in style. That's what happened to me just the other morning. It was the first day of the new millennium and I woke to find that mulattoes had taken over. They were everywhere. Playing golf, running the airwaves, opening their own restaurants, modeling clothes. . . . The radio played a steady stream of Lenny Kravitz, Sade, and Mariah Carey. According to the racial zodiac, 2000 is the official Year of the Mulatto" (12). Senna, too, hints at how this preference corresponds to racism: "pure breeds (at least the black ones) are out and hybridity is in. . . . Major news magazines announce our arrival as if we were proof of extraterrestrial life. They claim we're going to bring about the end of race as we know it" (12, 13). If hybridity is bringing an end to the black race as such, who is celebrating, and why? And how do otherwise liberal-minded writings about mixture inadvertently help to resuscitate dreams of whitening America?

Maria P. P. Root argues that the contemporary fascination with racial mixture is an effect of the "biracial baby boom," which followed the U.S. Supreme Court's 1967 repeal of the last remaining antimiscegenation laws in *Loving v. Virginia*. According to Root, "the contemporary presence of racially mixed people is unmatched in our country's previous history. Interracial families and multiracial individuals are changing the face of America and the meaning and utility of race" (xiv). Root's description of the "changing" face of America, like *Time* magazine's special issue, seems to herald a cataclysmic transformation of race in America and locates this shift in the past two decades. While it may be true that "for the first time in history, the number of biracial babies is increasing at a faster rate than the number of monoracial babies" (Root xiv), I would argue that mixture has been central to the definition of race for all of America's history. Indeed, Paul Spickard argues that there was "proportionately more interracial mating in the colonial era than at any later time in American history" (237).[4] Yet it is characteristic of the present moment that mixed-race individuals are being counted and that we are rethinking our categories for describing race.[5] As Jan Weisman suggests, "being 'mixed' is—in stark contrast with earlier, disparaging portrayals—now often exalted as being the embodiment of the multiculturalist or postmodern ideal" (159). The valorization of hybridity on both popular and academic fronts has increased the zeal for counting the number of mixed Americans.[6] According to Joel Williamson's study, *New People: Miscegenation and Mulattoes in the United States,* this current interest is not unique. In 1850, for example, at the height of pre–Civil War racial tensions, "mulatto" became an official census category, and mulattoes were counted and studied obsessively for decades until the gradual reinstitution of monoracial standards for defining American identity (5, 94–98).

Mixed-race Americans have long been credited with the capacity to blur the lines of racial differentiation. Historical studies and works of fiction from nineteenth- and early-twentieth-century America often celebrate mixture as a way to transcend racial division. Yet today this fluidity is described as "new," as a sign of millennial or postmodern transformations to America's face. As Root puts it, "The dialogue that multiracial people and their families have opened . . . may be part of moving to a deeper level of change to make the borders between race more permeable and eventually less discernible" (xxvii). Most contemporary studies of mixture, including Root's *The Multiracial Experience* (1996), focus on the past twenty years as a period of increasing mixture, fluidity, and change in racial definition and suggest that this recent shift might coincide with a decline in racism. Products of the 1960s "biracial baby boom," such as Karla Brundage, come from parents who "believed . . . that by having an interracial child, along with others in their generation, they would be one step closer to ending racism" (Brundage 117). In the wake of this progressive optimism, however, American attitudes toward race may be retreating. The nineteenth-century fascination with mixture corresponded with racial segregation, "sciences" of purity, and white supremacy; how do we know that history is not just repeating itself? It is thus imperative to measure these contemporary representations against the history of mixture in the Americas to see to what extent historic taboos and fears of difference remain in force underneath the changing categories by which we organize race in America.

I am interested in mixed identities—racial, cultural, sexual, and national mixtures—because of the ways in which they challenge universalizing notions of selfhood and highlight the complexities of subjectivity. As the half-Anglo, half-Mexican mestiza Chicana lesbian poet-playwright-essayist Cherríe Moraga says in "The Welder" (1981),

> I am a welder.
> Not an alchemist. . . .
>
> I understand the capacity of heat
> to change the shape of things
> I am suited to work
> within the realm of sparks
> out of control.
>
> (Anzaldúa and Moraga 219–20)

Or, as the U.S.–Afro-Caribbean lesbian poet-essayist Audre Lorde writes in "From the House of Yemanjá" (1978),

> My mother had two faces and a frying pot
> where she cooked up her daughters
> into girls . . .
>
> I bear two women upon my back
> one dark and rich and hidden
> in the ivory hungers of the other . . .
>
> I am
> the sun and moon and forever hungry
> the sharpened edge
> where day and night shall meet
> and not be
> one.
>
> (*Unicorn* 6–7)

Both of these poems imagine identity as multiple, molten, fluid, and they describe the formation of identity as the fusion of differences. For both Moraga and Lorde, this fusion of differences is racialized and sexualized. Lorde describes her different identities as dark and ivory, sun (male) and moon (female). Elsewhere, Moraga calls herself a "thoroughly hybrid/ mongrel/mexican-yaqui/oakie girl . . . a lesbian monster. . . . Mongrel is the name / that holds all the animal I am" (*Generation* 99–100). As they mix, negotiate, and incorporate these different components by welding and cooking, Moraga and Lorde change the shape of identity. They do not, however, assimilate differences into one unified whole: Moraga is not an alchemist, Lorde is not "one." They retain the sites of friction where different racial, sexual, and national elements meet, forming sparks and sharp edges.

Mestizaje, as I use the term, highlights the mixture of identities in the Americas and the friction that occurs between them. Although *mestizaje* derives from a specifically Latin American context, its fusion of African, indigenous, and European heritage describes race dynamics throughout the Americas as a whole. Carole Boyce Davies's study of women's writing of the African diaspora, *Black Women, Writing, and Identity*, borrows formulations of mestiza consciousness for analyzing black women's identities. Yet Davies qualifies her relationship to the Latino dynamic: "Still, I am conscious of the way in which 'mestizo' or 'mestiza' can be used as oppressive separation in Latin American communities in order to distance one from darker-skinned peoples and others who identify as 'African,' 'Afro-,' or 'Black.' The point is that all of these terms carry their internal contradictions" (16). *Mestizaje* can be a paradigm for these "internal contradictions," since it draws attention to heterogeneity and since the term itself is defined differently in the United States, Latin America, and the Caribbean.[7] The differing racial makeup of different nations assigns multiple faces to *mestizaje*, as do the individuals who identify as mestizo. Like Davies, I begin with theories of *mestizaje* as the framework for my analysis of African-American, Caribbean, Latina, and Chicana texts because this concept retains the sense of dissonance. Mestiza writings often include models for negotiating these contradictions, embrace racial multiplicity, and retain an awareness of the historical implications of border crossings and mixture. In her assessment of the political value of *mestizaje*, Chéla Sandoval writes that "*mestiza* feminism comes to function as a working chiasmus (a mobile crossing) between races, genders, sexes, cultures, languages, and nations. Thus conceived, *La conciencia de la mestiza* makes visible the operation of another *metaform* of consciousness that insists upon polymodal forms of poetics, ethics, identities, and politics not only for Chicana/os but for any constituency resisting the old and new hierarchies of the coming millennium" (352). As a "metaform" and an inclusive paradigm, *mestizaje* can serve as a model for the fusions, negotiations, frictions, and border crossings between races in the Americas.

Mestiza theory provides models for imagining identity beyond singular categories at the same time that it retains a sense of cultural specificity, politics, and resistance to hegemony. Sandoval posits mestiza differential consciousness as a solution to the ambiguity of politics under postmodernism: "This paradigm is the compass sought by Jameson that can enable 'cognitive mapping' under first world, postmodern cultural conditions. Indeed this paradigm can be recognized as a theory and a method for mobilizing oppositional forms of consciousness in the postmodern first world" (359). *Mestizaje* illuminates the racial, sexual, and national tensions traced yet often obscured in writings of the Americas. And internalized on the individual level, *mestizaje* can present a multiplicity of possibilities and fluidity of identifications.

This fluidity is, however, tempered by a memory of the oppressions wrought within mixture. *Mestizaje* embodies a historical narrative of the production of mixture, the often coercive intermingling of bloods—on the national level as well as the individual level—through the rape of indigenous and African women by men of European descent. These rapes continue as a dominant theme in the work of mestiza writers. For example, in her poem "I Was Not Supposed to Remember," Moraga claims,

> I was not supposed to remember being she
> the daughter of some other Indian some body some where . . .
> cast-off half-breed I wasn't
> supposed to remember the original rape

(*Generation* 98)

Mestizaje, for Moraga and for others, reflects a simultaneously racial, sexual, and national memory, an embodiment of colonization and conquest. The sex at the origins of miscegenation led to the sexualization of racial taboos against mixture—an obsession with sex and women's bodies as the site of potential racial transgressions—which explains how race, nation, sex, and sexuality are so intertwined in representations of mixed-race subjects. Given the racism and sexism embedded within this history, it is not surprising that Latina, Chicana, African-American, and Caribbean feminist writers have attempted to redefine mixed-race identity, transgressing the white man's transgressions, revising the racial and sexual behavior imposed by Euro-American norms, and crossing the divisions erected between black and white, the United States and Latin America, masculine and feminine, male and female, gay and straight. These writers build their identities across these lines, just as mixture places their bodies on both sides of cultural borders.

This book historicizes attitudes toward mixed identity in the Americas. I explore the social, political, and theoretical implications of racial mixture in different historical contexts where it was a significant concern. I focus on the two identifications used most frequently for describing mixed peoples in the United States, mestizos and mulattoes, comparing and contrasting the racial histories of the Southwest and the Southeast that have formed these paradigms. Despite many similar representations in literature and race theories, these two identities are conventionally opposed. Staging a dialogue between them, however, highlights the centrality of mixture in the development of racial identities both north and south of the southern U.S. border. As this border is fetishized in writings about America, U.S. racial dynamics are usually contrasted to and often held above mixture "south of the border" in Mexico and the Caribbean. In contrast, this book highlights identities and histories that these Americas share. Comparing these two paradigms enables one to see how racial identities develop in relation to each other, as black-white miscegenation in the southeastern United States was historically proscribed with reference to "impure" mestiza fluidity in Mexico and the Caribbean. In addition, this comparison shows how racial identities develop in relation to national and political agendas, as *mestizaje* was historically idealized as a harmonious blending to facilitate Mexican nation-building, whereas mulatto mixtures were conceived as a violation of an essential black-white binary to solidify the racial hierarchy at the foundation of U.S. slavery and Jim Crow. I juxtapose racial histories from these locations to shed light on the shared racial narratives that the mulatto-mestizo opposition obscures: the actual inharmoniousness of the historical production of *mestizaje* as well as the inaccuracy of any definition of mulatto mixture based on simple binary opposition. Both mulattoes and mestizos mix multiple different racial lineages (most of which, like U.S. African and Spanish heritages, were already racially mixed) as well as national, cultural, linguistic, and gendered identities.[8] This work is thus international, interracial, intercategorical, interhistorical, and interdisciplinary, juxtaposing paradigms past and present from different regions of the Americas to trace genealogies of mixed identity. The different political, racial, and generic strands in this project meet in the contemporary work of Latina, African-American, and Caribbean writers such as Moraga, Lorde, Gloria

Anzaldúa, Rosario Ferré, Michelle Cliff, and Ntozake Shange. I will situate the much-celebrated racial and sexual complexity of these works within larger historical traditions.

This book returns briefly to the colonial period to examine the historical origins of racial mixture in the Americas. My literary focus, however, begins in the mid–nineteenth century, immediately following the annexation of New Mexico and preceding the U.S. Civil War, because this period is one of intense racial analysis, nationalist sentiment, and abolitionist debate in the Americas. Many of the racial paradigms that still hold today were negotiated and solidified during the nineteenth century. I trace a lineage from nineteenth- and early-twentieth-century writing to contemporary texts to point out both their similarities and their significant differences. Considering contemporary racial paradigms in the context of their precursors will show the historical contingency of these paradigms and will show how past theories prefigure or challenge post–civil rights and postmodern theories.

Trinh T. Minh-ha describes the "fashionable preoccupation" with difference and marginality in the academy today. Recent theories "recycle" as theoretical subversion that which is everyday reality for peoples engaged in border struggle (*Moon* 156). Contemporary academic discussions have directed much attention to the heterogeneity of races, sexes, genders, and nationalities that meet in the Americas. Since this diversity was masked for decades by the illusion of a singular Anglo-American culture, the recent work of dismantling that artificially imposed illusion is of paramount importance.[9] Yet the diversity itself is not new, nor is the celebration of difference, marginality, and hybridity that is (once again) radicalizing American studies. Difference has been grasped as an academic cause in the wake of postmodernism, the civil rights movement, and the rise of ethnic and gender studies, each of which has valued "difference" in its own way. Negotiating difference, marginality, and hybridity, however, reflects a historical fact rather than a theoretical vogue, for many Americans.

Along U.S. borders, more than a century of literary and historical texts records an interest in identities not founded on a single cultural center. Within Afro-Caribbean and African-American literature, one can trace mixtures of African, British, and U.S. cultural practices. Mexican-American writers strategically invoke Spanish, English, or both to suit different political needs. Mulattoes and mestizos challenge our perceptions of race, too. As a result of the uncertainty of classification surrounding mixed identity and the frequent difficulty of ascertaining racial ancestry

by appearance, race becomes unmoored from any essential biological definition. This racial fluidity—which, in certain contexts, allows mixed-race
individuals an opportunity to pass and to construct a racial identity—
predates contemporary theories of racial constructivism.[10] For centuries,
mixed Americans have built decentered identities, considered characteristic of postmodernism, from the realities of their political situations rather
than from an academic trajectory through modernism and deconstruction.[11] As Rosaura Sánchez says, Chicano identities, though similar to
postmodern subjectivities, retain a foundation that postmodernism lacks:
"decentered subjectivity, and a focus on discursive formations, however,
have not erased historical referentiality" for Chicanos, whose identities
refer to specifically Mexican-American origins (10).[12] From this alternate
trajectory, we can reconceive "postmodern" theories of identity without
requiring a foundation of those theoretical or aesthetic movements that
were unique to a few privileged cultures.

The similarities between mixed identity and postmodern identity invite
a dialogue between the two, but dialogues between margin and center
too often occur according to the terms set by the dominant culture.[13]
Trinh criticizes the ways in which marginalized identities are "raised up
for the sake of Western vanguardism and its desire to conserve itself
as sovereign Subject of radical knowledge" (*Moon* 156). Today, as the
inhabitants of America's margins are bringing their code-switching and
signifyin(g) resistance to the literary forefront, their work is often reduced to examples of a dominant theoretical trend and their voices, writings, and histories are often framed—and eclipsed—by the terminolo-
gies of "bigger" (white male) names: Jacques Derrida, Michel Foucault, or
Mikhail Bakhtin. Chandra Talpade Mohanty critiques this trend in writings about mestiza consciousness: "Unlike a Western, postmodernist notion of agency and consciousness which often announces the splintering
of the subject and privileges multiplicity in the abstract, this is a notion
of agency born of history and geography" (Mohanty, Russo, and Torres
37). Mixed-race multiplicity, unlike postmodern multiplicity, is rooted in
agency, politics, and material conditions (38). These conditions form the
foundations of this book, as I put these so-called marginalized writers at
the center and base my argument on multiethnic literatures, histories, and
paradigms.

It is not coincidental that *mestizaje*, in particular, receives so much attention today. So-called Latin music, Mexican food, and Mexican folk art are

becoming increasingly popular as American consumer culture fetishizes its own margins as sources of sexy, spicy, and "new" American commodities. This neocolonial consumption often erases the origins of Latino culture and appropriates its products as deracialized, depoliticized, and dehistoricized "American" trends. Contemporary philosopher Jean-Luc Nancy warns mestizos, "Your difference, your differences, arrive in a world that pretends to be reclaiming differences in general, but that can always trap those differences into its indifference" (118). Yet even as it is deployed as a universal emblem for new frontiers of Americanness, *mestizaje* potentially undermines universalist identity categories and retains a memory of the historical circumstances at the origins of mixture in the Americas: the violent racial and sexual oppressions, the strategic uses of mixture as a means of colonization, and the racist desires of the colonizers to "whiten" the "Other" with their own blood.

The current popular culture obsession with changing racial topographies and contested racial allegiances reflects a continued discomfort with "impurity." It is important to contextualize this intrigue across different genres of American representation and to combat the rhetoric of purity by foregrounding the empowering political accomplishments of some fluid identities. In providing a genealogy of representations of racial and sexual fluidity, I seek not only to clarify the belatedness of hybridity as model for identity. Analyzing earlier texts in which hybridity coincides with overt racist and sexist oppression can serve as a warning for today: celebrations of mixture and fluidity often correspond to attempts to reinforce "pure" racial and sexual categories. The continued intrigue surrounding racial, sexual, and national border crossings draws attention to the persistent barriers that many individuals feel compelled to cross.

Literature and popular culture are the primary media through which conceptions of American identity are, and were, solidified. For this reason, I juxtapose literary, popular, and historical representations of mixture and measure them against each other. Together, literary, popular, and historical texts established models—such as the rape of women of color, miscegenation, passing, and boundary crossing—that reappear in future texts. I am particularly interested in historiographic interpretations, which, like literature, enact cultural biases from the writers' present as they dramatize historical paradigms. Literature and history are inseparable in investigating how and for whom these paradigms functioned. The writers I discuss repeatedly bring history into literature, and vice versa, crossing the boundaries conventionally set between disciplines, time periods, and nations.[14]

Feminist novelists and critics have been at the forefront of the effort to rewrite narratives of racial mixture because sex and race oppression intersect in the history of interracial mixing. In nineteenth-century literature, the innocent biracial heroine, a product of racially imbalanced sexual violations, became a paradigmatic victim. Mulattas and mestizas—in the feminine—have been targeted as the source, the cost, and the evidence of mixture, and they serve a significant symbolic function in writings that discuss the implications of mixture in the Americas. For these reasons, women writers have had a stake in rethinking women's relationship to biracialism and in imagining ways for biracial characters to escape victimization. I study texts by women writers as well as texts that center on mixed-race heroines to tease out the unique relationship between women and racial mixture.

Mixture is a central focus of the "canonical" traditions of nineteenth- and early-twentieth-century literature by African-American, Mexican-American, and Caribbean writers (such as Frances E. W. Harper and Cirilo Villaverde), so the African-American, Mexican-American, and Caribbean texts I choose to study from this period have already received significant critical attention (unlike texts by their white contemporaries, Elizabeth Livermore and Dion Boucicault) with the rise of African-American studies, Latina/o studies, and Caribbean studies.[15] Similarly, many outstanding recent texts by African-American, Afro-Caribbean, Chicana, and Latina women writers have gained critical visibility (including works by Toni Morrison, Jamaica Kincaid, Sandra Cisneros, and Cristina García) in terms of their intersections with current political and theoretical concerns (racial identity formation, postmodernism, postcolonialism, and transculturalism). Yet few critics attend to the connections among all of these works, the central role of mixture in racial definition, and the similar models of identity these writings present despite their different historical and cultural contexts. My choices of contemporary texts, then, are not necessarily those that have gained the most critical attention; instead, I choose those that respond most directly to the central issues that marked earlier texts' interest in mixture, such as boundary-crossing identifications, uncertain genealogies, women's role in racial definition, and sexual taboos. In analyzing contemporary writings, I will consider how they are in dialogue with previous models and with current theoretical visions.

Chapter 1, "Mulattas and Mestizas," begins with a look at histories of race dynamics in the Americas, juxtaposing representations of mixed identities in the United States and in Mexico. Many historians suggest that mulattoes in the United States experienced alienation in a bipolar, segregationist system, while *mestizaje* in Mexico formed the mainstream. This chapter interrogates this historiographic opposition between mulatta and mestiza experiences. Despite U.S. racism's attempts to segregate society into black and white, the racial mixture that the United States shares with Mexico consistently challenged those attempts. Although the two regions' dominant racial paradigms differed dramatically, both were founded on a reaction to interracial mixture and a preoccupation with fluidity. I follow my survey of histories that inscribe these tensions with an analysis of literary texts from the southeastern and southwestern United States that celebrate mixed-race fluidity, passing, redefining racial status, and fluctuating perceptions of racial identity. I trace a genealogy of mixed-race literature from 1850 to the present, highlighting the ways in which contemporary writers Gloria Anzaldúa, Sylvia López-Medina, and Ntozake Shange echo racial narratives of the past, both those that have received little contemporary critical attention (María Amparo Ruiz de Burton's *Who Would Have Thought It?* [1872], Josephina Niggli's *Mexican Village* [1945], Elizabeth Livermore's *Zoë; or, The Quadroon's Triumph* [1855], and Dion Boucicault's *Zoe, the Octoroon* [1859]) and those writers who have been at the center of much recent critical debate regarding their contributions to African-American literary history (Frances E. W. Harper, Pauline Hopkins, Nella Larsen, and Jessie Redmon Fauset).

Chapter 2, "Creoles and Color," considers the ways in which Caribbean race histories bridge mulatto and mestiza dynamics. Historically, the Caribbean has been seen as having the greatest racial mixture in the American hemisphere, and this mixture has led to an even more fluid race dynamic. Focusing in particular on racial histories of the British and Hispanic Caribbean, I examine the differences and the similarities between U.S. and Caribbean race relations, interrogating historians' attempts to displace the subversion of racial hierarchies away from the United States and onto the Caribbean. This chapter analyzes the contemporary writing of Puerto Rican prose writers Rosario Ferré and Ana Lydia Vega; the U.S.-Puerto Rican poet Aurora Levins Morales; and the Jamaican-American poet, novelist, and essayist Michelle Cliff, all of whose portrayals of racial fluidity—both mulatta and mestiza—echo the critically significant Cuban abolitionist novel *Cecilia Valdés* (1882), by Cirilo Villaverde.

Chapter 3, "The Transitive Bi-," considers the relationship between biracial and bisexual identities. I begin with an analysis of different sex and gender paradigms in the Americas that destabilize Euro-American heterosexist norms. I then examine the correlation between racial and sexual fluidity. As early as William Wells Brown's *Clotel* (1853) and William and Ellen Craft's *Running a Thousand Miles for Freedom* (1860), writers have simultaneously challenged race, sex, and gender categories. The subversion of racial classification often produces, or is produced by, a subversion of sex and gender. Despite this correlation, however, many mixed-race writers are reluctant to embrace marginalized sexualities, either homosexual or bisexual. I provide examples and possible explanations for this resistance in the writings of Paule Marshall and Cherríe Moraga. I then give extended readings of four contemporary texts by mixed-race women in which fluidity of race, sex, and gender overlap and interact: Judith Ortiz Cofer's *Silent Dancing* (1990), Audre Lorde's *Zami* (1982), Ruth Behar's *Translated Woman* (1993), and Michelle Cliff's *No Telephone to Heaven* (1987).

The dehumanizing racism that lay at the foundation of many nineteenth-century writings on mixture suggests an urgency for examining more closely the subtexts of contemporary popular writings on the "browning" of America, "the new face of America," and the like. Chapter 4, "Millennial Mixtures," investigates the function of mixture in contemporary popular culture, analyzing representations of Tiger Woods, Tyra Banks, the "New Face of America," and the multiracial movement. I compare contemporary news stories and popular magazines with nineteenth-century popular culture writings on mixture, revealing disturbing connections between race dynamics at the end of slavery and at the end of the millennium. I analyze the current aesthetic fascination with mixed-race writers, sports heroes, and fashion models, along with the movement to include a "multiracial" category in the 2000 census, in the context of this history and a recent spate of (often alarmist) news articles about the radical transformation of American ethnicity at the end of the millennium. I end with readings of recent novels by Cristina García and Alice Walker as they represent the current struggle between the fluidity and the containment of mixed identities.

The wealth of material I have found about racial mixture does not lend itself to neat and even categorization, just as mixture itself defies such categorization. If facility of reading was not a concern for me, I would have written one seamless, twisting (and extremely long) chapter, to emphasize the ways in which the different regions, time periods, and identities I discuss are inextricably intertwined. I am reluctant to draw borders where borders are fluid. For clarity, however, some demarcation was necessary. I have attempted to create divisions where they represent the least unnatural impositions or the least artificial separations, but inevitably I echo the same racial and national borders that my project defies. These borders should be considered institutional constraints rather than hard-and-fast divisions.

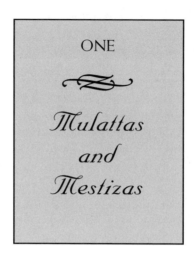

ONE

Mulattas and Mestizas

Paule Marshall's novel *Praisesong for the Widow* describes the origins of Thomasina Moore's uncertain racial identity: "He forced my mother / late / one night. / What do they call me?" (19). Her light skin enables her to pass and to perform in the chorus line at the Cotton Club. "She had the color that qualified" (19). She moves fluidly from the white cultural realm of nightclubs and cruise ships to the African-American cultural realm of "snakehips" and Harlem dance halls (26). Yet her color does more than give her access to these performances of privilege. Marshall inserts this question into her narrative about Thomasina's symbolic complexion. The dancer's "near-white of a blanched almond" skin (19) tells a story of both privilege and rape.

Marshall describes Thomasina's color as dual—not only racially dual but socially dual as well. Her light skin is "both sacred—for wasn't it a witness?—and profane" (19). Witness to what? Perhaps color bears witness to one's status in the hierarchy of the chosen or the damned. Or maybe it testifies to past profanity, the corruption of racial purity or the sexual violation of a black woman by a white man. Thomasina's access to the upper echelons of the color hierarchy, the "sacred" aspect, was produced in the traditional scenario of the white man's access to the black woman's body, the "profane" aspect. Her mixed race also bears witness to the decentering of racial hierarchies that occurs when the white man crosses the color line and leaves offspring on both sides. Thomasina's skin reflects the admixture of the violator and the violated and embodies both sides of the racial power imbalance that enables the mobility and the transgressions of light-skinned people. As a product of her duality, Thomasina transcends the limitations of any single racial identification, but she cannot escape the haunting origins of her identity.

The simultaneous violation and privilege surrounding the mulatto reflects the historical and cultural variations in biracial signification, ranging from scapegoating biracial subjects as traitors to their "true" races to celebrating biracial subjects as race leaders or representatives of racial transcendence. I would suggest that the ambiguous position of the biracial subject confounds any sense of "truth" in racial identity, recasting race as an uncertain and shifting field of differences: "What do they call me?" Americans have been asking for centuries what to call biracial individuals, fearful of the often ominous history inscribed in their mixture and the unsettling of racial differentiation that they represent. The need to ask and the fear of asking reflect a loss of racial definition and a lost sense of origins, yet Thomasina learns to turn to her advantage this loss and the tragedy of the scenario that produced it.

Just as biracialism leads African-American writers to think about the nature of racial identity, contemporary work by Chicana/o writers often centers on the issue of racial mixture. Being Chicana/o by definition means belonging to more than one race: Spanish, Native American, and often African- and Anglo-American, too. *Mestizaje* originally was the Latin American term for the racial and cultural fusion produced by the conquest and the colonial domination of the so-called New World, in which European colonizers mixed with the darker-skinned colonized subjects. In different regions of the Americas, *mestizaje* refers to different histories of mixture and different degrees of stigma or valorization. Recently, *mestizaje* has been celebrated as a marker of intercultural identification in general.

Mestizaje describes the product of mixture while invoking its origins. The term returns us to centuries-old history—conquest, rape, slavery, and cultural imperialism—as well as turning us toward new configurations of identity for the future. Chicana feminists Gloria Anzaldúa and Cherríe Moraga imagine mestiza identity as a radical incorporation of differences, a fluid shifting between languages, races, nations, and cultures. *Mestizaje* thus bridges narratives from America's past with contemporary academic rhetoric about identity. *Mestizaje* rests on a "foundation" of multiple, shifting components yet remains attached to history, cultural specificity, and a powerful politics of resistance, unlike many nonfoundational theories of identity that are inhibited by abstraction.[1] *Mestizaje* often transcends its potentially tragic origins (conquest, rape, "the death of the subject") and enables resistance to hegemony, a critique of imperialism, and powerful reinterpretations of self and culture.

Moraga emphasizes the power of the biracial offspring of rape. In her poem "Whose Savior?" she describes the physical hybridity that unifies mestizas like "familia" and fuels their rejection of whiteness:

> I hate white people.
> White blood.
>
> Hate the rape carved into this one's
> delicate nose, that one's shock
> of blonde wooly hair/hazel
> eyes, the pink spots
> that blotch my cheeks and hands
> in the bitterest of winters—
> secret signs surfacing
> making few people safe
> brothers
> familia.
>
> (*Generation* 102)

Like the conquest of the Americas, this poem begins with rape, but after the dash, after the recognition of the "signs" of racial mixture, Moraga introduces the family, the coalition of these mixed peoples, and the revolution that their identities signify. The signs of mixture (like wooly blonde hair) decenter whiteness, along with black and brownness, as pure racial categories. And the hatred in this poem decenters the cultural authority of whiteness with a vengeance that recalls Toussaint L'Ouverture, José Martí, Malcolm X, and other mixed-blood revolutionaries (*Generation* 112).

The figure of the tragic mulatto stands in direct contrast to contemporary celebrations of multiculturalism, postmodern hybridity, and Latina/o *mestizaje*. If mixed-race identity arouses pride for the Latina/o *raza*, why have relatively few African-Americans celebrated the biracialism of the mulatto? Is the mulatto not a border figure and a cultural translator as much as the Mexican-American mestiza? Does Thomasina Moore's ambiguous color reflect only one single, tragic narrative? This chapter will investigate the different relationships between mixture and identity for

Mexican-Americans and African-Americans. While Mexican and Chicana/o histories feature *mestizaje* as a central component in defining national identity, African-American identity has been built on greater racial polarization. Mulatto identification thus represents racial transgression for both African-American and Anglo-American identity.

While tragedy is a common fate for the mulatto character in literature, some writers have examined the potential privileges and increased access afforded biracial African-Americans. Yet few authors have envisioned mulatto characters who possess the revolutionary potential of Anzaldúa's mestiza consciousness. In her influential collection of essays and poetry, *Borderlands/La Frontera* (1987), Anzaldúa claims that "la conciencia de la mestiza" is the future of America. In her almost utopian vision, Anzaldúa celebrates mestiza identity because of its synthesis of differences, its commitment to flexibility, and its "uprooting of dualistic thinking," which present an "evolutionary step forward." She hopes that mestiza consciousness will ultimately lead to "the end of rape, of violence, of war" (80–81). Anzaldúa thus constructs a teleology, with *mestizaje* acting as a catalyst for the resolution of social conflicts. Rather than being embedded in tragedy, this mixture would herald an end to tragedy. Anzaldúa does invoke the rape at the origin of some mixed identities but suggests that mestiza fluidity will undermine the race and sex privilege that enables these rapes. She is perhaps too optimistic, but I am interested in the origins of and the power behind this optimism.

Anzaldúa's work reflects recent trends in race studies and postmodern theory, championing hybridity and the multiplication of difference as theoretical concepts, but her theories are also rooted in a long-established Mexican tradition of endorsing racial mixture as a social policy. To outline the historical precedence for contemporary celebrations of *mestizaje*, I will survey some of the different attitudes toward mixed identity in the Americas, revealing the common tendency to theorize mixture as a resolution to social problems. It is important to recognize that racial mixture has been celebrated in both antiracist and racist histories.

During the nineteenth century, at the same time that Jim Crow laws were regulating racial segregation in the southeastern United States, *mestizaje* was used as a means of solidifying national identity in Mexico (and the future southwestern United States).[2] While these historical developments might seem opposed, both revolve around the existence of racial mixture. I juxtapose attitudes toward *mestizaje* in the Southwest with writings about mulatto identity in the Southeast to highlight the shared impulse behind these different responses to racial mixing in the Americas. Although the social structures of Jim Crow society condemned the intermingling of the races, those very structures are based in part on the actual frequency of mixture. Official policy and social reality similarly diverged in Mexico. Although *mestizaje* was officially accepted as the normative Mexican identity, both light-skinned and dark-skinned Mexicans often shunned mestizos. And racial rhetoric that appeared tolerant on the surface was often based on racism. Spanish officials initially endorsed mixture with the darker-skinned native peoples only to achieve Spanish imperialist goals. In this way, racial hierarchies existed in tension with racial fluidity. Despite its ambivalent history, *mestizaje* is an enabling concept because it suggests ways in which race dynamics in the United States could be reexamined with greater attention to such contradictions. Moreover, because of *mestizaje's* current theoretical vogue, it is important to trace the ambivalent history behind it.

This chapter begins by surveying histories of mestizos and mulattoes in the Americas, analyzing the subtexts of critical and historical writings about mixture. I then turn to literary representations that employ similar rhetoric. In particular, I focus on the works of women writers. Since women were often positioned at the origins of racial mixture—as mothers, rape victims, or intercultural guides—women writers have had a unique investment in reimagining narratives of mixed identity. I first analyze representations of the Southwest, where *mestizaje* figures prominently in nineteenth- and early-twentieth-century women's writing. Both Anglo-American writers such as Susan Magoffin and Susan Wallace and Mexican-American writers such as María Amparo Ruiz de Burton, Jovita González Mireles, and Josephina Niggli draw attention to mixture, yet their depictions contrast according to the dominant rhetoric of their different cultures. Writings about *mestizaje* by contemporary Chicanas (Gloria Anzaldúa, Cherríe Moraga, and Sylvia López-Medina) resemble the models established by their less visible foremothers. I follow my literary analysis of *mestizaje* with an analysis of literature that treats comparative fluidity among African-Americans in the United States. Beginning with nineteenth-century abolitionist texts by both white and black, female and male U.S. writers (Lydia Maria Child, Elizabeth Livermore, and William Wells Brown), I contrast the tragic mulatto heroines of white writers with the more empowered and fluid identities of characters created by African-American writers. I then trace a lineage of empowered biracial heroines in the works of African-American women writers (Frances E. W.

Harper, Pauline Hopkins, Nella Larsen, and Jessie Redmon Fauset) before concluding with a reading of Ntozake Shange's 1994 novel, *Liliane,*
which presents the most fluid dynamics of all the African-American texts
I discuss.

Mestizaje and Histories of Race in Mexico

According to Moraga, "We light-skinned breeds are like chameleons,
those lagartijas with the capacity to change the color of their skins." Her
identity changes with her environment, Puerto Rican in Brooklyn, "Spanish" in Harlem, Cuban in Mexico, Italian, Jewish, "colored mixed with
cowboy" (*Generation* 116). Like Thomasina Moore, Moraga's mixed-race
background allows her to be at home in many different places. Moraga
continues, "I know full well that my mestizaje . . . is the catalyst of my
activism and my art" (127). The mixture of races within the mestiza ideally provides her with resources from different cultures (language, history,
gods and goddesses) and insight about the differences between the races
that meet within her. [3]

Many Chicana theorists, such as Anzaldúa and Moraga, have used the
concept of *mestizaje* to forward a radical critique of subjectivity. *Mestizaje*
challenges the stability, the singularity, and even the very identity of identity. Yet while some writers celebrate hybridity as the foundation of a new
subversive consciousness, there are reasons to be cautious about this new
wave of theorization.

First, the critical vogue surrounding *mestizaje* can be attributed to its confluence with postmodern celebrations of hybridity as much as its potential for political and antiracist critique. Mixture has decentered identity
for centuries, but that long history has been effaced when *mestizaje* is absorbed in the wake of postmodernism. Jean-Luc Nancy indicates the ease
with which the difference of minority groups can be co-opted within the
discourses of the dominant culture. *Mestizaje* eventually becomes a sign
for hybridity, in general, as happens in Nancy's own writing. Nancy (a
white Frenchman) claims to be a mestizo himself as a result of the shifting processes of all identity. He problematically assumes the authority
to redefine *mestizaje* as "nothing to do with mixed blood or mixed cultures," removing the term from its political/material foundations and its
specific American differences (123). Nancy's essay exemplifies a tendency
that Paula Moya notes among postmodernists to "reinscribe, albeit unintentionally, a kind of universalizing sameness (we are all marginal now!)

that their celebration of 'difference' had tried so hard to avoid" (126). When uprooted from its cultural origins, hybridity becomes an alternate type of essence, a raceless abstraction that effaces the differences between identities. Yvonne Yarbro-Bejarano, too, draws attention to "the expense of generalizing moves that deracinate the psychic 'borderlands' and '*mestiza*' consciousness from the United States/Mexican border and the racial miscegenation accompanying the colonization of the Americas" ("Gloria Anzaldúa's *Borderlands/La Frontera*" 13–14). Decontextualizing theories that emerge from actual borderlands risks idealizing sites of continued oppression.

Second, the degree to which academic theories (postmodern or otherwise) have embraced *mestizaje* is suspect in that it privileges people of color who have been "lightened" by mixture. The celebration of *mestizaje* often overlooks the continued oppression of darker-skinned peoples as the dominant culture seeks out the familiar (the whiteness) within the Other. A typical example of this sort of racism can be found in Rodrigo Chávez González's 1937 study, *El mestizaje y su influencia social en América*, where he posits *mestizaje* as a means of "improving" Indian races by mixture with Spanish blood: "No hay que tenerle miedo al mestizaje. . . . El mestizaje es la terapeútica para la patalogía indolatina [There is no need to fear *mestizaje*. . . . *Mestizaje* is the therapy for Indian-Latin pathology]" (121).[4] This racist celebration of *mestizaje* reflects the tendency that contemporary Caribbean historian Antonio Benítez-Rojo warns against: *mestizaje* can become a paradigm for conquering, whitening, and subsuming a darker-skinned people (*Repeating Island* 26).

Finally, theories of *mestizaje* often mask essentially conservative and exclusive definitions of race and identity. Mixture has the potential to overturn conventional thinking about race, but *mestizaje* itself is often used as a totalizing paradigm, assuming a fixed, even though mixed, biological foundation of identity. Indeed, José Vasconcelos's seminal 1925 treatise on *mestizaje*, which was central to the definition of Mexican identity and national unity in the early twentieth century, provides the foundation for essentialist, universalist, and masculinist definitions: "la raza definitiva, la raza síntesis o raza integral, hecho con el genio y con la sangre de todos los pueblos y, por lo mismo, más capaz de verdadera fraternidad y de visión realmente universal [the definitive race, the synthetic race or the integral race, made with the genius and the blood of all of the peoples and, for this, more capable of true fraternity and of real universal vision]" (60). And this biological fusion absorbs all difference, leaving no racial particularity to fragment the mestiza nation: "ya no será la raza de un solo color, de rasgos particulares [the race will no longer be of one color, of particular features]" (Vasconcelos 60). In her essay, " 'Chicana! Rican? No, Chicana-Riqueña!' Refashioning the Transnational Connection," Angie Chabram-Dernersesian critiques such essentialist deployments of *mestizaje* that have, in effect, fetishized mixture as an ideal and exclusive category (272–73). Writing of the ways in which *mestizaje* has come to signify an exclusively Chicano and biologically racial identity in the United States, excluding national, sexual, and class-based identifications that inflect race, Chabram-Dernersesian writes, "It is ironic that while we live in a period which prizes the multiplicity of identities and charts border crossings with borderless critics, there should be such a marked silence around the kinds of divergent ethnic pluralities that cross gender and classed subjects within the semantic orbit of Chicana/o. So powerful is the hegemonic reach of the dominant culture that fixed categories of race and ethnicity continue to be the foundation, the structuring axis around which Chicana/o identities are found" (273). Fixing *mestizaje* as a racially bounded and essential category of identity shores up common ground for Chicano identity politics yet also echoes historical attempts at Mexican nation building centered on a supposedly shared and effectively hegemonic racial ground. Like Chabram-Dernersesian, I advocate instead an antiessentialist *mestizaje* that, "rather than inscribing monocausality, a one-dimensional view of oppression, . . . forecasts an articulation of other intersected and overlapping categories" (275).

AnaLouise Keating describes Anzaldúa's use of *mestizaje* as a tactical means of deconstructing identity categories, even oppositional ones, from within: "Anzaldúa's new mestiza represents a hybrid, a complex mixed breed who can neither be reduced to a single category nor rigidly classified according to a specific set of traits" (30). To resist exclusion and essentialism, mixtures themselves must be regarded as partial, variable, and internally mixed (following Trinh Minh-ha's suggestion that we emphasize differences within individuals rather than fetishizing differences between them). In David Theo Goldberg's somewhat playful terms, "The reiterative revisability of hybrid heterotopias confronts the command of homogeneity with the material and discursive conditions of its horizon, exploding the confines of fabricated identities again and again into something new" (79). Moraga enacts this continual internal revision and invokes the expanding horizon of her own identity in "The Breakdown of the Bicultural Mind." She cites her multiple heritages that exceed any given identity—Spanish, French, Native American—and describes the significance of her mestiza flesh as something constantly changing: "I am a trespasser. I do not need signs to remind me. My immigrant blood is a stain I carry in the fading of my flesh each winter. But I am made of clay. All our ancestors know this. It is no myth, but wholly evident in the slow dissolving of my skin into the red road of this river. *Where will you take me, immigrant and orphaned?*" (*Generation* 131). This *mestizaje* confronts its own alien elements and imagines identity as perpetual travel (dissolving into the road, asking "where will you take me?") rather than a reiteration of origins. It rejects false claims to legitimacy, closure, and immutability.

Although *mestizaje* does not necessarily translate into the idealistic up-heaval that Anzaldúa and others envision, it does present a critique of white superiority. Since whiteness itself is wrought within *mestizaje*, it is impossible to isolate any exclusive whiteness or monocultural American-ness—the illusions on which U.S. racism is built. For centuries, Mexican and Latina/o writers have recognized this subversive potential. Accord-ing to Coco Fusco, Caribbean and Latin American thinkers are ahead of their northern counterparts in terms of decentered visions of race and America: "In the North, . . . a deeply embedded ideology of essentialist separatism . . . has continuously deferred recognition and affirmation of this country's and its people's racial and cultural hybridity. In the South, at least two centuries of ideological celebration of hybridity (the many discourses of *mestizaje*) often brings Latin American intellectuals to reject binary understandings of race" (23–24). Fusco establishes a binary North America–South America opposition here, but her insight regarding "the many discourses of *mestizaje*" (which could apply to both North and South) allows for a deconstruction of all such binaries based on the multiple hy-bridities on all sides of American borders. Furthermore, travel, immigra-tion, and cultural exchange between the different Americas (North and South, island and mainland) have begun to undo the effects of regionally different racial histories.

Although mulatto and mestizo identities certainly differ—originating in different countries as the product of different races, cultures, and histo-ries of conquest and slavery—each can shed light on the other. Strategies for taking control of the differences within one's identity are often obvious for mestizos, who more frequently move between languages, nations, and cultural borders, and are often denied or suppressed in histories of mulat-toes. Yet examining the two together draws attention to more covert tac-tics employed by some mulattoes. More important, a comparative study of different racial mixtures in the Americas should complicate reductive assumptions about bipolar, black-white division in the United States.

Both the United States and Mexico originally depended on the labor of darker-skinned peoples, and the prevalence of mixture in both regions reflects the degree to which the enslaved or colonized races were sexually subject to the dominant "white" races. Despite the shared facts of the two countries' racial mixtures, their institutionalized cultural imperialism, and their histories of violent racist domination, the southwestern and southeastern regions of the United States developed very different manifestations of racism. While African-American mixture originated in large-scale African slavery and Jim Crow segregation, Mexican-American mixture was built on a smaller-scale, more racially diverse system of slavery and a multiracial drive for independence that invoked *mestizaje* as a means of unifying the nation. Vasconcelos famously emphasizes this difference in *La raza cósmica* (1925), opposing *mestizaje* in Mexico and Latin America to the U.S. obsession with purity: "North Americans have held very firmly to their resolution to maintain a pure stock, the reason being that they are faced with the Blacks, who are like the opposite pole, like the antithesis of the elements to be mixed. In the Ibero-American world, the problem does not present itself in such crude terms. We have very few Blacks, and a large part of them is already becoming a mulatto population. The Indian is a good bridge for racial mixing. Besides, the warm climate is propitious for the interaction and gathering of all peoples" (26). This idealization of the effects of *mestizaje* attributes U.S. segregation to the supposedly more insurmountable racial barriers between white and black and ignores the actual mixtures prevalent in the United States: between Americans of European, African, native, and Asian descent.

The beginnings of *mestizaje* can be explained by a gender imbalance. Most of the Spaniards who came to the "New World" were male: military men, younger sons seeking their fortunes, and Catholic friars. Impelled by political obligations to produce children and expand the colony, Spanish men often took native concubines. At first, even the Catholic Church endorsed marriages between Spanish men and daughters of Amerindian noblemen, "porque desta manera muy presto podrán ser todos los caciques españoles [because in this manner all of the leaders will quickly become Spanish]" (Instituto 60). These interracial marriages facilitated the Hispanicization of the natives, increased domestic stability in the colony, and legitimized the unions of colonizer and colonized along with their offspring.[5] Antonia Castañeda's feminist analysis of the colonization of

America also describes how Spain initially promoted intermarriage with Amerindian noblewomen to improve relations with the American natives and to "advance particular political, military, religious, or social interests" (79). Spaniards in Mexico who married women from noble native families were often rewarded with official posts or *encomiendas* (land on which to establish an estate with Indian tribute and Indian labor) (Meyer and Sherman 209). The native woman comes to represent territory, and the conquest of the "daughters of the land" was an important component of colonization (Castañeda 79). Sexual domination lies at the heart of interracial mixture. For example, the conquest of Tenochtitlán in 1521 was supposedly made possible with the assistance of La Malinche, the "Indian princess" taken by Hernán Cortés as lover, translator, and mother to his mestizo child.[6] In this scenario, the colonized women became the (willing or unwilling) vehicles through which the Spanish men literally infiltrated the colony with their blood and semen. Thus begins the valorization of *mestizaje* as a strategy for colonization in Mexico (and the future southwestern United States) and the intertwined asymmetries of race and sex relations in the development of mixed Americanness.[7]

This intermixture contrasts with the United States, which was settled by a larger percentage of family groups who were political, economic, and religious refugees.[8] The conquerors of the North remained apart from the Native Americans to a degree that would not have been possible in Mexico. In "The Birth of the Mestizo in New Spain" (1939), historian C. E. Marshall contrasts the "self-sufficient" European settlements of North America, where "the Indians were brushed aside by land-hungry settlers," with the Spanish colonies, where "the essential fusion of conqueror and conquered" created a new society of interdependent "races of many colors" (161). While this opposition is oversimplified, eliding both the intimate relations between the colonizers and the Native Americans in the United States and the massacre of Amerindians by Spaniards in Mexico, it is true that intermarriage with Native Americans was more foundational in Mexican society than in the United States. By the time large numbers of African slaves were forced into the racial fabric of the United States, a Eurocentric society had already been established. In contrast to this relatively stratified racial division, slavery in Mexico was based on both Indian and African labor, and all three races mixed. Even the "pure" Spanish colonizers were the mixed descendants of Latins, Moors, Visigoths, and Jews.

While the majority of Mexico's agricultural work and mining during the colonial period was provided by unpaid Amerindian labor, a large number of slaves were imported from Africa, as well. Since these slaves were more expensive, they were more valued by the colonists, who often trained African slaves for skilled artisan labor or put them in charge of Amerindian workers as overseers in factories, ranches, or mines (Meyer and Sherman 214; Conniff and Davis 48). Many blacks did experience forms of slavery similar to those in the United States, but Mexico had a smaller number of black slaves (only about six thousand by 1800) and a higher incidence of slave revolts and maroon communities established by runaways.[9]

In their historical study *Africans in the Americas,* Michael Conniff and Thomas Davis contrast African-American experiences in Mexico and in the United States, claiming that Spanish colonies lacked the racial divisiveness and violence of U.S. race relations because of more flexible social categories, smaller black populations, nation-building rhetoric that repudiated racism, and sustained genetic mixing over centuries. "Prejudice and discrimination still exist, but they are so subtle and veiled" in the more "multicultural" "Latin-style" systems (291). Most blacks in Mexico mixed with Amerindians, mestizos, and Spaniards. In the nineteenth century, at the end of the colonial period, only about ten thousand Mexicans "could be considered blacks," although there was a large population of Afro-mestizos (Meyer and Sherman 217). Conniff and Davis claim that, "for the most part," Afro-mestizos assimilated into "the prevailing mestizo culture" (273). This gradual erasure of pure and separate races reflects the dominant Mexican national policy, and the imported Africans provided an additional cultural and racial element to Mexican *mestizaje.*[10]

Conniff and Davis argue that the codified segregation and binary race divisions produced by large-scale slavery in the United States were not possible in the Spanish colonies, where interracial blending thwarted racial divisiveness (313). Rather than centering on black-white differentiation, inequities of power were negotiated at every gradation of difference. Racial identity was more complex in Spanish America because color alone was not enough to locate an individual's identity in one race or another. Instead, race came to be identified with religion, culture, and behavior. According to Conniff and Davis, "persons were defined as white, for example, not only by phenotype but also by their European language, Christianity, class, formal learning, and style of life" (312). The term *casta* was used to designate status based on these multiple factors. This "social race" was the foundation of hierarchies, since the multiple different shades of brown formed by Spanish American *mestizaje* problematized color-based hierarchies.[11]

Within the fluid dynamic of the Spanish colonial *casta* system, it was relatively easy for individuals to elevate their racial status. Although the Spaniards imposed a regimented hierarchy of *castas* based on different degrees of racial mixture, this artificial system was difficult to implement and had little or no impact on public perceptions of race, which were instead based on appearance, context, profession, or family. For the mixed *castas*, race was largely a matter of social opinion and varied with context.[12] As early as 1529, Pope Clemente VII said of Spanish America, "la hermosura de las virtudes limpia en los hijos la mancha del nacimiento, y con la limpieza de costumbres se borra la vergüenza del origen [the beauty of virtue cleans/purifies the stain of birth in children, and with the purity of customs one erases the shame of origin]" (Rosenblat 15). In this edict, race and legitimacy are determined by manners rather than fixed at birth. In the eighteenth century, one could buy status, and, as Angel Rosenblat suggests, race became a matter of class: "El régimen de castas tendía a disolverse en usa serie de diferencias económicas [The *casta* regime tended to dissolve into a series of economic differences]" (180).[13] Alejandro Lipschutz and Jack D. Forbes also discuss the ways in which mestizos with financial privilege became accepted into the whiter ranks and bought certificates verifying "purity of blood" (*limpieza de sangre*) (Lipschutz 320–23; Forbes 90).[14] In "Black Pioneers: The Spanish-Speaking Afroamericans of the Southwest," Forbes writes that race "was not definite by the late eighteenth century and many people were of such a mixed character that they were simply *de color quebrado*" (82). Although Forbes translates *quebrado* as "all mixed up," I would translate it as "broken," indicating the fractures within and the ultimate breakdown of the Spanish *casta* hierarchy.

As Mexico became predominantly hybrid, nineteenth-century proindependence discourse embraced *mestizaje* to build national unity.[15] Conniff and Davis claim that some emerging nationalist ideologies "approved of racial mixing as a way to create homogeneous, hybrid citizenries" and to eliminate racial divisions (313, 270). Despite this attempt to define a unified Mexican identity, mestizos were still often marginalized by both indigenous Mexicans, for whom mestizos served as a reminder of rape and racial domination, and lighter-skinned Mexicans, who frequently still adhered to an older social code that privileged whiteness (Vigil 113). Many light-skinned mestizos passed for Spanish and reinforced the conflation of *limpieza de sangre* and class status. A light-skinned mestizo aristocracy developed. Although the complex hierarchy of racial categories was officially abandoned in 1822, when Mexico gained its independence from Spain, it continued to be used in social circles, marriage records, and institutions that implicitly supported the "pigmentocracy" (Vigil 113, 176). Official rhetoric and racial mixture contradicted such color-based hierarchy, but social interactions often continued to follow a racist pattern. Darker-skinned mestizos who were unable to take advantage of social fluidity and join the aristocracy were often classed with Amerindians, blacks, or mulattoes, forming a caste that defied racial categorization (Meyer and Sherman 211). Celebrating *mestizaje* as an ideal often remained at the level of rhetoric, as individuals were still ranked by arbitrary color divisions.

T. R. Fehrenbach's history of Mexico, *Fire and Blood*, contrasts this hierarchical structure of central Mexico with the situation in northern Mexico (the present-day southwestern United States). On the sparsely populated northern frontier, the caste system that developed elsewhere in Mexico was difficult to implement. Carey McWilliams's influential history, *North from Mexico* (1990), draws attention to the racial diversity of the initial settlers in what is now the southwestern United States, decentering the image of the lone European exploring the American wilderness. [16] Of the original "Spanish" colonizers of Los Angeles, two were "Negroes," eight were mulattoes, nine were Amerindians, one was of Chinese descent, and one was mestizo. Although all had Spanish names like Rodríguez and Variegas, only two were in fact racially Spanish (McWilliams 44). [17] In California, the legends of "pure" Spanish ancestry were a "fantasy," and only a very small percentage of the distinguished *gente de razón* were actually of pure Spanish descent (McWilliams 88). In addition, according to McWilliams, the "Spanish" elite of California intermarried with American, British, Scottish, German, and French adventurers who embraced Hispanic culture and even Hispanicized their surnames (89–90). Thus, by 1848, when the United States took over the territories of northern Mexico under the Treaty of Guadalupe Hidalgo, the "Spanish" culture of California was truly racially and culturally mixed. [18]

In New Mexico, Mexican migrants adopted Native American forms of agriculture, which, along with Mexican and indigenous adaptations of Spanish culture and religion, helped to form a thoroughly syncretic society (McWilliams 72–73). As McWilliams describes it, "the culture of the Southwest, in 1848, was a trinity: a whole consisting of three intricately interwoven, interpenetrated, thoroughly fused elements"—Spanish, Mexican, and Indian cultures (42). Even McWilliams's blending of religious and sexual imagery in this description is probably accurate, for religious conversion and interracial breeding were the primary means by which the Spaniards colonized the Americas. When Anglo-American culture and laws entered the southwestern United States in the nineteenth century, three racial groups had already intermingled to such a degree that no single strand could be unraveled and labeled as belonging to one race or the other (42). The New Mexicans colonized by the United States were thus already accustomed to domination, adaptation, and amalgamation. Fehrenbach fuses Mexican rhetoric (*mestizaje*) and U.S. rhetoric (the myth of the melting pot) in his description of these New Mexicans: "The Bajío had become a genuine melting pot, where *indios* merged into *mestizos* and *mestizos* tended to be accepted slowly into the 'white' race." This region became "neither distinctly Spanish nor Indian" (276), as is consistent with U.S. melting pot ideology. In Fehrenbach's account, the people who settled what is now the U.S. Southwest "forgot" both Aztec and Spanish ways, moving beyond the racial divisions of the South in their formation of a new vaquero culture (combining native styles of food and dress), a new "bronze race," the future *raza* that Chicanos now celebrate (280). Fehrenbach's history thus traces an evolution from Spanish and Aztec cultural origins to twentieth-century racial terminology.

Many historians diminish Mexico's racism by contrasting Mexican race dynamics with those of the United States.[19] A 1960 conference sponsored by the Instituto Panamericano de Geografia e Historia, *El Mestizaje en la Historia de Ibero-America* [*Mestizaje* in the History of Ibero-America], elicited many such romanticized views on the absence of racism in Spanish America. For example, in a fairly suspect argument, Wigberto Jiménez Moreno contrasts the European colonization of Mexico with that of the northeastern United States, claiming that since New England was colonized by Puritans, who feared the corrupting influence of heathens in their New Jerusalem, and Mexico was colonized by Catholics, who professed to believe that all men are brothers, racism was installed in the foundations of New England colonialism but not in Mexico's colonial society. According to this interpretation, Puritans emphasized the racial distinctions of the Old Testament, but Catholics emphasized the lessons of social equality in the New Testament. Jiménez Moreno denies antinative racism and celebrates Mexico as a model of racial harmony, claiming, "el mexicano de hoy siente que el indígena es uno de los factores que han dado a México una fisonomía inconfundible, y México es precisamente uno de los países más equilibradamente mestizos en el Continente [the

Mexican of today feels that the Indian is one of the factors that has given Mexico unmistakable features, and Mexico is truly one of the most harmoniously mixed-race countries on the continent]" (Instituto 85).[20]

Similarly, in the same conference proceedings, John Gillin claims that racism in Latin America never reached the same proportions as in the United States. Gillin gives as an example the Latin American usage of *negra* or *negrita* as a universal term of endearment rather than a pejorative. This usage of *negra* reveals at least a desire to value blackness. However, it also potentially sexualizes racial difference, removes race from context, and reduces the complexity of color to a quality of desire, presenting insufficient proof for an absence of racism. Like Jiménez Moreno, Gillin is optimistic about the blurring of racial distinction and the erasure of racial hierarchies, asserting that "the prejudice against race mixture . . . has been blurred in most parts of [Latin America] during the past 150 years" (Instituto 77). A comparably optimistic view of race relations is simply not found in studies of race in the southeastern United States. While I agree with the assertion that Mexico has been culturally syncretic and racially heterogeneous since its foundation, Jiménez Moreno and Gillin use dubious reasoning to prove these conclusions and falsely idealize Mexico as a place without racism. Since these two histories emerged during a time of increasing civil rights sentiment, perhaps the historians' commitment to racial equality made them unwilling to see the hierarchies that persist in the face of mixture in Mexico and Latin America.

U.S. historians have also demonstrated this tendency to idealize *mestizaje*. Two early women writers in New Mexico make similar assumptions that predate the 1960 conference. In her 1948–49 lectures on race relations, historian Erna Fergusson claims that racial mixture in the Southwest produced a healthy social system and that all racial prejudices were imported from the Southeast after the United States took over New Mexico ("Race Relations"). In addition, Fabiola Cabeza de Baca Gilbert's tales of early-twentieth-century New Mexico suggest that all "nationalities merged into one big family. . . . There was no discrimination as to color or race" (84). Indeed, color ceases to function as a signifier of race in Cabeza de Baca Gilbert's account: she claims that anyone who spoke English was included as a white American (148–49). As both women idealize New Mexico as a model of harmonious interracial fusion, they eclipse the reality of friction and intolerance. The idealism in both accounts is enabled by *mestizaje's* inconsistency with the binary racial definitions already established in the (eastern) United States. If *racism* refers strictly to a black-white problem, it does not apply to the Southwest, according to this logic.

So the path toward contemporary celebrations of *mestizaje* was blazed long ago, by Spanish colonizers, by Mexican nationalists, and by twentieth-century historians, despite the fact that those with lighter skin often held most of the power. Carlos Morton writes that "in Latin America October 12, Columbus Day, is celebrated as El Día de La Raza (The Day of the Race), or the day when all of the races started 'mixing.' . . . We do not honor the elitist 'conquistador,' but rather celebrate La Raza (The Family) as a whole" (20). This claim attributes to Latin Americans a resistance to the histories of the dominant culture. He suggests that Latin Americans honor the mixed legacy of colonialism rather than the moment of conquest itself and defines *raza* as a natural grouping based on shared genetic history ("family") rather than a social structure built to enable colonial domination. By honoring "all the races and creeds who contributed to [America's] creation from Tierra del Fuego to Alaska these past five centuries," instead of Columbus and the conquistadors, Morton decenters European icons and moments of historic violence and focuses instead on creative processes and border-crossing multiracialism (20).

Black, White, Mulatto, and Jim Crow

While *mestizaje* was frequently encouraged in Mexico, miscegenation was rendered taboo in the United States to maintain the ideal of black and white racial stratification at the foundation of U.S. slavery. Social and economic hierarchies today still echo the barriers erected by centuries of slavery and Jim Crow segregation. Slavery officially rendered these racial barriers immobile, but both blacks and whites frequently crossed them. Most frequently, white men crossed the line in illicit relations with slave women. Whereas in Mexico similar relations were often legitimized by marriage, in the United States, this crossing was an open secret, a common practice that few publicly endorsed. This sexual violation produced racial mixture just as in Mexico, but the U.S. mixture was not condoned by church or state, as it was in Mexico. Some people, like Henry Clay, argued that the "amalgamation of the races" would lead to the abolition of slavery (William Wells Brown 55), but racist white Americans, and even some abolitionist African-Americans, like William Wells Brown, condemned this amalgamation as "evidence of the degraded and immoral condition" of racial and sexual dynamics in the United States (55). The epitome of degradation, for Brown, was the enslavement of the racially mixed products of this corruption, particularly the fair mulatta.

In *Clotel* (1853), which has been called the first African-American novel, Brown describes free mulatto women who own homes, spend their own money, and receive gifts through the affections of white men. Significantly, these fair women crossed the line between the races almost as much as white men did. His heroine, Clotel, whom Brown claims is Thomas Jefferson's daughter by a slave woman, has "a complexion as white as most of those who were waiting with a wish to become her purchasers" at a slave auction (62). Clotel's white lover buys her, and they have a daughter together, but they never marry, and he later leaves her for a light-haired, blue-eyed statesman's daughter (82). Clotel is tragically returned to slavery, but she temporarily escapes by passing as a white man, crossing boundaries of both race and sex difference (167–69).[21] She ultimately frees herself by jumping to her death in the Potomac. While the novel retains tragic associations, racial fluidity and border crossings underlie Clotel's tragedy. Brown thus constructs a paradoxical image of the mulatta: she is deprived of life and liberty at the same time that she is freer than the darker slaves, able to transcend borders of racial difference, and skilled at escaping both prison and sexual strictures. The rigidity of racial barriers corresponds to—responds to and elicits—the subversion of them.

When emancipation officially removed these barriers in 1863, African-Americans were still systematically denied the rights that new laws supposedly granted. Only a few African-Americans who successfully manipulated, subverted, or masked racial identity succeeded in overcoming those (in)visible barriers. Prohibitions against miscegenation, in part a response to the actual frequency of black and white mixing, led to official policy requiring separation of the races (during slavery by caste, during Jim Crow by location). Although many of the laws aimed at preventing miscegenation were also used against Native Americans and Latina/os in regions of the United States where those groups presented a visible challenge to white supremacy, such laws were primarily directed at relations with African-Americans. According to C. Vann Woodward, in the 1890s, when the rise of industry, the decline of the economy, and urban flight east of the Mississippi were changing the nature of American identity, black Americans became the target of blame for the changing quality of life in the United States (51–53). Increased mobility of African-Americans between the 1850s and the 1890s presented an affront to prewar social codes, leading white Americans to develop laws to replicate the earlier caste system (Williamson, *Origins* vi). Through racist public policy, the recently emancipated African-Americans were visibly scapegoated and purged from American public identity.

As with *mestizaje* in the Southwest, sex/gender was a primary axis along which black-white racial segregation was negotiated. Joel Williamson suggests that the first Jim Crow laws, such as those requiring separate train cars, were aimed at "protecting" white women, the symbol of vulnerable American purity (*Origins* 15). Unlike Mexico, where *mestizaje* served as a means of homogenizing the nation, U.S. national coherence was built on the exclusion of nonwhite Others through segregation and through xenophobic immigration and naturalization laws. These exclusions were formed around the specter of mixture. This tension between the flexibility of racial barriers and the reinforcement of segregation continued into the twentieth century. I will use the mestiza model—fluidity produced by racial mixture—to focus attention on ruptures in black-white segregation and to highlight the actual fluidity that underwrote Jim Crow.[22]

Barriers to fluidity in the southeastern United States were not only legal but psychological as well. The symbolic associations of whiteness with purity and blackness with evil and filth fueled the taboo against interracial associations. Furthermore, with the rise of the social sciences and the drive to categorize group identities, the emphasis on physical traits (head shape, skin color, stature) directed ethnocentric anxieties toward groups with the most visible differences. People of African descent were the object of much study, most of which aimed at proving a correspondence between physical difference and mental or spiritual difference, a correspondence based on the supposed connection between visible phenomena and natural laws. In a manner of self-fulfilling prophecy, racist studies strove to prove that the fear of racial difference was founded on natural, essential hierarchies in which Africans were a separate and lower species. The social construction of race emerged from studies that artificially and arbitrarily linked social traits to physical ones.[23]

In the nineteenth century, increasing interracial mixture lead to anxiety about the uncertainty of racial difference and the vulnerable foundations of white privilege. This anxiety produced further segregation and artificial codification. In literature, writers such as Thomas Dixon dwelled on the visible difference of black Americans, perhaps to combat the actual blurring of boundaries. In *The Clansman* (1905), for example, Dixon describes "Old Aleck" as "so striking a negro in his personal appearance, he seemed . . . a distinct type of man." Dixon describes his head as "mashed," his bow-legged walk as "a moving joke," and his "protruding stomach" as like "an elderly monkey's" (248–49). Descriptions of such visible characteristics were meant to prove the essential inferiority (even animality) of the emancipated slaves. As Dixon's Abraham Lincoln explains, "There is a physical difference between the white and black races which will forever forbid their living together on terms of political and social equality" (45). This insistence on polarization corresponds to the threat of miscegenation, so potential black rapists, reaching toward the exalted purity of white women, form the visual foundation for Dixon's racist essentialism. Emancipation threatened the social perceptions in which white supremacy and white purity were invested by allowing the freed slaves to share geographic, political, and social space with whites. In response, Dixon and other writers produced didactic fiction with vehemently racist depictions to foster racial segregation and to inspire racist fears regarding the physical proximity of black Americans.

In *American Anatomies*, Robyn Wiegman analyzes this modern construction of race as a visible distinction, "a profound ordering of difference instantiated at the sight of the body" (24). Wiegman claims that visual apprehension is not an objective criterion but rather a contingent and acculturated phenomenon. I would argue that not only did social taboos affect the visual experience of race, such as Dixon's, but the actual unreliability of skin color as a social indicator would have thwarted attempts to build social hierarchies on apparent race.[24] Wiegman asks, "But if the truth of race could escape the visual, if the hallmarks of corporeal signification were increasingly and ultimately unstable, if the binary structure of racial thinking could dissolve at the sight of the body, how then could the necessary clarity of differentiation be found to ascertain once and for all the hierarchy of being?" (47). I would answer that faced with the visual uncertainty of racial differentiation caused by mixture, mechanisms such as the social sciences, eugenics, Jim Crow laws, social codes, and racist literature worked to replace the solid foundation that racist hierarchies lacked in the corporeal world. Eroding racial distinctiveness produced the interest in comparative anatomies, the increasing attention toward the raced body as an object of study that Wiegman locates in the nineteenth century.

In 1885, George Washington Cable displayed some of this anxiety about the blurring of the races. He insisted that for the plantation hierarchy to function, "the difference between master and slave [was] never *lost sight of* by either" (10, emphasis added). That is, some visible distinction must exist between the races. Although Cable wrote to advocate the civil rights of freed slaves, he betrayed some anxiety about potential social amalgamation, and he never "lost sight of" black-white differentiation. He carefully distinguished between civil equity for black Americans (which he supported) and social equality or intermingling (which he did not advocate) (53–54). He then denied that miscegenation occurred to any significant degree, noting the supposed absence of racial intermixture in Oberlin, Ohio; Berea, Kentucky; and other "nests of ["negrophile"] fanaticism" (102–3). He claimed that miscegenation did not occur because of "the ordinary natural preferences of like for like" and because the "two races . . . have no wish to . . . mingle their two bloods in one stream" (103). In this way, he projected his own racial agenda onto the nature and the desires of humanity and distanced hybridity or "racial confusion" from his America by attributing it to more barbarous times and peoples (111). Significantly, even his criticism of racism was consistent with his insistence on retaining a separation of the races: as he condemned those who act as if black Americans have zero social value, he claimed that all racial fractions—two, four, six, and eight—still divide into zero (9). While Cable criticized the devaluing of African-Americans, he also denied the existence of any distinction between mixed race and black, effacing the intermediate existence of mulattoes.

Much legal, social, and scientific attention was dedicated to the mulatto as a threat to racial differentiation based on visible characteristics.[25] The social and legal status of mulattoes was initially ambiguous, but, particularly in the nineteenth century, laws were created to solidify their social and racial position (Williamson, *New People* 61–67). Two major studies of mulattoes in the United States reflect different attitudes toward black-white racial mixture. Joel Williamson's historical study *New People: Miscegenation and Mulattoes in the United States* (1980) explores the impact of racial mixture on American identity in the past two centuries.[26] Edward Byron Reuter's *The Mulatto in the United States* (1918) compares and contrasts U.S. attitudes toward racial mixture with those in the rest of the world. Williamson considers Reuter's book to be the only previous wholly relevant sociological text on the subject of mulattoes and miscegenation (*New People* xi). This claim juxtaposes Williamson's research in the 1970s with Reuter's in the first decades of the twentieth century. While Reuter's work follows decades of sociological and pseudoscientific studies of racial difference and the negative effects of racial mixture, Williamson's follows a period of revaluing blackness and the erasure of the term *mulatto*. Reuter's study reflects the culmination of the belief that mulattoes represent a mixture of two unassimilable and distinct races, while Williamson's follows the virtual disappearance of racial "purity" and hence of mixed race as a distinctive identity. The two studies thus span the twentieth-century evolution of attitudes toward racial mixture. Both studies provide valuable insights into the history of mulattoes and the history of historians' attitudes toward mulattoes.

Both Williamson and Reuter consider the United States to be anomalous in its treatment of biracialism. Reuter opposes a supposed tolerance for racial mixture in Latin America to the psychic black-white polarization in the United States. Williamson emphasizes instead mulattoes' failure to develop into a permanent racial and cultural category, as mestizos did in Latin America. In my view this failure is, in part, a product of the U.S. psychic polarization. In the United States, mulattoes were initially a sign of sexual transgression, proof of the failure of taboo to prevent miscegenation. While Spaniards in Mexico were encouraged to mix with native women as part of the colonial project, African-American women in the United States had no such link to the colonized land and were perceived as essentially separate from American nationality and corporeality. As a result, mulattoes were not embraced as a group until their existence could no longer be denied. Mulattoes were first recognized by the U.S. census in 1850. They existed as a distinct census category for less than one hundred years, and by 1920 *mulatto* was officially equated with *black* (Williamson, *New People* 2). Today since most "black" Americans are of mixed race, the category *black* has come to signify the racial mixture that characterizes African-Americans.

Williamson provides more of the history of the development and disappearance of mulattoes as a distinct racial category, so I will discuss his 1980 text first, inverting historiographic chronology to restore historicity to mulatto identity. Williamson contextualizes this brief recognition of mulattoes as a distinct race, tracing the origin of *mulatto* as a social category (as opposed to census category) back to the first Africans brought to America in the 1600s. According to his argument, in the seventeenth and eighteenth centuries, mulattoes were valued as intermediaries between whites and blacks, planters and slaves. Mulattoes, both free and slave, were seen as a third class, elevated above the status of black Americans and more likely to be employed as domestics and artisans rather than field hands (*New People* 14–15). Like the mulatto characters in *Clotel*, a racially mixed elite enjoyed a position of relative social and political freedom.

During the 1850–1915 period, however, "the dominant white society moved from semiacceptance of free mulattoes . . . to outright rejection" (Williamson, *New People* 62).[27] During this time in which the lines between the races were being renegotiated, whites became increasingly anxious about sharing social status with people of color. More mulattoes were kept in slavery, particularly during its final decade, to ensure their difference from whites. The definitions of *black* and *white* changed, as the United States moved toward the one-drop rule. In eighteenth-century Virginia, for example, anyone who was at least three-quarters white was legally accepted as white. This law often meant that visibly (even socially) "black" Americans officially enjoyed the political status of whites. Yet later laws ensured that black was never white: Virginia lowered the fraction of "black blood" that defined someone as black from one-sixteenth in 1910 to one drop in 1930. After 1930, mulattoes became black for legal purposes. At the same time, most southern states created laws forbidding interracial marriage and miscegenation. Community vigilante groups, such as the Ku Klux Klan, which began in the 1860s, developed to enforce segregation. William L. Andrews also argues that "the appearance of the Ku Klux Klan, the rise of Jim Crow legislation, the disfranchisement of the blacks, and the establishment of white political domination of the South" represent the South's attempt to ensure that the "future American" would be Anglo-Saxon rather than mulatto (20). The South attempted to do away with mixture altogether.[28]

During this "changeover period" (to borrow Williamson's term), a mythology of race developed, with a proliferation of popular lore and "scientific" studies about mulattoes. These discourses often extended proslavery arguments past emancipation "to keep Negroes in their subordinate role" (Williamson, *New People* 95). "Muleology" compared racial mixing to the unnatural breeding of mules, which renders the offspring unable to reproduce itself (96). One such pseudoscience, an early form of "neurology," claimed that all bodily functions were governed by electric signals. Late-nineteenth-century neurologists determined that those signals ran in opposite directions in blacks and whites, so the product of their mixture had confused signals and jangled nerves. Philosophies about racial mixture predicted that mulattoes would die out in a few generations, because they were thought to be an ephemeral, weak, and unstable breed. Such philosophies that denied a future to mixed identities eased the minds of the racist South, which Williamson characterizes as "embattled," "tense, anxious, [and] strung-out" regarding the decline of slavery and of official racial stratification (*New People* 74). Despite social, legal, and scientific barriers to the mixing of races, miscegenation continued, and mulattoes did not die out. As Williamson put it, "miscegenation ground on day by day, probably hour by hour, and perhaps minute by minute in continuous unrelieved and willing toil, beneath sun and moon, in heat and cold, white men with black women, black men with white women, a mass of arms and legs and torsos, ever writhing like some multilimbed, many-colored Indian goddess in a steady, rhythmic, and fluid copulation with herself" (93–94). Williamson's prose at this juncture loses its rational, measured, historical tone, echoing the irrational sciences produced by the "embattled" and "strung-out" South. This remarkable description mirrors the frantic anxiety and desire regarding miscegenation that is characteristic of both the nineteenth century and more recent writings on mixture, like the 1993 issue of *Time* magazine discussed in the introduction. Williamson's imagery renders miscegenation sexually corrupt by conflating it with orgylike group sex, incest, and even autoeroticism (the goddess copulates with herself). The vision is grotesque; the excess of limbs suggests deformity. Furthermore, he problematically associates this sexual perversion with an Indian goddess, invoking negative stereotypes of dark women's sexuality. He describes this sexual process as labor—continuous, grinding toil—illuminating how the South's economic structure was founded historically on the reproduction of slaves (which assigned a commercial value to sexual relations with female slaves) and the reduction of both male and female slaves to the level of cogs in a machine. This rhetoric, perhaps unwittingly, demonstrates the parallel between the "unrelieved" "grinding" labor forced on slaves in the fields and the continually enforced miscegenation whereby planters attempted to impregnate their slaves since birth had become the only means of expanding the slave labor force after the slave trade was banned.

To make sense of its new, fluid racial universe, the post–Civil War South needed to develop a new structure that assigned every person to a specific, fixed place. Williamson claims that "the dichotomous nature of western civilization" made the South "furiously intolerant of anything that was not distinctly slave or free, black or white, male or female" (*New People* 74). While mulattoes had always challenged such binaristic thinking, emancipation more completely threatened racial dualism in the South, uprooting all individuals from their antebellum roles. Says Williamson, "The simple existence of mulattoes after the war militated against the white man's sense of identity. . . . The white sense of self depended in part upon maintaining that separateness" (95). Here, Williamson describes how identity itself was based on seeing oneself in opposition to another and how removing the enslaved Other from southern consciousness thus problematized the definitions of whiteness, of freedom, and of identity.[29] Although true racial polarity never existed in the South (beyond the level of myth and illusion), emancipation removed the ground from underneath the dream of racial opposition and symbolically opened up southern identity to legal transgression.

The disappearance of visible cues to the racial organization of the South rendered blackness a matter of behavior as much as of appearance. Race was redefined as a philosophical or psychological category. In the early twentieth century, Williamson claims that even "pure" whites could be called black depending on their "inner morality": "Thus by the early twentieth century the color line actually reached into the white world to include white people who behaved in a black way" (*New People* 108). This claim renders *black* a fluid designation that can be applied to people regardless of their race. As a result, *white* sometimes can equal *black* (Williamson, *New People* 2). Indeed, Williamson's preface essentially does away with the racial categories *black* and *white*: "In the broad sweep of recorded history, black was never totally black, and white was never entirely white. . . . Scientific scholars generally agree that there is actually no such thing as race, that mixing has been universal and perpetual and that human traits so overlap that it is impossible to describe the characteristics of one 'race' to the exclusion of all others" (*New People* xiii). What Williamson does not clarify is that although the fictitiousness of *black* and *white* renders these terms ideally mutable, American society has built hierarchies based on them for centuries, with very real effects. Williamson's work does reveal, however, the ways in which racial mixture profoundly influenced our current notions of identity, of difference, and of Americanness.

In his study, Reuter compares and contrasts the situation of mulattoes in the United States with that of mixed-race groups in other countries. It is interesting to note the degree to which his statements of more than eighty years ago still inform race relations today. In a characterization that prefigures postmodernism in its emphasis on communications, networks, border crossings, and the blurring of differences, Reuter attributes the increase of "race admixture" to the increasing ease of communication and travel (along with the rise of urbanization), and he foresees that no "pure" races "of any consequence" will remain in the world as a result of new meetings between races and cultures (16, 160). He also notes that amalgamation "usually . . . tends toward the elimination of any problem that the presence of the unassimilated alien may have created" (17). In his view, confrontations that arise from the meeting of racial differences would be resolved by mixing elements of the different groups. This position is noteworthy for its optimism, which approaches that of Anzaldúa, though the continuance of black-white tensions after centuries of racial mixing in the United States disproves Reuter's bold prediction.

Reuter claims that interracial harmony has not yet been achieved in the United States because black Americans and white Americans have been polarized, with one group symbolizing poverty, disease, dirt, and ignorance while the other is assumed to signify purity and cultural superiority. The "half-caste" product of two such "non-assimilable groups" will remain an "alien" in both groups (18). Reuter's statement reflects the racist connotations that have been attached to the terms *white* and *black,* and as long as those connotations remain, the biracial products of the two will be unable to fit into either of those diametrically opposed symbolic categories. The long history of slavery in the United States maintained and reinforced racist polarization to so great an extent that it became embedded within U.S. culture (attitudes, language usage, laws, and literature) (93). And the taboo against miscegenation worked in tandem with the psychic opposition between black and white. As a result of this preference for pure distinctions, Reuter concludes that "psychologically, the mulatto is an unstable type" (102). This statement coincides historically and rhetorically with the development of muleology, which hypothesized the imminent demise of the weakened products of racial mixture.

Yet racial difference is not necessarily insurmountable, in Reuter's vision. He cites as an example the various racial hybrids that have blended successfully in Latin America, forming a single mixed-blood race with little racial antipathy (24, 22, 50).[30] This theory that successful amalgamation can reconcile differences resembles both the rhetoric of *mestizaje* and postmodern celebrations of hybridity.[31] Like the historians discussed earlier in this chapter, Reuter opposes successful Latin American hybridity to U.S. racism, but he suggests that the only difference between the two regions is the degree and persistence of black-white psychic opposition. According to Reuter's propositions, increased communication between Anglo-Americans and African-Americans could lead to a decrease in racial antinomy, and mulattoes could then follow the Latin American model of reconciled differences.

Reuter's racist bias, however, falsely assumes that all mulattoes desire only to become a part of the white race. He claims that "the ideal—the center of gravity—of the hybrid group is outside itself" (315). It is interesting to think about the implications of a group's center existing outside itself. While I maintain that the biracial subject has no single center, Reuter's model curiously decenters the mulatto at the same time that it tries to erect whiteness at the center. His praise of "superior mulattoes," however, defeats his Anglocentrism. His argument recalls that of so many racist others who claimed that "white blood" improved African-Americans,[32] but his examples—including William Wells Brown, Sojourner Truth, W. E. B. DuBois, and Ida B. Wells (183–216)—certainly do not reinforce a white American center. Rather, these writers and activists used their positions of visibility to endorse the causes of black Americans, keeping whiteness on the margins (or "outside") of their identity.

In *Playing in the Dark*, Toni Morrison claims that the polarization of African-Americans and Anglo-Americans in the United States led to a psychological and intellectual interdependence of blackness and whiteness based on opposition, hatred, and fear. The whiteness of American identity was based on the existence and the exclusion of blackness, the Other, the "not-me" (38). Without this differentiation, whiteness alone bears no meaning (59). This argument complicates the singularity of any racial identity (since each cannot stand alone) and reveals the centrality of blackness to American whiteness. Racial opposition is thus a product of the relationship between the races. To project "not-me" and "not-free" onto blackness, however, a clear line would have to exist between black and white. Perhaps the biracial thwarting of black-white separation denies whiteness the distance it requires from blackness to establish oppositional privilege. The racism that emerges at the threatened black-white border might result from white Americans' attempts to define separate group integrity.

I would argue that the attempt to segregate black and white in the United States rests on a fluidity comparable to *mestizaje* in the Southwest and Mexico, but this fluidity is obscured by historically different racial definition, legal segregation, and historians' insistence on viewing U.S. race relations through binary division. As Victor Valle and Rodolfo Torres claim, the majority of Americans are mestizos "under the skin," but *mestizaje* occurs in the interstices of mainstream U.S. culture, outside the illusory boundaries that the dominant center attempts to draw around American identity (148, 152). Indeed, perhaps mixture is the defining racial characteristic in the United States. This brief historical survey explains why such different racial sentiments and narratives emerged from the Southeast and the Southwest, despite their shared foundations on mixture. While mulatto identity fuses two racial halves whose historical connotations have been based on legal opposition and sexual anxiety, mestiza identity fuses racial components whose mixture has been more openly acknowledged throughout Mexican history. While miscegenation in the eastern United States produced a barrage of legal, literary, scientific, and philosophical texts decrying and defying the breakdown of black-white polarization, *mestizaje* reflects centuries of tactical interracial negotiations, political alliances, and obligatory fusions that formed American culture in the Southwest.

Celebrations of *Mestizaje* in Chicana Literature

In a sense, the United States has always been a mestizo nation, a product of immigration, colonization, miscegenation, and the international exchange of cultures, commodities, and ideas. This mixture, however, is often obscured by a mythology that universalizes Euro-American culture. The United States thus has much to learn from its mestizo citizens, who negotiate differences of race, language, and culture on a daily basis. Historically, mestizo Americans have been negotiating the multiple elements of their heritage and redefining culture and identity in powerful ways. In literature, they have shown how mestizo subjectivity can be shifting, fluid, and strategic. A writer uses Spanish to convey one attitude, English to convey another, and a hybrid mixture of the two to convey yet another. She can refuse to privilege Anglo-American standards by not translating Spanish phrases or by subverting English rules of grammar. In their intercultural negotiations, mestiza writers have challenged our definitions of language, genre, and literature itself.

The most well known contemporary Chicana texts, including Gloria Anzaldúa's *Borderlands*, Cherríe Moraga's *Loving in the War Years*, Ana Castillo's *Sapogonia*, and Sandra Cisneros's *Woman Hollering Creek*, explore the varied dynamics of *mestizaje*. These texts interrogate mestiza issues such as the guilt involved in the production of mixture, the changing attitudes surrounding people of mixed race, and the potential power of mixture. Yet these writers are not the first to celebrate *mestizaje*. Their works should be considered within the long tradition of Mexican-American writing that has explored the complexities of mestiza identity.

Examples of Mexican-American attitudes toward *mestizaje* prior to the Chicano "revolution" of the 1960s are relatively scarce, and many literary writings from earlier in the century are only recently being discovered or rediscovered. Literary historians from the Recovering the U.S. Hispanic Literary Heritage Project, the New Mexico Federal Writers' Project, and other institutions have recovered early texts that address *mestizaje*. These narratives that depict racial mixing in the southwestern United States reflect attitudes that contrast with U.S. anxieties about miscegenation and tragic mulatto scenarios. An analysis of these writings suggests that for the predecessors of today's Chicanos, racial mixing was accepted as the foundation of society. I am especially interested in early writings by and about women, examining whether they were targeted as objects of racial anxiety, victimized as the mothers of racial mixture, or scapegoated by advocates of racial purity.

A Mestiza Nation: Early Representations of Mexican-American Mixture

After the United States took over northern Mexico, many Anglo-Americans traveled throughout the region and published accounts of the peoples and cultures there. Most of the writings published in the nineteenth century about New Mexico were written by Anglo-Americans, who often measured the races of the Southwest with their own bipolar, ethnocentric expectations. In the 1847 diaries of her trip *Down the Santa Fe Trail and into Mexico*, Susan Magoffin records her shock and distaste regarding New Mexico's racial and cultural identities. Magoffin was accompanying her husband, Samuel, on the "bloodless conquest" of the northern Mexican territories, a battle of cultural conflicts, coercion, and political negotiations prior to the resolutions of Guadalupe Hidalgo. Magoffin is repulsed by the exposed bosoms of the Mexican women ("none of the prettiest or the whitest" [95]), and she ridicules the Spanish women who covered their faces with "white paste" (102), as if to whiten their too-dark skin. The ethnocentric Magoffin sees mestizas only in relation to whiteness and tries to "improve" the Spanish ladies of Santa Fe with her Anglo-American manners.

William W. H. Davis's 1857 depiction of New Mexico, *El Gringo; or, New Mexico and Her People*, reflects a self-consciousness about race (indicated by reference to himself as a "gringo," a derogatory term for white men among New Mexicans) and a racist anxiety about *mestizaje*. He describes the racially mixed New Mexicans as "destitute of manly attributes," in part because they have inherited what he regards as the worst qualities of the races that combine within them: the deceit of the Indian, the Spaniard's "spirit of revenge," and the "fiery impulses" of "the Moor" (217–18). This description not only is built on racial essentialism but also assumes an essential sex/gender alignment that is subverted by racial impurity (rendering mixed men unmanly). According to Davis's argument, as long as racial mixture occurs, "there is no present hope of the people improving in color," assuming that "improvement" corresponds to light skin and that New Mexicans, like the women Magoffin reviles, must want to be white (216). In a similar racist depiction, Susan Wallace writes in her 1888 accounts of her travels through New Mexico, "The restless energy of the Spaniard, the quick preception of the Moor, even the cunning of the roving Apache, appears to be lost in the sluggish current which lazily beats in the pulses of the modern Mexican" (60). Significantly, both of these examples were written at the same historical moment as many tragic mulatto narratives of the Southeast, and these works reflect a similar anxiety about racial mixture and the breakdown of "essential" racial differentiation. The racial perceptions of these travelers to the Southwest reinforce New Mexican historian Erna Fergusson's argument from her lectures "What Are New Mexicans?" and "Race Relations" that any racism in New Mexico was imported by outsiders' racist standards. Fergusson might claim that Magoffin, Davis, and Wallace imposed alien southeastern judgments on mestiza fluidity.

These racist attitudes reflect the clash between U.S. and Mexican race dynamics that occurred in New Mexico during the mid–nineteenth century. Mexican *mestizaje* was extraordinary to Anglo-Americans who came from a region where miscegenation was illegal and races were officially segregated. In contrast, early Mexican-American writers did not suppress or record anxiety about racial mixture. Many women writers, such as Nina Otero Warren, Jovita González Mireles, and Josephina Niggli, recorded the New Mexicans' mixture of indigenous and Spanish beliefs, stories, and folk practices to preserve the region's unique culture. In this endeavor, these authors performed the function of ethnologists, writing about the experiences of Mexican-Americans for a predominantly white readership. As such, these women often served as intermediaries between the different cultures of the post–Guadalupe Hidalgo southwestern United States.

In "Cultural Ambivalence in Early Chicana Prose Fiction," Gloria Velásquez Treviño suggests that many earlier Mexican-American women writers used American conventions to gain the readership of white Americans, while mid-twentieth-century writers used elements of both Mexican and American literary traditions, synthesizing Anglo-American plot conventions and stereotypes with Mexican traditions of storytelling and folklore (15, 21, 29, 59, 65). According to Velásquez Treviño, those writers who emphasize their Mexican lineage resist total assimilation within or colonization by Anglo-American culture (68–69). Many of these writers recover their Mexican and Native American pasts to displace the "fantasy heritage" of racial purity that Euro-American culture had created to facilitate colonization (70). While some texts challenge the myth of a pure Spanish culture in the United States, others buy into the myth of European origins to satisfy Europhilic readers.

J. Frank Dobie and the Texas Folk-Lore Society fit into the first of those two categories. The Folk-Lore Society's early-twentieth-century analyses emphasize the importance of racial hybridity in the foundations of Latino culture. For example, Jovita González Mireles describes *Tejanos'* cultural origins as multiple and shifting. In "Folk-Lore of the Texas-Mexican Vaquero" (1927) she claims, "On one side, he descends from the first Americans, the Indians, on the other, his ancestry can be traced to the Spanish adventurer and conquistador" (7). It is significant that González credits the Indians with being the first Americans, rendering the Spaniards the outsiders or latecomers. She thus rejects that fantasy of pure Spanish origins to which McWilliams claims so many inhabitants pretended. Ironically, although Texas born and Texas bred, the vaquero is considered an outcast, an "undesirable alien," by the Anglo-Americans who have only recently migrated to Texas ("Folk-Lore" 7). The injustice of the true insider being cast to the margins by a lighter-skinned invader is thus repeated twice, first with the Spaniards and the Amerindians and then, beginning in the 1840s, with the Anglo-Americans and the Mexicans. The dominating culture's claims to centrality thus lack foundation: they are the foreigners who alienate the "real" Americans. These changing qualifications of Americanness put into question any singular cultural authority.

Furthermore, the "original" Texans were themselves biracial. "From the mingling of [Indian and Spanish] races a unique type has resulted" (González, "Folk-Lore" 7), with racial characteristics of both ancestries. According to González, the *Tejanos* inherited from the Indians a "love for freedom [and a] dislike for law and restraint." From the Spanish, they inherited a "sincere religious feeling, which mingled with pagan superstitions and beliefs has added flavor and color to the . . . borderland" (7–8).

Though these descriptions echo the essentialism of Wallace and Davis and describe the production of mixed identity as if it were a culinary recipe, at the same time González rejects symbolic discourses that favor purity, whiteness, hierarchy, and assimilation.[33] *Tejano* culture, in this view, is not original but is rather the product of mingling, of added flavor and color: it is a construction or fusion of multiple elements.

Ironically, some of González's personal writings reflect a hint of anxiety about racial mixture. In a short narrative about the first day of school, "Bienvenida a la escuela" (Welcome to School), she writes of a joke that her brother played on her to punish her for her vanity: "En son de broma me dijo que él diría a mis amigos que mi color no era natural sino que lo había comprado en una tienda de cosméticos por cinco dolares [In a joking manner he told me that he would tell my friends that my color was not natural, but that I had bought it in a cosmetics store for five dollars]" (manuscripts 16.1–2, n.d.). This story demonstrates that color is an artificial symbol of status and can be bought or concealed with makeup, playing on the eighteenth-century Mexican practice of purchasing certificates of "purity of blood," by which one could buy lighter skin in legal terms (Forbes 90). This story also assumes (by satirically undermining) a distance between González and the dark-skinned mestiza women whose pasted white faces so repelled Magoffin in New Mexico. The financially privileged, university-educated González probably experienced a gap between her own mestiza experiences and those of the *Tejanos* about whom she wrote (cowboys, shepherds, and domestic servants). Perhaps in her personal accounts she was unable to achieve the analytic distance about racial mixture that marked her ethnographic writings about others. González counteracted her own, potentially anglicizing, privileges with a self-conscious dedication to Mexican-Americans.[34] Significantly, she later became a political advocate for Chicanos, suggesting a relationship between the recovery of her mixed racial tradition and the liberal politics of defending Chicano social equality (Velásquez Treviño 76).

María Amparo Ruiz de Burton's *Who Would Have Thought It?*

One of the first published novels by a Mexican-American woman, María Amparo Ruiz de Burton's *Who Would Have Thought It?* (1872) romances the idea of racial mixture without celebrating it as clearly as do twentieth-century writers. This novel embraces many of the sentimental and romantic values of popular Anglo-American women writers of the period— purity, modesty, and white-skinned beauty—yet projects those values onto a character whose racial identity is contested throughout the entire novel. The heroine, Lola, is first referred to as an orphaned "nigger girl" whom the white New Englander Dr. Norval brings into his family (16). The Norval family debates the extent of her blackness: Mrs. Norval "shiver[s] in disgust" at "how black she is!" while the Norvals' daughter, Mattie, points out that Lola is not "so black" since her palms' "pink shade" makes them an even prettier white than Mattie's are (17). Lola's racial origin is a source of mystery throughout the novel, as she is called "black," "Indian," "Spanish," "Mexican," "mongrel," and even "Pinto." This conflation of all nonwhite races suggests an equality between black, Mexican, and Spanish that defies U.S. black-white polarization (along the lines of *mestizaje*) while refusing to privilege mixed over black. Although Dr. Norval insists that Lola's blood is "better" than their own, this status is anything but certain beyond his word (25). Ruiz de Burton values Lola's racialization in European terms, insisting that Lola's mother, Mrs. Medina, is Mexican of "pure Spanish" descent and that Mr. Medina is of Austrian descent, with blonde hair and blue eyes. Yet Lola's paternity is never clarified. Mrs. Medina had been captured by "savage" Indians, and Lola was born some time after the capture (203). Her supposed father, Mr. Medina, did not even know of her existence. While Rosaura Sánchez and Beatrice Pita claim in their introduction to the novel that Mrs. Medina was kidnapped while she was pregnant and that Lola's father is the Austrian, the novel does not provide evidence for this paternity (xix). Indeed, once Mr. Medina returns to claim Lola, Ruiz de Burton describes him as "the gentleman whom Lola called Father, but who did not seem to be such, for his hair was very light and his eyes were blue, whilst Lola's were jet black. Moreover, he seemed too young to have a daughter eighteen years old" (250). Although Ruiz de Burton does not directly suggest that Lola is not Mr. Medina's daughter, she does make clear that Lola's mother was raped by the Apache man who took her as his wife.

What seems most important here is not the question of true paternity but the fact that Ruiz de Burton leaves paternity, and hence Lola's racial identity, mysterious. Even Lola's physical appearance fluctuates, with her black skin turning out to be paint that wears off gradually over the course of the novel. For several chapters, Lola's skin is black with white spots, at which stage Mrs. Norval asserts that the girl must be either a spotted Pinto or victim to a cutaneous disease (78–79). Lola narrates the Indians' attempt to keep the Medina women from being discovered, and thus rescued, by staining their skin black: "the Indians never permitted the dye to wear off our faces. As soon as it become a little lighter, they immediately made us paint ourselves over again" (100). Not only is Lola's blackness an artifice, but her whiteness, too, is described as artificial, "bleached" by the effects of the "Indian paint." Her shoulders eventually become whiter than "anything," as Mattie questions, "Can anything be whiter than Lola's neck and shoulders?" (232).

Although Lola's skin ultimately is "white and smooth" after the paint wears off, and she confesses that the dye caused her much shame by making her "an object of aversion" (100), the ambiguity of her color complicates any simple theories of white superiority. The "aversion" toward Lola's blackness or spottedness comes from the more detestable characters in the novel, and the heroine remains racially ambiguous. There is even a mock-up of this romance in the subplot, where various Yankees battle over the love of the fair quadroon, Lucinda, who may or may not enjoy hearing allusions to her African origin (59, 185–86). Mixture is a key component of the novel. Ruiz de Burton has chosen to center her romance on a character whose race is not only unknown but also fluid, changeable, and artificially "stained"—a true precursor to the socially constructed and fluctuating identities of postmodernism. Sánchez and Pita argue that Lola's blackface allowed Ruiz de Burton to critique racism without challenging racial purity (assuming that Lola's whiteness is unquestioned when she becomes engaged to Julian Norval): "the thorny issues of racism and miscegenation are conveniently sidestepped" as "the child's whitening . . . work[s] out social contradictions while at the same time containing them" (xx–xxi). But I disagree: *Who Would Have Thought It?* does not contain anything. Everything remains unresolved—the planned marriage of Julian and Lola, Lola's paternity, and Lola's own attitudes toward her color or ancestry—as certainly as the title of the novel is a question.

Significantly, this romance is set not in the Southwest but in the Northeast, in the context of the Civil War. So the overt cultural conflicts in the novel are between North and South, black and white, leaving the conflicts between Mexicans and the United States relatively unspoken. Rather than debating the justice of taking over the New Mexico territories after Guadalupe Hidalgo, the characters in *Who Would Have Thought It?* discuss the friction between Yankee and southerner, racism and abolition (18–19, 215, 241). Surely the situation in the Southwest is present here, in the person of Lola, but all activities in the Southwest—Mrs. Medina's capture, the women's time with the Apaches, and even Dr. Norval's travels—occur prior to the novel's chronology, outside the bounds of Ruiz de Burton's narrative. Why does she put so much silence, mystery, and masquerade at the foundation of her novel?[35] Was she, as Sánchez and Pita suggest, hiding her social critique? And why would she be so coded and polite in this novel, when *The Squatter and the Don* (1885) overtly criticizes U.S. imperialism in the former Mexican territories of the Southwest? Perhaps the explanation lies in the Civil War and the racial dynamics of the Southeast at the time of abolition. In the 1850s and '60s, two simultaneous conflicts arose in the definition of American racial identity: in the Southwest after the Treaty of Guadalupe Hidalgo and in the Southeast surrounding the emancipation of slaves. Both transformations involved accepting as "American" peoples with darker skin, yet even more threatening to the race-stratified United States was the visible presence of racial mixture that both regions shared. Ruiz de Burton pulls the two together and shows how the conflicts in the Southeast and the Southwest result from a fear of as well as a fascination with the mixing of dark and light races. Her framing of the narrative makes this parallel less than plain, however, as it was to most Americans of the period, for whom the frequency of miscegenation was an open secret. Perhaps her choice to relocate Lola in the East (in New England and Washington, D.C.) reflects an attempt to open the secret just a bit and to expose the masked racial fluidity at the center of U.S. nationality.

Josephina Niggli's *Mexican Village*

Josephina Niggli also draws attention to interracial mixing. *Mexican Village* (1945) is another of the first novels written by a Mexican-American woman in the United States, and it lays the ground for many conventions of the literary tradition that follows it.[36] Unlike Ruiz de Burton, Niggli writes from a Mexican-American tradition dominated by pastoral narratives, *corrido* ballads, and oral folklore, and her novel blends that oral folk tradition with more conventional narrative styles (and many of the character types from González's sketches). *Mexican Village* contains ten separate narratives, each set in a different location and involving a different family, and weaves oral narration, songs, monologues, poems, letters, and prayers through these ten stories. The characters who come together in these narratives and in the town of Hidalgo are from different races, different classes, and different countries. These separate sections have the effect of emphasizing the diversity within the Mexican village and the impossibility of reducing Mexican civilization to one cultural element.

Strength in this Mexican village emerges from a variety of national cultures. Although the Spanish Castillos hold the most wealth in Hidalgo and perform the ceremonious functions of aristocracy, the family is in decline, and the truly powerful characters are mixed. The strongest individual in Hidalgo is Tía Magdalena, the "eagle witch" *curandera*, who believes she controls every character's fate through herbs, potions, and spells. The eagle half of her identity descends from the Aztec tradition, while the label *witch* derives from the Christian condemnations of native religions that accompanied European colonization. Lolita, another strong female character, is a gypsy from Spain. She consults a witch woman to free herself from a vow of chastity made before the shrine of St. Veronica. A bargain with the witch enables Lolita to marry the candy maker Rubén (235, 260–61). In exchange, Lolita goes into the mountains yearly to perform a witch dance (266). The success of Lolita's plot suggests that the witch's power is greater than Catholic power, since the witch supposedly nullifies the chastity vow to St. Veronica, subordinating European traditions to Mexican-Indian ones. In addition, the half-Irish, half-Mexican Anita O'Malley, a "wild" rebel and a dancer with "purple red of polished mahogany" hair and olive skin, has the power of Lilith and a "pagan" fire burning in her body that makes men sacrifice their lives out of love for her (147, 171). This woman's strength, too, comes from a powerful fusion of Euro-Christian descent and pagan wildness.

The main protagonist in *Mexican Village*, Bob Webster, is a culturally and racially mixed bilingual (with a *Tejano* accent) U.S. American of Spanish and Mexican descent who has come to Mexico to run a quarry.[37] Bob shares physical and racial traits with Spaniards, Amerindians, and Anglos. Bob's father, a U.S. man with blonde hair and blue eyes, denies his son because he manifests the "Indian" blood of his Mexican mother (40, 449–50, 467). Yet the plot reveals that Bob actually descends from the noble Castillo line, a supposedly pure Spanish family, and in his blood the Spanish mixes with Mexican, Indian, and *Yanqui* (a Mexican spelling of *Yankee*) (476). Significantly, when in Europe, a French woman calls Bob an Indian, assuming that all Americans are Indians (29). This assumption and Bob's identity highlight the racial ambiguity of American identity and the inaccuracy of any name applied to this nation of immigrants.

When Bob first arrives in Hidalgo, he is an "outsider," a traveling *Yanqui* with an unpronounceable name (3). Yet his face shows that he has Mexican blood, and after association with the Indians, chameleon-like, he begins to look like a Huachichil (26–27, 53). Like Lola in *Who Would Have Thought It?* his mixed identity changes to blend with his new context.

Like Ruiz de Burton, Niggli draws together U.S. and Mexican mixtures in the body of a border-crossing character. In the end, Bob chooses not to claim the wealth of his Spanish ancestry, changes his name to Roberto Ortega (his Mexican birth name rather than his father's name), and associates himself with the "illegitimate" *Tejanos*, "whose blood was a pleasure rather than a disgrace" (468, 470). While initially his racial hybridity brings him tragedy and alienation from his white father and the Castillo inheritance, Bob ultimately rejects the tragedy of his illegitimacy and finds pride in his multiracialism. He chooses his mother's Mexican heritage and Spanish name over the light-skinned heritage and American name of his father, denying purebred patrilineage.[38] In the eyes of his sister, Sofía, Bob becomes a "true Mexican" (471). Yet Bob has been a true Mexican all along: inclusive of multiple races and nations (since Bob is a U.S. American by birth). According to Velásquez Treviño, Bob builds his identity on the foundation of two cultures, *mexicano* and *yanqui* (129). This statement reveals the fact that identity can be built and rebuilt on changing foundations, and Bob's is a truly constructed, fluctuating identity—Spanish, Indian, *Yanqui* outlander, true Mexican.

Contemporary Mixture: Anzaldúa, Moraga, and López-Medina

These affirmations of *mestizaje* from the first half of the twentieth century prefigure Gloria Anzaldúa, Cherríe Moraga, and Sylvia López-Medina, suggesting that these contemporary Chicana writers should be studied in the context of the earlier work. Too often, contemporary Chicana writers are studied only within Euro-American frames of reference, obscuring (or colonizing) the Mexican-American models that predate them. Anzaldúa, for example, is frequently cited as an example of postmodern feminism.[39] Although her destabilizing theories, her affirmation of marginality, and her fragmented literary aesthetic do share many attributes with postmodernism, her political and cultural subjects ally her with a much older tradition. Furthermore, her subversion of genre and her narrative code switching, considered characteristic of postmodernism, also emerge from the Mexican tradition of *corridos* and *pastorales*. The multiple cultures of Anzaldúa's work resist circumscription by Euro-American academic discourses.

In *Borderlands/La Frontera*, Anzaldúa writes from the *Tejano* tradition, from the point of view of a mestizo people who became foreigners in their homeland "overnight" when the Anglos "migrated illegally into Texas" and converted it into a U.S. republic (6). This description recalls Jovita

González Mireles's description of the vaqueros: the mestizos were forced from the center to the margin by Anglo outsiders. Anzaldúa relates this displacement of Texas's cultural and racial center with reference to both Mexican and Anglo-American narratives. She cites the Mexican *corrido* "Del peligro de la Intervención":

> Ya la mitad del terreno
> les vendió el traidor Santa Anna,
> con lo que se ha hecho muy rica
> la nación americana.
> [Santa Anna sold them half of the land, with which
>   the American nation has made itself very rich.]

(Borderlands 6)

And she cites William H. Wharton with regard to the same event: "The wilderness of Texas has been redeemed / by Anglo-American blood and enterprise" (7). The friction between these opposing views is characteristic of Anzaldúa's "borderlands" methodology and *la conciencia de la mestiza*, which sustain contradictions. Significantly, both quotations emphasize the historical fact that Anglo-American wealth is founded on land that was taken over from Mexico, a fact that positions Mexico at the foundation of U.S. national identity. By choosing to quote narratives from both sides of the Mexican-U.S. conflict, Anzaldúa situates her work as a product of both traditions. Positioning Wharton's statement alongside the *corrido* reflects the actual *mestizaje* of American traditions and the cultural borderlands on which American nationalism is defined.

Like González before her, Anzaldúa reclaims the folk origins of *Tejano* culture. When Anzaldúa read her first pocket Western as a child, she was surprised that the only Mexicans in the book were servants, *cantineras,* or villains because she "knew that the first cowboys (vaqueros) were Mexicans, that in Texas we outnumbered the Anglos" (Anzaldúa and Moraga 200). From a perspective on vaquero culture that resembles González's, it is ironic that the "Mexican and Indian were vermin" in Anzaldúa's twenty-five-cent book. Both González and Anzaldúa are anxious to combat the racist mythologies of Anglo-American literature and to affirm the racial mixture of the first American cowboys.

In this tradition, both Anzaldúa and Cherríe Moraga examine the origins of their biracialism and the role of their foremothers in the creation of racial identity. Like Niggli and like writers of U.S. mulatto fiction, Anzaldúa and Moraga emphasize the importance of mixture in their political practices, their relationships to history, and the frictions within their racial experiences. In opposition to the story of the tragic mulatta, the source of shame or tragedy for these Chicana women is not the existence of darker ancestors but ties to lighter, colonizing ones. Both writers value the *india* in their identities, the powerful, dark-skinned women from whom they descend. They reject the adoption of Anglo culture to pass in the white world (which Moraga confesses she often did when she was younger), and they consider themselves to be strengthened by their resistance to internal colonization.[40] For both, gendered identity, rather than "fitting" into the categories defined by Euro-American feminism, "is grounded in the Indian woman's history of resistance" (Anzaldúa, *Borderlands* 21). They differentiate themselves from feminists who base their theories on the Euro-American tradition, and they insist on the resistance of their colonized, darker-skinned ancestors.[41] La Malinche, Coatlicue (the goddess of fertility and death), Coyolxauhqui (the moon goddess), Cihuacoatl (the snake goddess), and others present indigenous foundations for Anzaldúa's and Moraga's feminisms and divergent models for their continual (re)definitions of *woman*.[42]

Yvonne Yarbro-Bejarano responds to critics who cite this invocation of goddesses as essentialist or as an idealization of Aztec cosmology by suggesting that Anzaldúa in particular uses these figures for "imaginative appropriation and redefinition . . . in the service of a new mythos" ("Gloria Anzaldúa's *Borderlands/La Frontera*" 19). Anzaldúa's Coatlicue, for example, presents a model for negotiating contradiction, transition, and redefinition, not a nostalgic insistence on cultural origin. In a 1994 interview, Anzaldúa clarifies her invocation of Coatlicue as part of a forward-looking process, "this birthing stage where you feel like you're reconfiguring your identity and don't know where you are" (*Interviews* 225). In this description, the indigenous goddess of birth and decay opens up identity as a "stage" with no stable definition or fixed endpoint. Rather than essentializing an originary *indigenismo*, Anzaldúa uses Coatlicue to theorize the fluidity of mestiza identification.

In their oft-cited anthology *This Bridge Called My Back* (which has been foundational for feminisms by women of color), Anzaldúa and Moraga split mestiza experience in two, decentering any hegemonic or monolithic sense of mestiza identity. Moraga bemoans the pale skin inherited from her Anglo father and reclaims her mother's Mexicanism despite her own apparent whiteness, but Anzaldúa emphasizes the fact that she is dark and has never experienced the privileges of light skin. Moraga considers the real tragedy of her race to be her whiteness, and she turns to her mother as the source of the racial darkness that is invisible in her.[43] As she distances her Chicana political identity from her white-looking body, she sorts through her memories to discover which aspects of her life have been based on privileges corresponding to light skin (Anzaldúa and Moraga 34). While Moraga is "La Güera" (the blonde/white/light one) and her racial appearance draws attention to the presence of the colonizing white patriarch in her family, Anzaldúa claims a different racial family story in "La Prieta" (the dark one). For Anzaldúa, her darkness does not come from her mother's line, as with Moraga, Bob Webster, and a host of other biracial characters. Her grandmother is the racial judge, a representative of one of the first Texas families, with Spanish and German blood, a "hint of royalty lying just beneath the surface of her fair skin, blue eyes and the coil of her once blond hair." She inspects the newly born Gloria for "the sign of indio, or worse, of mulatto blood," concluding "too bad mihijita was morena, *muy prieta,* so dark and different from her own fair-skinned children" (Anzaldúa and Moraga 198). Anzaldúa's mother cautioned her to wear her sombrero to keep her face from darkening to the color of an Indian's. While Malinche supposedly betrays her people by joining forces with the Spanish Cortés, and while Moraga's Mexican mother betrays her family by marrying an Anglo man, Anzaldúa's mother betrays her daughter by not teaching her to love her dark skin. "I am terrified of making my mother the villain in my life rather than showing how she has been a victim. Will I be betraying her in this essay for her early disloyalty to me?" (199). Each scenario targets the mother as the source of guilt or complicity with lighter-skinned colonizers, and both Moraga and Anzaldúa position themselves within that chain of guilt by examining their complicities with racism. Moraga and Anzaldúa share similar roles in the female inheritance of racial guilt and racial ambivalence, yet their different colors lead them to part ways in their writing.[44]

Continuing in the tradition of celebrating *mestizaje,* contemporary Chicana literature has imagined in fiction what Anzaldúa and Moraga describe in theory. Although not sharing Anzaldúa and Moraga's theoretical fame or Sandra Cisneros's, Helena María Viramontes's, and Ana Castillo's fame as fiction writers, Sylvia López-Medina more directly builds on the

genealogies of mixture of earlier Mexican-American literary and histori-
cal narratives in her novel, *Cantora* (1992). In this "cultural kaleidoscope,"
López-Medina claims that mestizos in the United States are set apart,
observers but not "lost in the tangled forest of U.S. culture" (vii, viii).
While it is usually mestiza culture that is described as "tangled," this description attributes the tangle of cultures to the United States and locates
U.S. mestizos apart, assigning them a sort of cultural integrity that the
United States lacks. Although they are mixed, it is as if mestizos resist being circumscribed, colonized, or absorbed by U.S. nationality, retaining
just enough outsideness to have a clear perspective on the tangled whole.
López-Medina describes this vantage as "living on the edge of irony" (viii),
a liminal space like Anzaldúa's borderlands where cultures meet yet retain
critical distance, intermingle without subsuming each other.

Rosario, the heroine of *Cantora*, is mestiza, with the blue eyes of a French
soldier and the Mayan cheekbones and "wild" energy of Native American maternal ancestry (16, 22). Like Niggli's Anita O'Malley, Rosario's
strength and wildness are linked to this mixture. To preserve her multiple
heritage, Rosario chants in a French and Spanish dialect the names of her
ancestors (140). López-Medina, too, incorporates elements of the oral
tradition into her novel and assigns a central role to women in the formation and retention of multiracial identity. She emphasizes genealogy but
does so to remember mixture, not to prove *limpieza de sangre*.

When Rosario falls in love with Alejandro, her father deems the match
unacceptable because Alejandro is an *indio* (161). Rather than accepting an
arranged marriage, Rosario runs away from her patriarchal home, choosing poverty and a dark-skinned husband. Similarly, her granddaughter,
Amparo, rejects her family's preference for arranged marriages and hand-
chosen colonial-style bloodlines.[45] At the end of the novel, Amparo gives
birth to a bastard baby and denies the importance of patrilineage. Much
like Bob Webster, Amparo claims that the baby's unknown father does
not matter because she will always know her mother (306). Since half of
the baby's origins remain uncertain, her racial and familial connections
are established solely through her mother.[46] Moreover, since her baby is
half unmoored from her parentage, Amparo symbolically thwarts future
attempts to construct a genealogy. When Amparo travels to Mexico, she
recovers records of her family's lost origins and symbolically "frees" her
family by opening its racial secrets (182, 223–26, 300).[47] Indeed, the book
opens with Amparo's family tree. In this way, López-Medina seems to suggest that travel and freedom coincide with the acceptance of the secrets

within family history: the mixed, the bastard, and the transgressive. Yet Amparo also learns that the traveling is worth more than the genealogy, as the legacy she leaves her fatherless child is one of ultimate genetic and ancestral uncertainty. This uncertainty is not, however, a secret, a source of shame, or a "shadow" (306); it is mestiza.

Zoe vs. Clotel: 150 Years of Tragic and Heroic Mulattas

Just as *mestizaje* has been central to Mexican national discourse (and thus to the southwestern United States as well), the situation of mulattoes is one of the narratives that has dominated U.S. literature. Since racial mixture was often considered taboo in the United States, the actual prevalence of mixture has been a source of intrigue that has carried a powerful mystique for readers and writers from antebellum society to the present. While in the nineteenth century mulattas symbolized the taboo associated with intercourse between two presumably unassimilable races, many contemporary texts engage the recent vogue enjoyed by multiculturalism and hybridity. This section will consider the link between taboo and vogue, nineteenth-century and contemporary views on mixed-race African-American identity.

Zoe and the Mother of Mixture

Many cultures have worked out their racial anxiety through a legendary woman. Often, like Pocahontas or La Malinche, this woman is positioned between cultures, translating between the colonized and the colonizer, mediating the process of colonization. Both Pocahontas and La Malinche became lovers with one of the conquering men and have thus assumed symbolic responsibility for fusing the cultures of the colonizer and the colonized. They represent both sides of the colonial conflict and the crossings between sides. The women's bodies are targeted as the source of new mixed races.

Racial meaning is produced in the bodies of women for U.S. African-American culture as well. In a subversion of the traditional patrilineal system of inheritance, a child's race (and thus social status) followed that of the mother, both during and after slavery.[48] Since most mothers of mixed-race children were black, the law ensured that biracial children were classified as black, guaranteeing slave status to the products of master-slave rape and reserving the designation *white* only for those of "pure" ancestry. The mother takes on the full burden of racial parentage and comes to symbolize racial origin. During slavery and the Civil War, when families were frequently fragmented and scattered, the search for the lost mother parallels the search to resolve uncertain racial status.[49]

In nineteenth-century abolitionist fiction, white writers such as Lydia Maria Child, Elizabeth Livermore, and Dion Boucicault often used mixed-race heroines (mulatta, quadroon, octoroon) to interrogate the injustices of slavery. As women, these heroines represented this link to racial definition as well as the potential locus of future violations and mixture. Since mixture was intertwined with rape, the mulatta earned sympathy as a paradigmatic victim of racist corruption and as a symbol of the defilement of women. Female characters could be modeled after sentimental heroines from domestic fiction of the period, surrounded with the familiar cues of chastity, piety, morality, and purity. The virtuous mulatta defied racist stereotypes of the overly sexual black woman and gained the attention of readers trained to applaud the literary signals of Christian domesticity.[50] She functioned somewhat like *Time*'s contemporary "new face of America" in her duplicitous whiteness and apparent innocence. She attracted and fascinated. Her beautiful, near-white appearance masked the open secret of her impurity and displaced the taboo of her history.

Most writers also provided elaborate detail about their heroines' near-white appearances to suggest a racial affinity with white readers. Diane Price Herndl questions this affinity in her essay, "Miscegen(r)ation or Mestiza Discourse?": "In making their heroines practically white by birth and mostly white by conventionality of attitude, do [Helen Hunt Jackson and Frances E. W. Harper] enslave racial identities to 'a prescribed, conventional, and imposed form,' as James Olney argues, or do they open up the possibility of real intercourse between white women and women of color?" (264). Herndl ultimately answers that "both are true," using Anzaldúa's mestiza consciousness as a model for sustaining this ambiguity (264). Herndl's choice of the word *intercourse* to describe the relationship between white readers and near-white characters is telling (though perhaps unintentionally so). The blood coursing through white readers' veins also courses through the mixed-race heroines' veins, suggesting an intercourse of identity and drawing attention to the interracial sexual intercourse that mingled this white blood with others'. Authors fueled their abolitionist arguments by invoking the conventions of "pure white womanhood" and positioning a woman with these conventions inscribed on her skin and her "attitude" at risk of enslavement or defilement. This risk unjustly threatens the heroine's purity of attitude, which was celebrated to eclipse the impurity of her race and to render her defileable (rather than already defiled).

The name *Zoe*, based on the octoroon and quadroon literary models created by Boucicault and Livermore, became a shorthand for this tragic heroine trapped between racial worlds and locked out of domestic harmony because of "one drop" of "black blood." Although her African heritage is invisible on the surface, enabling her to be misread as white, there is always some lingering evidence to document its presence. Despite her virtual whiteness, the "truth" is always discovered. Yet this heroine is never truly black, either, and readers are seldom tortured for long by witnessing her treated as such. Zoe's racial mixture ultimately leads to an irresolvable conflict of identity and lifestyle that often results in her death. As suggested by the pseudoscientific muleologies, Zoe's embodiment of interracial differences was conventionally self-annihilating. (In this sense, though antiracist in intent, tragic mulatta narratives could ease the fears of racial purists by promising the demise of interracial identity.) This non-threatening tragic mulatta opposed the feared vengeance and ambition of the male mulatto, like Robert Norwood in Langston Hughes's play *Mulatto*, who enters the front door by force and takes his seat in the father/master's house through patricide.[51] According to Werner Sollors, the near-white mulatta potentially represents "a national symbol and a Christ-like mediator" (300). She is posed as both innocent product and humble mediator at the crux of U.S. race drama.

Although these white writers sought the abolition of slavery, their mulatta heroines are certainly ambivalent. Their popularity in melodrama reflects the intrigue surrounding impurity. Mulatta fiction satisfied the nineteenth-century fascination with miscegenation, illicit relations, and sexualized taboo. And the tragic endings envisioned by most white writers suggest a certain paternalism, assuming that mixed-race African-Americans were inevitably victimized. The sacrifice of the tragic mulatta served as a vehicle for condemning slavery. To maximize reader sympathy, any possible resistance or transcendence was dismissed in favor of ultimate suicide or violation. Furthermore, the emphasis on their whiteness codes tragic mulattas according to the terms of white supremacy, reinforcing the notion that only white beauty and white sentimental virtues redeem mixed-race women, and the fact that they are not quite white keeps them from leading successful lives.

While many writers attempted to erase their Zoes' difference according to the terms of white culture, the presence of "black blood" destabilizes racial order and hierarchy, undermining conventional racial forms.[52] The Zoes' existence disproves the myth of an impassable gulf between the races. They are a "living reminder" that black and white members of plantation families are related, "of one blood," and that racial lines "cut across real blood ties" (Sollors 300). In Sollors's words, Zoe "is at the crossroads of consent and descent" (300). She signifies a breakdown in the order, a lack of consent, an impure family member. Not only does Zoe serve as a reminder of white men's transgressions, but her mixed identity itself crosses the line between black and white and shows where their differentiation becomes impossible.

Since the tragic mulatta was such a popular and influential literary convention, she reappears in many texts, from the antebellum period through the present, either with the name _Zoe_ or with different names but familiar attributes.[53] Many writers—black writers in particular—emphasize her subversion of racial hierarchies, but nineteenth-century white writers more often elided this threat. Although she appears by many names in the texts I analyze, I use the name _Zoe_ to refer to the traditional model. The type was familiar enough to most readers to invoke a consistent set of character traits—near-white beauty, virtue, tragedy—and beliefs about racial difference or the lack thereof.

White Writers and Tragic Mulattas: Child, Livermore, and Boucicault

While William Wells Brown's _Clotel_ contains perhaps the most famous tragic mulatta heroine, this influential novel follows a pattern designed previously by Lydia Maria Child and adopted later by many other women writers of race melodrama, including Elizabeth Livermore and Pauline Hopkins. Nineteenth-century black American writers shared an investment in creating agency for African-American characters, and many such authors used mulatto identities to explore agency and mobility. Yet the literary products of such white writers as Child, Livermore, and Dion Boucicault often confine biracial characters within restrictive, one-dimensional roles that fail to leave room for agency, escape, or subversion. For example, Xarifa, an educated, cultured, golden mulatta in Child's 1846 story, "The Quadroons," is seized from her luxurious home and the arms of her white harp teacher, sold at a public auction to a "profligate" master with gross language and rude hands, and becomes a "raving maniac," dashing her brains out against the wall after her "pure temple was desecrated" (71–76). Her master sees her only as a "useless expense" (76). While Child creates this violent tragedy to enlist reader sympathy for the abolitionist cause, she does not see a way out for her mulatta characters, who are condemned to suffer in a rigid racial hierarchy. Child allows them no means of independent agency. Indeed, in "Scale of Complexions" (1834), Child would put an end to racial amalgamation and place "defenceless blacks under protection of law and public opinion" (*Oasis* 200). Although her call to end the rapes that produced so many biracial Americans is undoubtedly admirable, she would protect oppressed races by further denying their agency and confining them within the paternalistic control of white society.

Unlike Clotel, Child's Xarifa is weak and unable to transcend black and white racial distinctions. In the same vein, Livermore's *Zoë; or, The Quadroon's Triumph: A Tale for the Times* (1855), a sentimental tragedy of a light-skinned woman from the Caribbean island of Santa Cruz, creates one of the first literary Zoes. Although this text has received little critical attention and has been out of print for quite some time, its depiction of the ambiguous status of a mixed-race woman is very revealing. In her introduction, Livermore articulates her goal as freeing "the African" and realizing in "him" "poetry, music, high art, and full reflection of God's love" (1: v). Here, the standards of value are derived from Anglo-American literary values of the period. To emphasize Africans' and Euro-Americans' sameness, Livermore chooses a near-white heroine.[54] Yet while deemphasizing racial difference in Zoë's person, Livermore also dwells on Zoë's difference. There is a tension between sameness and difference that complicates Zoë's identity: "There was a marked difference between Zoë's countenance and that of [Anglo-Saxon] girls," but "Zoë was no darker than many a *white* Creole and she was entirely free from the most peculiar and repulsive African indications" (1: 36).

In describing Zoë, Livermore invokes stereotypic attributes of women of color such as passion and strength, yet Zoë's strength comes from her religious zeal, which thus increases her value in the cult of true womanhood and distinguishes her from racist stereotypes. Her "fiery temperament" and "strong affections" are one with her "religious aspiration" (1: 98–99). Livermore describes Zoë as "different" and "weird" and in the same sentence claims that she looks and talks as beautifully as an angel (1: 106). The duality of her biracialism leads to duality in Livermore's descriptions, such as "cherub changeling" (1: 106), in which Zoë's cherubic whiteness redeems her changeling darkness. In another passage, Livermore describes Zoë's hair as "pagan" and "fiery" yet tamed with an iron to "becoming obedience." Significantly, when smoothed, the curly locks are described as "dutiful Christians" (1: 146–47). Just as Christianity supposedly tames Zoë, it also subdues the wildness of her hair. Zoë's complex identity yokes black and white racial stereotypes, complicating the distinction between them. Livermore encourages her readers to look past color while paradoxically emphasizing the mask presented by Zoë's racial difference: she is an "angel of light, hidden from the eyes of the vulgar by a dusky envelope, only to give more loving lustre to the spirit" (2: 271). Race is thus a permeable confinement: dark skin veils the lightness within identity but allows the "lustre" to shine through. This is how Zoë can appear dark and light at the same time.

During her childhood, Zoë is sent to Denmark, where she is trained to act as a lady with virtue and Christian morality. Zoë mourns her separation from her mother, and significantly, while in Denmark she cannot remember her mother's color (1: 189). Echoing U.S. legislation that attached children's race to their mothers, exile from her dark mother reflects Zoë's exile from her race. Livermore also foreshadows the bias of historians—Reuter, Williamson, and others—by using the Caribbean as the origin of her character's racial mixture and contrasting that "dark" environment to the all-white society that Zoë meets in Europe. While in Denmark, she comes of age in a supposedly raceless environment, and she has no sense of racial identity. "Her differences of person from the other girls she attributed to a West-India climate as also her love for the hot summer sun and aversion to the winter's snow and cold" (1: 102).[55] All concern for color here is displaced from the racialized subject onto the objective and uncontrollable realm of climate. Livermore attributes differences of color to the natural environment of the region (whether hot or cold), disregarding the history of slavery and colonial domination that determined the Caribbean's racial appearance.

It is significant that Livermore chooses to set this conventional American race melodrama outside the United States. She thus displaces the abolitionist argument and the race debate onto others, distancing the guilty United States from the conflict. By using Europe to symbolize the absence of racial divisiveness and the Caribbean to reflect the heart of rebellion, mixture, and daily interracial clashes, Livermore projects the opposing sides onto a cross-Atlantic face-off. As a result, her white U.S. readers can perceive themselves as moderates, in the middle of two continental extremes. Zoë does not gain any sense of her racial identity or of the oppressions associated with race until she returns to the American hemisphere, where she falls into the U.S. racial classification

of quadroon. Although the bulk of the narrative, including Zoë's first encounter with U.S. racial definition, is displaced from the United States,
Livermore attributes racism to U.S. racial categories. While sailing near
Bermuda, two "negro" women working on the ship offer Zoë some lemons.
Zoë instantly identifies with the quadroon woman: "What a new world is
dawning upon my vision, through the simple errand of two poor peasant
women! I thought it was my second self I saw with the huge burden of my
griefs of years made visible" (2: 57). The "new world" that she discovers
is the "burden" of American race dynamics. According to Zoë, this new
racial identification changes essential aspects of her identity: "I have called
myself an Ethiopian, and glorified in the title, for it spoke of fervor and
enthusiasm and poetry. But the degraded negro! That is different. Why,
he is despised wherever he abides. He is a slave, an outcast. Am I of the
slave's origin?" (2: 57). As an "Ethiopian" in Europe, Zoë's mixture was poetic and interesting, but as a "new world" "negro," it is degraded, outcast,
and linked to slavery. The change of geographic location and racial label
throws Zoë's identity into crisis, and, from the U.S. perspective of racial
stratification, her mixed heritage becomes "a twisted knot" and a "tangled
skein" "thrown" at her (2: 57–58).

Livermore contrasts American racism with British and Danish tolerance
(2: 148). By removing Zoë in her youth from the racial barriers of the
Americas, Livermore explores the potential of allowing identity to expand without regard to racist distinctions. Yet even in Denmark, Zoë is
thwarted by her teacher, Miss Ingemann, who believes in strict separation of the races and considers it a waste to educate Zoë as a lady when
she would be better suited to be a cook (2: 59, 1: 147–48). The limitations imposed on Zoë are compared to "fetters" (2: 266), implying that
some sort of slavery has followed her to Denmark despite her legally free
status. The Danish government does not allow its colonists to overstep
the racialized limitations marked out for them, so Zoë's intellect is not
permitted to soar. Zoë does indeed end up working as a pastry cook,
fulfilling Miss Ingemann's prophecy, and Zoë's fate is ultimately tragic
(2: 261–62).

Although Livermore criticizes the boundaries imposed on Zoë because
of her race, the fates of the author's mulatto characters support the racist
opinions of her characters Mrs. Strophel and Jane Rutgard: Zoë's death is
a result of seeking too much out of life and attaining too much education
for her own good (2: 305). Disappointment is the inevitable outcome. Zoë
is like her father, the ambitious George Carlan, looked down on by whites

for his encroachment on their aristocratic rights and dignities and scorned by blacks because of his mixed caste, haughty bearing, luxuriant surroundings, and economic successes (2: 7). When Zoë first returns to Santa Cruz and wants to bond with "her people," they resent her for her "outlandish education" and her father's superiority (2: 242). Livermore implies that Zoë's education clashes with the race of her birth and that no amount of European cultivation can help Zoë to transcend her troubled origins. Despite the advantages of her cultural elevation, Zoë is not permitted to realize her high aspirations, and she is doomed to assume the role attributed to her by Miss Ingemann because of race. In contrast to William Wells Brown, Livermore establishes an essentialist connection between race and achievement, and Zoë's mixed race achieves nothing but disappointment.

In the end, Zoë meets the stereotypical fate of the tragic mulatta. A male cousin of her wealthy white friend, Hilda, proposes a "lawless union with Zoë," because in that society a white man has no other sort of unions with women of color. Zoë reacts to this threat of defilement by contemplating suicide and raving on a hill during a hurricane, in King Lear fashion. She imagines "her people" ground to dust, boiled in cauldrons, tormented on treadmills (2: 254–55). In the man's offer, Zoë witnesses her own degradation and that of all people of color, and this tragic fate seems inevitable. After her encounter in the storm, Zoë's health declines, and the novel predictably ends with a drawn-out deathbed scene. For Zoë, death is "the quadroon's triumph" of the title and the ultimate freedom of her soul from "the bonds which enthrall it" (2: 302–3). Livermore casts death as Zoë's destiny and the only source of liberation for the mulatta. The writer surrounds her dying heroine with Christlike imagery: she dies at sunset, with "the face of an angel." At the moment of her death, a former admirer miraculously appears, then disappears, leaving a parchment on which is printed, "But when that which is perfect is come, then that which is in part shall be done away." Zoë's death thus foretells the coming of a more perfect world. Livermore implies that Zoë's death is a self-sacrifice for the good of her people. Hilda promises at Zoë's deathbed to plead for the cause of all people of color: "Thy people shall be my people, as thy God is my God!" Zoë's only material achievement is the enlistment of support from her white friend, who promises to carry Zoë's manuscript, a narrative of her people, to America for publication (2: 303–4). While the white Hilda travels freely between nations, as does the manuscript, for Zoë the most suitable place is in heaven. In this limiting race dynamic, mulattoes are bound by birth to tragic endings.

In this vision, the mulatta is unable to find any place in this world because her betweenness exiles her from both black and white society. Livermore foreshadows Reuter in her invocation of the "greater fragility of constitution said to be inherent in the mixed race" (1: 20). Zoë is weak because of her mixed origins, which deny her a place in a racially divided society. Livermore thus uses U.S. standards of black-white racial separation in her depiction of European and Caribbean race dynamics. Since Zoë is neither black nor white, she has no place in a system based on rigid divisions of color. The fact that Zoë can find no place in Livermore's novel suggests that the dichromatic system cannot accommodate Caribbean subjects, mixed-race Creoles such as Zoë. Yet in subsequent tragic mulatta novels, similar situations occur on U.S. land, with U.S. subjects, suggesting that racial mixture in the United States problematizes black-white distinctions just as much as in the Caribbean. Attempts such as Livermore's to displace mixture from the United States onto the Caribbean are thus made in vain.

Another one of the original Zoe figures comes from Irish immigrant Dion Boucicault's drama *The Octoroon* (1859). Significantly, this play, which focuses on the issue of racial uncertainty, begins with the image of ruptured lineage. Old Pete, a cheerful slave on the plantation Terrebonne, claims that the "darky" children "nebber was born." Instead, "one morning dey swarmed in on a sassafras tree in de swamp" (3). The lack or denial of mother, even in Old Pete's playful jest, signifies a lack of origin and thus the impossibility of proving these children's racial status. The mulatto heroine Zoe is beautiful, timid, and loved by all. Her color is so fair that she has to summon proof to convince George, one of the many white men who love her, of "what I am" (16), with "what" being her racial status, which then determines her identity, "I." The lightness of her appearance obscures her real racial identity. To reveal the "ineffaceable curse of Cain" that marks her, she points to the "bluish tinge" on her fingernails and to the "white" of her eyes (16). These bodily markings suggest the coloring of a white blue blood, but Zoe inverts traditional expectations for whiteness: instead of white fingers and blue eyes, she has blue fingers and white eyes. Only hidden at the roots of her hair is the mark "dark, fatal" (16). Throughout the play, Boucicault repeatedly returns to Zoe's pallor and flushed cheeks as indicators of her physical whiteness and to her fainting horror at the possibility of being enslaved as evidence of her "white" feminine demeanor.

Boucicault also describes Zoe's worth in economic terms. She receives an annuity from her "natural" father and is "worth her weight" in sunshine, signifying both her moral value and her potential economic value on the slave market (5). Boucicault describes in great, voyeuristic detail the auction scene, in which Zoe is sold to the evil Irish M'Closky for twenty-five thousand dollars (20, 21, 29). The price of these fair women is always high, and the primary tension lies between her moral values and her trade value. Zoe proves that the former sum is greater, as she poisons herself to avoid any unsanctified sexual associations with M'Closky. As a result of these Christian values, the familiar qualities of domestic fiction outweigh racist stereotypes. Zoe's adoption of sentimental ideals subverts the stereotype of licentious black women, freeing her from limiting racial identities. Just as white blood endows her with ambiguity, flexibility, desirability, and the power to move up in the racial hierarchy through liaisons with white men, the sentimental influence further distances her from stereotypical blackness. Her spiritual transcendence mirrors the fluidity of light-skinned mulattoes who pass into white society and eases the anxiety surrounding that fluidity by casting the mulatto as a superior, "more than black" type. In the process, a new stereotype develops in which the mulatta heroine must be pious, virtuous, and tragically condemned to distance her from darker women. While still defined on white cultural terms, echoing the pattern set by Livermore, Boucicault's Zoe employs those terms to void her market value and to deprive M'Closky of his concubine. The only way for Zoe to escape defilement is for her to take her own life, repeating the tragic endings of earlier Zoes.

Turn-of-the-Century Representations: Harper and Hopkins

Other chaste, beautiful mulatto women appear in the more academically visible works of Frances E. W. Harper, Pauline Hopkins, and Charles Wadell Chesnutt. With the rise of African-American studies, these writers have been reclaimed as important originators of the African-American literary tradition, a tradition that I consider to be embedded with decentered identities. Indeed, the canon of turn-of-the-century African-American literature is mulatta literature, and the most studied authors of this period contribute to mulatta mythology. I focus here on the women writers for the ways in which they prefigure the race, sex, and gender fluidity of contemporary feminist texts.[56] Harper's *Iola Leroy* (1893) and Hopkins's *Contending Forces* (1900), *Hagar's Daughter* (1901–2), and *Winona* (1902) investigate racial dynamics in which a Zoe-type woman temporar-

ily transcends her legal racial identification. The racially mixed heroines
in these texts are decentered and empowered along the lines of Brown's
Clotel and in opposition to Child, Livermore, and Boucicault.

It is significant that these texts have attracted such extensive critical
attention in recent years, at the same time that racial constructedness became a major focus of postmodern and poststructural theories of identity.
Henry Louis Gates Jr., Houston Baker Jr., and others have directed attention to these works that reveal the signifyin(g) duality, the subversion of
racial hierarchies, the language games, and the instability of identity in
African-American culture, invoking poststructural terminology to show
how that culture has been "always already" poststructural.[57] Through the
mulatta character, turn-of-the-century African-American writers explored
the politics, mobilities, and instabilities of racial identity, and through
their work, the mulatta heroine evolved beyond the paradigms envisioned
by earlier white writers.

Several aspects of mulatta identity appeal to the theoretical frameworks
of contemporary critics in African-American studies: the production and
deconstruction of racial categories; the racial and sexual violence that it
embodies; the obsession with (unsuccessfully) reading bodies for race;
and the possibility of nonunitary, decentered, and fluid identifications. I
would argue, however, that it is not merely these theoretical concerns
that have sparked so much critical discussion over what has now become a canon of late-nineteenth- and early-twentieth-century mulatta
fiction. Harper, Hopkins, and Chesnutt in particular have received much
critical attention because of their ambiguous political messages. While
contemporary Mexican and Chicana/o critics often celebrate *mestizaje* as
a marker of racial, cultural, and national uniqueness, many contemporary African-American critics perceive *mulatta/o* as an assimilationist identity category. Some recent criticisms of the "mulatta canon" almost echo
nineteenth-century arguments about racial purity in their resistance to
mulatta/o identity as an embodied transgression of the color line. As
Kristina Brooks argues in an analysis of Hopkins, "Confronting turn-of-
the-century racism with visible proof that racial barriers were indeed artificially constructed and imposed, Hopkins uses a strategy [racial passing]
that, nearly one hundred years later, ironically leaves her open to charges
of elitism" (124–25). Mulatta/o mixture might have presented a radical
challenge to racist definition in the late nineteenth and early twentieth
centuries—eras obsessed with racial purity and white supremacy—but
such mixture is antagonistic to the racial definition that founds much

contemporary African-American resistance to white racism. In contrast to Mexican and Chicana/o nationalism, which encompass mestiza mixture, Black Nationalism, Black Power, and African-American studies are built on African-American particularism and an oppositional relationship between blackness and whiteness, an oppositional integrity that mixed-race identity defies. Mixture cuts right into the heart of identity politics.

For example, Baker's critique of Harper and Hopkins's "soothing mulatto utopianism" suggests that mulatta fiction is wrought with desire to please and desire for the "white Father" (*Workings* 23, 33). According to Baker, "texts that during the past century of Afro-American intellectual discourse have been placed under assimilationist quarantine" for supposedly accommodationist politics have had their ban lifted in the past few decades "to provide a historical lineage for late-twentieth-century Afro-American women's subjecthood. However, actual violence against such subjecthood is precisely what these newly circulating texts often seek so forcefully to transform into marks of beautiful distinction" (23). In this scathing characterization, mulatta fiction revels in the violence against African-American women that is read on mixed-race bodies. Baker finds in *Contending Forces* an "ironic transmutation of the mark, sign, and act of concubinage (read: 'rape') into a symbolic black code of beauty, grace, intelligence, and historically embodied prominence" (24). The mulatta's beauty, in this reading, reflects a self-destructive homage to rape.

Twenty years worth of critical study has obsessively debated whether African-American representations of mulattas buy into conventions of white supremacy or subvert those conventions from within. One fear among African-American critics seems to be that the masking of difference represented by mulatta fiction results from a latent shame about blackness and a reverence for whiteness. Defenders of the genre emphasize the constrictions that white racist domination of the public realm imposed on turn-of-the-century fiction, requiring covert literary strategies and allowing difference to emerge only under erasure.[58] The fact that representations of mulattas are central to any canon of African-American literature seems to be a source of embarrassment for some critics and a model for exploring and expanding identification for others.[59] Baker accuses mulatta fiction of "white-faced minstrelsy" and considers the genre to be working "in the service of the cultivation of *an approving white public opinion*" (*Workings* 26). Gwendolyn Brooks, too, in her 1968 afterword to *Contending Forces*, found Hopkins to be assimilationist: "To ask [blacks], to entreat them to address themselves, rather than whites, to cherish, champion themselves, rather than whites . . . was not her inspiration nor motivation" (Washington 434). Mary Helen Washington, Hazel Carby, and Deborah McDowell defend Harper and Hopkins in the name of black feminism, but these critics also seem a bit disappointed, as their search for the progressive political potential in mulatta fiction is infused with apologizes for its deficiencies: "Although neither of these novels meet today's requirements for feminist fiction, at least . . ."; "We may debate how effective [Harper's] novel was . . . , but we need to recognize that . . ."; "Ironically, despite the early writers' efforts to revise homogenized literary images, they succeeded merely, and inevitably, in offering alternative homogenization" (Washington 76; Carby 94; McDowell 38). Claudia Tate emphasizes the ways in which Harper and Hopkins were misjudged "by a scholarly tradition that was defensive about issues of race" and missed the symbolic political value of African-American women's domesticity (126). The consensus seems to suggest the mulatta fiction is consistently misread, misunderstood, or studied with insufficient critical methods. Perhaps this ambiguity is what makes critics return to the genre again and again, as if to resolve a particularly thorny mystery or to explain away a possible blemish in African-American literary history. The mulatta has attracted as much obsessive concern among African-American critics as it did among nineteenth-century white racists. Kristina Brooks aptly concludes that these fictions "require readers to engage in a continuous process of repositioning in regard to their own racial, class, and gender identifications—as well as their place in history—if they hope to understand the uses of fiction in a time of historical crisis, both Hopkins's and our own" (149).

My interest in the symbolic significance of literary mulatta identity parallels my interest in *mestizaje:* both mixtures break down the unitary aspect of any paradigm, those of the dominant culture as well as those of the marginalized culture. Mulatta fiction employs and challenges the markers used to signify white racism as well as those that signal African-American identity politics. Recent studies of Hopkins, for example, note her resistance to both white- and black-defined norms. In opposition to charges that she supported either accommodationist or progressive racial and political models, Hopkins's representations of mulattas were unruly, troubling any category of identity. They thwarted monoliths of the turn of the century as they thwart monoliths of contemporary criticism. Jennie Kassanoff argues that Hopkins's racialized and gendered identities "effectively deconstruct the monolith of the New Negro by questioning its contours and its limitations" (159–60). Rendered complex by interracial families, international histories, secret genealogies, shifting alliances, and even transgender identifications, Hopkins's mulatta characters emphatically resist circumscription by any model of African-American identity, an unruliness that might have precipitated her loss of control over the *Colored American Magazine* to Booker T. Washington in 1904. At the same time, as Lisa Marcus argues, Hopkins's near-white heroines address myths of white womanhood and subvert those myths from within by including African-American women within the image and the genealogy of "true [white] womanhood." In this way, Hopkins "genealogically reimagines America's national psyche and physiognomy" (Marcus 119). Like María Amparo Ruiz de Burton, Hopkins invokes sentimental conventions but subverts them by applying "true womanhood" to women with mixed or ambiguous racial identities and genealogies. According to Shawn Michelle Smith's study of Hopkins, "By reinscribing the focus of white obsessions [with racial mixture] as a potentially subversive site in definitions of racial difference, Hopkins utilizes her biracial heroines to undermine dominant ideologies of race" (189). In this way, an African-American writer could apparently buy into white racist obsessions, but her reinscription of these obsessions undermined racism. I would argue that the mulatta character is a fetish for both African-American and white American writers because of internal contradiction: she embodies both the taboo against miscegenation and the omnipresence of miscegenation; she reinforces white standards of beauty and propriety at the same time that she denies white supremacy by being not white. She supports and negates the frameworks of racism. Both black and white American writers, from the 1850s to today, have been drawn to the ways in which nineteenth-century mixture eroded the binary racial definition that had mediated identity for both blacks and whites in the United States. This obsession produced a prolific body of mulatta fiction that concerns sex, gender, and race, the myths of whiteness and femininity created by the dominant culture as well as those produced by resistant African-Americans.

Washington, Carby, and others also emphasize the ways in which the mulatta heroine in U.S. literature exceeds the dimensions of given literary labels. According to Washington, Harper and Hopkins "reverse the image of the tragic mulatto heroine, devising ways for their heroines to become political and social activists" (76). In borrowing traditional genres of white American fiction, such as the sentimental novel, black women writers reflect a unique investment in destabilizing that genre

from within, encoding the difference of African-American women's experience, responding to the unique sexual mythologies imposed on black
women during slavery, and finding agency for the doubly oppressed black
female character. Although these biracial heroines may seem to be tragic
mulattas, the empowerment they often possess, their political activism,
and their physical mobility undermine the tragedy of their racial position and resist any singular enclosure such as the home and hearth of the
white domestic novel. Carby also emphasizes mobility and subversion,
suggesting that the mulatta figure acts as an intermediary who "allowed
for movement between two worlds, white and black, and acted as a literary displacement of the actual increasing separation between black and
white" (90). The liminal biracial individual calls into question the separa-
bility of black and white at the same time that she moves between and beyond racial definitions. In response to Carby and Washington, Kimberly
A. C. Wilson claims that "since identity for the mulatto lies between existing precepts of racial singularity," she "deconstruct[s] essentialist notions
of race" (104). This early antiessentialism prefigures postmodern identity
theories that are still deconstructing racial definition.

Harper's *Iola Leroy* focuses on the mobility of mixed-race characters,
whose lack of visible racial identity enables them to transcend their positions. Iola Leroy moves between North and South, white and black, slavery and freedom. Although she has an opportunity to become absorbed
into the white race through marriage with Dr. Gresham, Iola casts her
lot with those Americans blacker than she and dedicates herself to the
education and improvement of the recently freed slaves. As a result, she
refuses to privilege the whiteness within her. While Gresham insists that
"the color line is slowly fading out" and sees "no use in [Iola's] persisting
that [she] is colored when [her] eyes are as blue and complexion as white
as [his]," Iola refuses to enter into society "under a shadow of concealment" where she might be mistaken as a white woman (Harper 232–33).
Iola resists the fading visibility of racial difference, reinforcing the color
line as she crosses it. She insists on racial identification, even though she is
given the opportunity to escape it. She considers the black blood in her
veins to be a political and social obligation rather than "an undetected
crime" (233). In these passages, race becomes in part an issue of choice,
an identity category that may be hidden or shifting, a construction based
on social perception. As a result of this lack of clarity, Iola affirms her
black allegiance all the more publicly.

Iola declares this allegiance at the occasion of Dr. Gresham's marriage proposal, and her black identification is clarified by her refusal of a white husband. Harper uses the marriage plot to signal and to depart from convention. The novel begins with Eugene Leroy marrying Iola's mother, Marie, with the full knowledge of her racial mixture, a subversion of the traditional scenario in which the white man unwittingly marries a light-skinned mulatta, and ends with Iola's marriage to Dr. Latimer, who chooses to identify as an African-American but has the potential to pass for white, and Henry's marriage to the dark-skinned Lucille (68–69, 256–66, 277–78). Harper thus charts a trajectory away from white ascendancy and tragic mulatta conventions and links racial identification to marital declaration: moments of passionate exchange and chosen (rather than inherited) family alliance. On the occasion of Henry's engagement to Lucille, Marie Leroy declares herself to be "not one who can't be white and won't be black" (278). Through this use of the double negative, Harper renders racial identity unstable: if the mulatto is not neither black nor white, she becomes whatever she chooses. Choosing a spouse highlights this racialized and gendered liberty.

Representing mulattoes as the natural leaders of the African-American race supports both racist mythologies (since it might imply that white blood makes them superior) and antiracism in *Iola Leroy*. Mixture itself spans the range of political and social possibility as it evolves from a source of tragedy to a means of empowerment and dedication to African-Americans. Washington says of *Iola Leroy*, "though it has a highly melodramatic plot, complete with idealized mulatto heroes, sudden reversals of fortune, the bad punished and the good rewarded, [Harper] gives its main character a more powerful and unambiguously heroic role" (77). Although Harper's characters suffer after the initial discovery of their mixed racial constitutions, this suffering renders the mulatta heroic and fuels her political activism (59). Harper thus invokes and then moves past nineteenth-century rhetoric that vilified or pathologized mulattoes.

In her novel *Contending Forces*, Hopkins asks, "Combinations of plants, or trees, or of any productive living thing, sometimes generate rare specimens of the plant or tree; why not, then, of the genus homo?" (87). This suggestion disturbingly invokes the pseudoscientific rhetoric of eugenics, but Hopkins levels harsh critiques at white Americans' obsession with purity, and her mixed-race characters prove the hypocrisy of this obsession. In violation of literary standards that resisted any direct discussion of sexuality—both the white sentimental tradition and the New Negro opposition to the physicality of slavery's racist images of African-

Americans—Hopkins overtly reveals the sexual origins of mixture and critiques the sexual myths used to justify lynching.[60] A speech delivered by her mulatto hero, Will Smith, asserts that by falsely accusing black men of interracial rape, white men are trying to displace their own guilt for their role in the creation of the mulatto race: "Rape is the crime which appeals most strongly to the heart of the home life. . . . Irony of ironies! The [white] men who created the mulatto race, who recruit its ranks year after year by the very means which they invoke lynch law to suppress, bewailing the sorrows of violated womanhood" (271). Based on these assertions, Hopkins suggests that white men have no grounds for claiming moral or genetic superiority over black men. Hopkins adds didactic assertions like Smith's to her representations of biracial female characters to emphasize the damage wrought by white men's violations, contrary to Baker's critique that she does not sufficiently flesh out the violence of her "mothers'" past (*Workings* 36). Despite the suffering imposed on her cultivated and virtuous mulatto characters, they triumph and, of course, marry in the end, becoming heroes on the domestic level if not on the political scale that Harper represents.

This empowerment is built on mobility and the discovery of origins. In *Hagar's Daughter*, Hopkins presents scenes—for example, the escape of the enslaved mulatta by jumping into the Potomac River—that are based on Brown's *Clotel* and repeated in *Iola Leroy*. This repetition of familiar events is characteristic of the formulaic genre that the tragic mulatta narrative became, and such repetition reinforces these texts' (often subversive) relationship to convention.[61] These intertextual duplications also prefigure postmodern fiction's penchant for echoing past narratives, cutting and pasting scenes from other novels into narrative amalgamations. Intertextuality is one means by which the genre succeeds: the invocation and revision of familiar tropes and figures drives the narrative and highlights the novel's relationship to literary history and social conventions. Since *Hagar's Daughter* was serialized in *Colored American Magazine*, the familiar scenes facilitated the connection between episodes of the novel and helped readers to perceive the serial fragments within a familiar historical and literary situation.

The link between lost mothers and lost racial origins is one recurring theme that Hopkins invokes in *Hagar's Daughter*, thus playing on the familiar association of maternal origin with racial certainty. The discovery of racial heritage occurs simultaneously with the discovery of the maternal line. Jewel and Aurelia, two mixed characters who pass for white, deconstruct the monolith of mulatta identity with their opposing racial and sexual embodiments. Jewel is a "fair fragrant lily," a "white angel of purity," and a "saint." In the same scene, Aurelia is described as a "tropical flower" with "dusky eyes" whose "bewitching" attitudes and "siren charms" are irresistible (and later destructive) for men (*Magazine Novels* 103–4). Both women compete for the same man, but Jewel is virtuous and chaste, while Aurelia is evil, deceptive, and plotting. Aurelia is "false to the core," with "no soul"—indeed, no real identity (194). Aurelia thus contains the negative associations of their shared racial uncertainty, while Jewel remains ethereal and free from corporeal impurity. When Jewel too turns out to be Hagar's daughter and of mixed racial origin, Hopkins's readers must question if racial mixture necessarily leads to deception and sensuality, as it does for Aurelia. The disclosure of Jewel's racial origins is rendered less tragic by her pleasure at being reunited with her mother. Her discovery is both sweet and tragic. Yet both women, fair and "tropical," are cast out of society because of their origins, and Jewel dies before her lover can accept her racial mixture (283).

Although Ellis Enson, one of the novel's heroes, advocates racial amalgamation as an end to racial separation and antagonism (270) (much like the Mexican nationalist endorsement of *mestizaje*), Hopkins provides no clear answers. Indeed, her purpose seems to be to expose the absence of clarity, the ambiguity of racial identity, and the elusiveness of racial origins. As Hopkins peels back layers of identity to reveal her characters' secrets, "black blood is everywhere—in society and out, and in our families even" (160). Again, the inability to separate or distinguish the races causes initial anxiety, and racial certainty becomes unmoored from each character as "cases of mistaken identity are common enough" (194). No one is "immune" (266). Even the whitest woman could discover a hidden racial identity. This possibility threatens to erase the binary opposition between blackness and whiteness, to deconstruct the certainty of difference. Soulless characters like Aurelia, who lack an essential definition at the core, can construct identities at will, but the implications of this decenteredness are sinister. The ultimate image is a complex, shifting network of racial lineage in which identity is always an unfixed unknown. Hopkins's rhetoric lacks Harper's idealism.

This complexity reaches its height in *Winona* (1902), which was also serialized in *Colored American Magazine*. Hopkins's heroine, Winona, crosses all axes of identification based on race, nationality, sex, and class. She too is a light-skinned mulatta whose maternal origins cause her temporary reenslavement, but in this text, the white father is a British man who lives as a Native American. Winona's identity is situated in opposition to U.S. definitions of race as well as U.S. nationality, as she moves from her island home in Lake Erie (on the border between the United States and Canada), to John Brown's separatist colony, to Canada, and ultimately to England. At one point during this journey, she cross-dresses and darkens her skin to pass for a mulatto male nurse, Allen Pinks, so that she can care for her white rescuer, Maxwell, while he is in prison. And Winona crosses class boundaries with the same facility as she crosses national and sexual boundaries: her ultimately recovered identity, as the missing heir to the Carlingford estate, moves her from poverty to wealth. In an extensive reading of the homoerotic subtext of the prison scene, Siobhan Somerville argues that "the often unstable division between homosexuality and heterosexuality circulates as part of Hopkins's exploration of the barriers to desire imposed by the color line" (11). When Winona, in the guise of Pinks, "gaze[s] down on [Maxwell's] Saxon face" and kisses him (*Magazine Novels* 387), the transgression of heterosexuality highlights the transgression of the color line, and vice versa. Since the mulatta is positioned between white and black norms of womanhood, the male disguise frees her from either convention. The blackface further distances Pinks from the chastity demanded of near-white heroines. Somerville also emphasizes this expansive aspect of the disguise: "Through her disguise, then, Winona is able to escape from the narrative expectations attached to the figure of the mulatta heroine by entering temporarily into the role of Western hero, or at least his male sidekick. . . . Whereas intimacy between a white man and a younger black man had been sanctioned within the space of the prison, that of a white man and a younger biracial woman remains culturally taboo" (105). In this reading, darker skin and masculinity allow Winona temporarily to escape the generic conventions of the mulatta narrative and the racial and gender expectations that coincide with it.

In a final flouting of readers' expectations, Hopkins surprisingly gives the last word of *Winona* to a minor character who has been introduced to readers only a few pages before, the black cook Aunt Vinnie. This voice from the margins of the novel (in terms of race, class, and narrative space) assumes center stage and issues the greatest threat to dominant racial mythologies and hierarchies: "White folks been ridin' a turrible hoss in this country, an' dat hoss gwine to fro 'em' you hyer me" (*Magazine Novels* 436). The "hosses" from the bottom of the hierarchy will dismantle the constructions imposed by "white folks," throwing the riders off of their high horses. Hopkins's use of dialect and her choice of speaker distance this revolutionary message from Winona, potentially marginalizing or trivializing its sentiment. Yet giving Vinnie the last word might also reflect yet another subversion of convention, ultimately refusing to privilege the aristocratic politics of the refined mulatta heroine. Readers are left not only with no singular image of Winona's identity but also with no clear sense of the novel's political message or moral center. I would argue that this lack of clarity is what enables Hopkins to transcend the political conservatism and white supremacy that Baker or Gwendolyn Brooks might attribute to her and to do so without alienating white readers of her period.

Mulattoes in the Harlem Renaissance

Of all of these mulatta characters, it is significant that only Iola Leroy and Winona fully escape the tragic endings typical for the Zoe type. Yet this character type has evolved in twentieth-century American fiction to include more "survivors," women with agency, power, and mobility. The literary mulatta has moved from the position of racial outsider, precariously situated between worlds and constantly at risk of discovery, to a position of belonging, embracing a flexible and self-consciously constructed biracial identity. Since World War I reconstituted global and social hierarchies, since large-scale immigration changed the racial and cultural makeup of the United States, and since the Great Migration brought hundreds of thousands of African-Americans from the sparsely populated rural South to dense urban centers, it has been more difficult to enforce or even to imagine racial separation. The earlier ideals of racial purity have been challenged by historical, social, and demographic realities. Within this supposed melting pot, increased contact between people of different races has overturned nineteenth-century racial fictions.

African-American feminists have reclaimed mulatta identity in empowered, socially mobile characters. The heroism of Iola Leroy resurfaces in Zora Neale Hurston's *Their Eyes Were Watching God* (1937): Janie, too, is the light-skinned descendant of a violated slave woman, and she ultimately refuses to compromise her African-American origins for the sake of economic prosperity.[62] As the illegitimate daughter of an illegitimate daughter (her mother's father was Nanny's master), Janie's identity is always partial and contested. *Their Eyes Were Watching God* traces shifts in her identity as she moves among locations, social classes, and marriages. Janie's identity is not only the product of sexualized racial domination, racialized sexual domination, and erased origins, it is also continually re-defined by mobility and choice. Flying "mule-angels" present the novel's paradigmatic hybrid heroes, transcending the sorrows of this world and riding around on people, subverting the master-mule relationship (57).

As with the earlier period, much critical debate focuses on the am-bivalent politics of the mulatta canon of the Harlem Renaissance. Baker, who celebrates Hurston's "reclaiming" of a southern black vernacular, lev-els a damning critique at Nella Larsen and Jessie Redmon Fauset, "the bone descendants" of their "white-faced" turn-of-the-century foremoth-ers' "mulatto utopias": "Rather than a vision of communal, white-faced self-containment and race leadership, the Harlem Renaissance writers ex-periment with the narrative possibilities of moving even closer to the patriarchal source of concubinage [through passing]. They dream of re-deeming 'shame' in the name and under the flag of *(in)corporated white rights*" (*Workings* 35). I would argue, however, that Larsen and Fauset are not en-dorsing passing or their characters' wish to be white. In *Quicksand* (1928) and *Passing* (1929), Larsen's depictions of passing emphasize moral ambi-guities, the betrayal of racial allegiance, and a potential threat to African-American families. Both texts' heroines seem ultimately to be punished for any white identification, perhaps echoing the demands of an emerg-ing discourse of black nationalism. Fauset's *Plum Bun* (1929) does directly invoke the nineteenth-century tradition but attributes an almost patho-logical quality its tragic mulatta plot conventions. Angela is tired of be-longing to a "tragic race," is "sick of tragedy," and thus decides to employ "the unique weapon" of her light skin to "cross over to the other side" (143, 136–37). Although racial mixture leads to mobility for Larsen's and Fauset's characters, the light-skinned woman who passes is depicted as betraying her obligations to the people of "her" race.

Mary Helen Washington argues that "the very choice of 'passing' as a symbol or metaphor of deliverance for women reflects Larsen's failure to deal with the problem of marginality" (164), presumably because pass-ing reflects a complete transversal, with no in-between. In contrast, I find an emphasis on interracial friction in Larsen's and Fauset's depictions of passing. In *Passing*, Clare returns to black society and meets with tragedy when her two worlds, white and black, confront each other in one Harlem apartment. In *Plum Bun*, passing ultimately creates more of a tragedy for Angela than does her "black blood," and she loses her sister and her lover by turning her back on the race of her childhood. Significantly, the sor-row following their loss causes her to lose her "colour" in illness so that her black eyes present the only "relief against that awful whiteness" (311). Ultimately, brown skin, exotic colors, and a longing for the passions of Harlem become more valuable when set against that "awful" whiteness that infects Angela while she passes (326–27). In the end, she achieves happiness by revealing her true race and siding with "coloured" people. Both Larsen and Fauset thus revise the assumption that blackness leads to tragedy for biracial subjects by suggesting that passing and whiteness lead to even greater tragedy, loss, and suffering.

These flexible biracial heroines stand in contrast to the possibilities that Langston Hughes envisions in his play *Mulatto* (1931), written within a decade of *Quicksand, Passing, Plum Bun,* and *Their Eyes Were Watching God.* While Robert Norwood is condemned to a position of racelessness because he refuses to associate himself with either race (18, 23), these biracial women are doubly empowered by their ability to move and play between two racial worlds and to mold their identity strategically. This difference may reflect a gendered cultural condition: since women's identities are more compromised socially and politically and are decentered through family obligations, women writers are more interested in the potential of shifting, unstable, multiple identities. It is possible that women have more to gain than do men from nonfoundational or postmodern strategies for agency, so more female characters are depicted in this manner. It is also possible that as targets of the search for racial certainty, women have had to revalue their role in the production of biracialism, using literature as a means of claiming power. In either case, women are at the center of racial ambiguity and the key to racial ancestry; literary interpretations have responded to this situation, with biracial women playing a pivotal role at the center.

Racial Decentering in Ntozake Shange's *Liliane*

Ntozake Shange's recent novel, *Liliane* (1994), epitomizes racial and cultural mixture, both in content and in manner of presentation. This text presents a culmination of centuries of racial mixture and the most fluid race dynamics of all of the texts I have studied. If at times the histories of African-American and mestizo cultures have seemed far removed from each other, Shange brings them into intimate communication. *Liliane* bridges *mestizaje* and African-American biracial paradigms, juxtaposing histories of U.S. and Puerto Rican racial definition and greeting multiracialism with a literal celebration in the end. Shange's vision of the dynamic convergence of races in the Americas reflects the contemporary popularity of hybridity as a theoretical model for radicalizing identity without diluting African-American identity politics (as Baker might fear). Like *Liliane*, this chapter concludes with a vision of optimism tempered by the history that precedes it.

While *Liliane* is in dialogue with contemporary celebrations of multiculturalism and hybridity, it also recalls earlier African-American texts that deal with racial mixture. In the tradition of Brown and Hopkins, Shange positions a woman with contested racial affiliations at the center of mixed-race dynamics. Liliane's bilingual Afro-Latino photographer lover, Victor-Jésus María, describes Liliane as "la gringa negra" (64). In this description, she belongs to the *negra* race because of her chosen identification, but her wealth, her education, and her social advantages class her with the *gringa* race (a contemporary Iola Leroy). She is both black and white, both inside and outside Victor-Jésus's *negro* world. In the sections narrated by Victor-Jésus, Liliane's racial ambiguity is filtered through the Spanish language and Victor-Jésus's Latino perspective. As a result, the descriptions of her racial identity transcend black-white U.S. dynamics at the same time that they record the different standards for defining racial identity in different cultural contexts. For example, for the Latinas who run the bodega where Liliane buys produce, "it was beyond their version of the world that *mi negra linda* [Liliane] wasn't a *morena* at all, but a regular niggah" (68). Victor-Jésus thus situates Liliane's racial identity between U.S. and Puerto Rican definition, just as her gender identity does and does not correspond to "real Latina" standards: "Y, if she's not gonna give me any babies, the least she could do is bring me an avocado, sí? Gotta keep her on her toes, ya know, a bit off balance, outta focus. It's not like we lived in some sorta black-and-white frame" (68). This transnational frame, then, expands perceptions of Liliane's identity, rendering it a bit "outta focus" from any single normative lens. Unlike Livermore's Zoë, this movement between the perspectives and the racial categories of different nations expands rather than constricts Liliane's mobility. She exceeds American boundaries, and her racial definition goes beyond race or skin color to include cultural and linguistic components: "She was driven . . . to learn every language, slave language, any black person in the Western Hemisphere ever spoke. . . . She felt incomplete in English, a little better in Spanish, totally joyous in French, and pious in Portuguese. When she discovered Gullah and papiamento, she was beside herself" (66). Just as skin color is not enough to unify Liliane with black Americans, the English language alone does not cover her identity. Only an amalgamation of international languages could describe the multiple ways of being black. Liliane fantasizes about pulling her paintings onto her body: "The colors pour onto my skin. I am now streaked blue-black, reds, yellow, luminous blue" (20). The multiple colors of her paintings resemble the multichromatics of *mestizaje*. Black-white paradigms always leave something out: desire for the red, the blue, or the black. Liliane wants more color because any previous identification has been lacking. She does not want to choose between races but rather to choose them all. The desire for more color also parallels Liliane's efforts to overcome her alienation from dark-skinned people, to prove that she is more than a *gringa negra*.

Shange portrays this ambiguity of racial association symbolically through a high school rivalry between the White Team and the Blue Team. Since the Blue Team "had the most niggahs on it," Liliane was forced by her parents to be "the White Team color bearer," to bear whiteness as a public identity (158). Liliane wants to attend the Blue Team party because she does not want to "associate with losers who were the White Team" (160). Yet to prove her belonging among the Blues, Liliane must withstand an outburst of violence as real racial conflict replaces the Blue-White rivalry and "a mess of race-crazed crackers" bursts in on the party (162). As a result of her ability to defend herself against the invading whites during the brawl, Liliane earns the friendship of Bernadette, who had "always figured she was some other kinda white girl" (164). This scenario depicts blackness as something that one must earn, with the adoption of certain cultural traits and political allegiances, rather than simply something with which one is born. Bernadette's statement reveals the uncertainty of racial identity, the constructedness of racial definitions, and the fact that there is more to race than skin color.

Like many privileged light-skinned literary characters, Liliane has relatively easy access to different nations, races, and cultures. She travels, speaks different languages, and sleeps with men who are African-American, French, and Latino. As she describes it, "Borders have never intimidated me. My passport is in order." (16). The only barrier before her is her fear of Anglo-American men. Liliane's father pretends that her mother died to cover up the fact that she left him for a white man. For Parnell Lincoln, a civil rights attorney, this "crossing over" is the one impermissible transgression since it values the black man less than the white one.[63] Yet Liliane overcomes this fear by repeating (and perhaps revising) her mother's action, by crossing over in an affair with the white motor-

cyclist, Zoom. Victor-Jésus describes Liliane as "territory as yet undis-
covered by European 'explorers,'" until her "violation" or "colonization"
by Zoom (134, 143). At first, Victor-Jésus criticizes this relationship as
being "too close to real life to be art" (134). Yet Liliane revises the historical narrative, which does become art in Shange's novel, and labels
Victor-Jésus's resistance "a remnant of precultural diversity socialization"
(139). Indeed, even Victor-Jésus notes the link between Zoom's name and
"proceso" (which "es la revolución"), highlighting the ways in which Liliane "zooms" past racial divisions and historical conventions, "defying the
laws of physics" in the process, as she rides off on a motorcycle with the
"Lewis and Clark of the avant-garde" (135, 136). As with contemporary
Chicana feminist revisions of the myth of La Malinche, Liliane is not just
indigenous land being passively colonized by a white man: she is part of
a process of reconfiguring identity and nationality.[64]

Liliane fictionalizes her white lover's identity when, to hide her transgression from her father, she tells him that Zoom is a very light black man.
By pretending that the white man is black, by claiming that it would be
better for him to be black, Liliane erases the authority, the superiority, and
the centrality of Anglo-American men. Her affair with Zoom echoes and
subverts the traditional conquest as she absorbs him into her multiracial
list of lovers, demystifying the taboo, the threat behind relationships with
white men. Even Liliane's initial fear of white men fails to put them at the
center of American culture. She describes racist dynamics as keeping the
races "tangled up and wound round ourselves" (178), and separating them
would cause them to die. Even as whites try to organize the world around
themselves, they become so "tangled up" with other races that there is no
clear racial center. Each is dependent on the other, and the relationship
is wound too tightly to unravel.

In the midst of this tangled dynamic, the distinction between white
and black begins to blur, as Shange questions the authority of whiteness
in American culture. First, whiteness is often no more than a construct,
something that can be taken on and imitated by people of any race. Even
white women "caked white flour on their faces to be sure they weren't
mistaken for quadroons or octoroons" (39).[65] As in *Iola Leroy*, the privileged, light-skinned African-Americans of Liliane's class have the option
of choosing to imitate this whiteness or to use their privileges to advance
the cause of blackness. Liliane's father and her friends' fathers dedicate
their efforts to civil rights, claiming that African-Americans are "at a crossroads" and that it is the responsibility of those who can see both ways to

guide the race down the correct path (40). In contrast, there are those
members of the black middle class who imitate white American culture so
well that it seems they should have statues of black "lawn jockeys" in their
front yards to complete the picture, even though "real little Negro boys
lived in these houses, wasn't no need to pay for fake ones" (165). With so
many opportunities for racial imitation, for the adoption of fakes, Shange
problematizes the authenticity of racial identity.

Society imposes a responsibility on "elite" African-Americans, like Liliane, to "crossbreed or intrafertilize and become the Beyond Belief Brood
(offspring) of the Talented Tenth" (108). The two ways of sustaining racial
eliteness are crossbreeding and intrafertilizing, outbreeding or inbreeding. Similarly, Liliane mentions that the two taboos in her family are
interracial sex and incest. In both cases, having sex with someone from
outside the group is linked with having sex with someone inside. Werner
Sollors notes this same phenomenon in the tradition of mulatto fiction:
"The themes of incest and miscegenation, of inner and outer boundaries
to sexual choices, easily get confused in American race melodrama, merging two fears into a single, overpowering one" (302). This confusion of
inside sex and outside sex is based on historical precedent as well. Historian Vernon Lane Wharton notes that when intermarriage between the
races was outlawed in 1876 in Mississippi, "such marriages were declared
to be incestuous and void, and the parties participating were made subject to the penalties for incest" (19). In Mississippi, inside and outside
were legally conflated (predating Derrida by almost one hundred years)
to place the taboo against intermarriage on the same level as the taboo
against incest.[66] Both sexual transgressions deconstruct whiteness, revealing its simultaneous incorporation and disavowal of difference.[67]

This dynamic is particularly apparent in Shange's description of the
Creole Malveaux family. While the Malveauxs "could have turned their
backs on their darker brothers" (107) (and pass for white, presumably),
they do not do so. Yet they are encouraged to turn either outside to
whites or inside to themselves—to crossbreed or intrafertilize—to remain above the race they try to "uplift." Significantly, the products of
this confusion between inside and outside ultimately face tragedy, but it
is a different tragedy from that of their literary forerunners. Sawyer and
Hyacinthe Malveaux, Liliane's friends, represent a trajectory away from
nineteenth-century standards of mixed-race definition: "Sawyer was born
into hell. Sawyer was the sixth generation of Creoles who decided not
to turn their backs on their darker brothers. Sawyer was a brother. And

Sawyer died" (112). Originating in the lightening of the race, Sawyer's identity ultimately moves through DuBoisian social consciousness to contemporary gangsta nationalism, where he dies "just like the little hoodlum boys" when someone from East St. Louis shoots him in the head four times (112). This microcosmic view of African-American history reflects how nineteenth-century standards and advantages for mulattoes no longer define contemporary race dynamics. Similarly, Hyacinthe grows a twelve-inch Afro while at Cornell and has to be institutionalized for mental instability. People say of her, "*Pauvre* Hyacinthe, delicate, mongrel-blooded, tragic mulatto didn't claim her birthright" (112). Shange fuses Hyacinthe's political empowerment and dedication to her race with the stereotype of the weak half-breed, the tragic mulatto, the unstable hybrid. From the anachronistic perspective of the Talented Tenth, the tragedy for the Malveaux children comes from their refusal to lighten the bloodline. While nineteenth-century literary tragic mulattoes suffer as they are caught participating in the white world, Sawyer and Hyacinthe encounter tragedy when they are caught participating in contemporary identity struggles within the black world (much like Clare in the context of Larsen's Harlem Renaissance). Shange criticizes the pretensions of the Beyond Belief Brood and condemns the myth of the tragic "mongrel" mulatto. She also undermines or deconstructs their supposed superiority, since it is based on a confusion of black and white, incest and miscegenation, inside and outside.

As a result of the general decentering of race and difference, the events around which the novel revolves are truly multilingual, multiracial, and multicultural, as Shange's characters stage funerals for dead Aztecs by the California roadside, enacted through the mixed rites of Franciscans, Yorubas, Nahuatls, and U.S. blues, attended by a black Cherokee, a blonde woman with dreadlocks, an Asian woman with orange braids, the courtesan of Shango, and a woman dressed in drag as a friar (133–35). It is significant that this hybrid group chooses the Southwest, a historical locus of mestiza fluidity, as the symbolic place to come together harmoniously to mourn the conquest of Native Americans, a narrative familiar to them all, while expressing the diversity of races, religions, and historical situations involved.

The novel ends in a party to affirm *la raza*, a wedding that invokes the "solemnity" of "the decision to continue *la raza* on purpose, for ourselves, not for profit" (287). Again recalling *Iola Leroy*, Shange makes a wedding an opportunity for choosing or declaring a race. Liliane's friends celebrate this power to define themselves by fusing divergent cultural elements, dancing "a *bomba* with a southern drawl, a *merengue* with Mississippi improvisation . . . the jump-up hitched on to a get-down blues" (287). Even the wealthy, light-skinned Granville, formerly a prime specimen of the Beyond Belief Brood, converts himself to *la raza* with "the determination of every Maroon, Garveyite, Panther Zapatista" (287). This manifestation of racial pride redefines *la raza* to include all people of color, uniting all races in one category, choosing the Spanish term for race perhaps because *mestizaje* has a longer history of celebration than that other mixed racial model, *mulatto.*

Through the symbolic device of Victor-Jésus's wedding photographs, Shange "guide[s] the lost and unrecovered gems of our folks to landscapes more appropriate to our nature . . . worlds [where] no persons of color ever look crazy" (281). In Victor-Jésus's pictures, all of the characters in the novel appear to be "recovered" from tragedy—even the ghosts of Sawyer Malveaux and Liliane's murdered friend, Roxie, are seen in the frames—and come together to celebrate in the end. This ideal vision breaks down barriers between the different racial, cultural, and class-based groups through which Liliane's story moves—even the barrier between life and death—much like Gloria Anzaldúa's utopian mestiza consciousness. Yet Shange, like Victor-Jésus, is aware that "the land I give us is *un poquito* metaphorical" (281). She concludes her novel with a tribute to the power of art (Liliane's, Victor-Jésus's, or Shange's), of "dreams, fields of fancy, and realms of the spirits" (281), to expand the horizons of perception beyond the historical barriers that make hybrid fiestas such as this one remarkable. The novel does not promise actual utopia, "but, *querido,* I promise to paint it for you. . . . Okay?" (288).

There are many possible outcomes to this general unmooring of identity from its terrestrial, biological, and historically tragic origins. One is liberating: exclusion becomes impossible. Identity becomes inessential, flexible, shifting, strategic. Yet identity also becomes uncertain. People such as Liliane have to fight for racial inclusion. So the narrative of mixed identity leads back to the unresolved debate between essence and construct, identity politics and postmodern identities. Or perhaps mixture bridges this debate. I would suggest that writers such as Shange and Anzaldúa, and even Ruiz de Burton and Hopkins, imagine decentered identities that enable resistance to monolithic or hegemonic conceptions of race and difference, while also imagining powerful identity politics rooted in culturally specific conventions and historical memories. Indeed, these writers use the process/*proceso* of decentering or of crossing boundaries as the transient foundation for identity politics. Shange's photographic image of *raza* captures one potential angle of mixture, ideally endowing it with revolutionary powers to redefine identity and community. Although this fiesta borders on the utopian, it also introduces strategies for rejecting Anglocentric identities, tragedies, histories, and paradigms.

TWO

Creoles
and
Color

Caribbean identity is built on both mestizo and mulatto mixture. While Mexican usage of *mestizaje* often elides the Africanist presence, this presence is more visible in the racial makeup of the Caribbean. In defining her Puerto Rican–American identity, Rosario Morales includes "the ebony sheen to my life," "the sound of african in english" (Levins Morales and Morales 56–57). She affirms "The Other Heritage" within her *mestizaje*: "I was just right just me just brown and pink and full of drums inside beating rhythm for my feet" (58). As she says in another poem, "Africa," "Though my roots reach into the soils of two Americas / Africa waters my tree" (55). She reminds us of the racial, national, linguistic, and cultural legacy of Africa in all of the Americas and celebrates the brown, the pink, and the black.

This Caribbean mixture bridges the two American race paradigms discussed in chapter 1, pairing the mediating mixture of *mestizaje* with a black-to-white racial spectrum. Moreover, it transcends racial categories to include an overt mixture of nations, languages, and color. This chapter analyzes histories, theories, and representations of Caribbean race dynamics, which often romanticize the islands as a place of uncomplicated fluidity. I retain that sense of fluidity insofar as it redefines race identity as a complex product of color, class, education, and other social factors rather than a fixed essence but temper the idealized image of the Caribbean with an analysis of the persistence of color hierarchies. The complexities of Caribbean identity, although often opposed to U.S. race dynamics, offer many insights regarding the construction of racialized identities in general and American identities in particular.[1]

Martinican poet and critic Edouard Glissant celebrates the "new," "open" identities of the Creole Caribbean, which subvert the "old and rigid sense of identity" ("Creolization" 274). In the Caribbean context, *Creole* literally means island-born (as opposed to European-born), but the term also connotes mixed race. Since mixture occurred so frequently on the islands, *Creole* is opposed to supposedly pure and rigid European identities.[2] I regard these open, "impure" identities as emblematic of the mixture that has defined all of the Americas for centuries.

Glissant claims that our views of civilization have been transformed "from the all-encompassing world of cultural Sameness, effectively imposed by the West, to a pattern of fragmented Diversity" achieved by peoples in resistance (*Discourse* 97). This "Diversity," which Glissant attributes to the Caribbean, is cross-cultural, antiuniversalist, antiessentialist, and dynamic, unlike the sublimation of difference established by "expansionist plunder" from "the West" (98, 253). In addition to the geographic opposition between the West and the Caribbean, Glissant also builds a theoretical opposition between universal essence and fragmented difference that coincides with a temporal opposition between the past of colonial domination and the Creolized, diversified present. The frequency of mixture in the early history of the Caribbean, however, suggests that this challenge to universal essence is long-standing, not a product of contemporary postcolonialism. The qualities that have empowered the islands' challenge to imperialist domination—geographic, racial, national, and linguistic heterogeneity—support postcolonial theories with a history of effective political resistance, breaking down Glissant's opposition between colonial history and contemporary antiessentialism.

According to Barbara Christian, "Ethnic and African American Studies in the United States are, in a sense, just beginning to catch up with the complexities of the very concept of identity, complexities acknowledged by Caribbean peoples, for in that region identity is seldom characterized by a simple or single label" ("Rough Terrain" 258). In the Caribbean, although Europeans have been the dominant, colonizing force, they do not constitute a majority. Furthermore, the mixture of peoples of African, British, French, Dutch, Spanish, East Indian, and indigenous descent in the close quarters of the Caribbean islands has absolutely de-centered *white* and *black* as pure and polarized racial categories. Unlike the racial history of the southeastern United States, no amount of literary or scientific mythology could support an illusion of binary racialization. Although racial and racist hierarchies dominate Caribbean history, the uncertainty of racial differentiation based on skin color alone has cre-ated a social structure in which other characteristics such as class, lan-guage, cultural practices, and beliefs have come to signify *race* as much as color. While the planter aristocracy in the southeastern United States was defined by its supposedly pure whiteness, the Creole aristocracy in the Caribbean encompasses a range of skin colors and relies on manners and social codes to distinguish itself.[3] Christian's statement suggests that the peoples of the Caribbean have long acknowledged this social contin-gency of racial identity, foreshadowing by centuries recent trends in race studies and postmodernism.

Yet in adopting the Caribbean as a model for these contemporary theo-ries, it is too easy to forget the histories of conquest, domination, slavery, and violation that produced this fluid multiracial dynamic. This chap-ter will juxtapose contemporary celebrations of Caribbean fluidity with the histories of racial violence and resistance in the Caribbean, situat-ing the Caribbean model of race dynamics in its originating context. The much-discussed nineteenth-century Cuban novel *Cecilia Valdés* em-bodies this tension between racial fluidity and oppressive hierarchies, and it played a central role in the formation of Cuban racial mythology. I in-clude a reading of *Cecilia Valdés* to establish a precedent for contemporary Caribbean literature on mixture and to show how this novel is in dia-logue with U.S. mulatto literature from the same period. After surveying representations of the Caribbean's race history, I analyze literary texts by contemporary Puerto Rican and U.S. Puerto Rican writers Rosario Ferré, Ana Lydia Vega, and Aurora Levins Morales, who tend toward an overly idealistic view in their literary depictions of the fluidities produced by Caribbean race history. I choose prominent feminist writers from either side of the "border" between the United States and Puerto Rico to high-light both the racial continuity and the internal national difference that bridge Puerto Rican identity from the island to the mainland. Finally, I conclude with an extended reading of literary and theoretical works by Jamaican-American writer Michelle Cliff, who offers a more histor-ically grounded and tempered version of the complexities of Caribbean identity.

Histories of Race in the Caribbean

In 1891 José Martí wrote, "No hay odio de razas, porque no hay razas [There is no hatred of races, because there are no races]" (21). The mixture within "nuestra América mestiza" challenges the foundations of racism (15). As a Cuban exile in New York City, Martí analyzed the seeds of a new America in which all racial differences would be surmounted (21–22). What led him to such an optimistic view at the same moment in history when Jim Crow was the official policy of the southern United States? I am interested in the tension between Martí's confidence in the impossibility of racial hatred and the actual persistence of racism.

In the Caribbean that was Martí's background, the color variations of racial hybridity challenged segregation, and the ambiguity of color as a signifier of race lead to an emphasis on the social elements—class, culture, language—that imbricated racial identity. While racial hierarchies did and do exist in the Caribbean, those hierarchies have a different appearance, different meanings, and different signifiers from U.S. racial hierarchies. To heighten an awareness of the complexity of American racialization, it is worthwhile to historicize this model of racial dynamics that more clearly transcend the black-white polarization to which U.S. racial definition has often clung.

Caribbean slave economies were dominated by large plantations that depended on huge slaveholdings to produce labor-intensive crops (sugar and coffee, for example). Unlike the situation in the United States, the small European population on the islands was insufficient to establish a separate, independent white culture. Interracial mixture began with the first intercultural contacts, since the Europeans depended on people of color for labor, trade, and communication. Early European settlers brought African slaves to the Caribbean, and these slaves were often the first to learn the native Arawak language. Spanish conquistadors frequently paid Africans to act as translators in early negotiations with the native Caribbeans, positioning the Europeans, the Africans, and the natives in an interdependent triangular relationship from the start. As a result of frequent interracial mixture, a white minority, and the diversity of nations that have met there, the Caribbean often serves as a paradigm for racial fluidity. [4]

Glissant claims that the black-white separation imposed in the United States was impossible on the islands, where all strata of the population were fused together in the confines of the plantation system ("Creolization" 272). In the process of creolization, the generations produced on the islands blended the different races. Glissant's U.S.-Caribbean opposition is emblematic of recent historical studies. According to historian Jan Rogozinski, "In place of the stark division into two races found in some other parts of the world, island societies developed an elaborate network of shades and hierarchies" (x). In his well-respected history of the Caribbean, Franklin Knight similarly opposes Caribbean fluidity and "simple" U.S. race divisions, describing Caribbean race dynamics as "confusing, sometimes hyphenated blends rather than in sharply distinguishable elements polarized as simply black or white, African, Asian, American Indian, or European" (309). Joel Williamson also claims the Caribbean fostered greater leniency toward racial mixture than did the United States (*New People* 2). Finally, Mark Kurlansky idealizes the "subtler dynamic" of racism in the Caribbean and suggests that the United States introduced "virulent new strains of racism" into the more harmonious islands (41–44).[5]

I want to challenge the illusory opposition that emerges from such comparisons, since they often idealize the Caribbean (reifying the racial mixture that was produced in conquest and violation) and oversimplify the complexity of U.S. race relations. Tied to this emphasis on Caribbean racial mixture is a tendency to attribute the harshest forms of slavery and the worst plantation systems to the islands. Miscegenation corresponds historically to both racial fluidity and violent racial oppression under slavery. There is a causal relationship between these seemingly contradictory racial processes: the domination of slaves under harsh plantation conditions often led to (and required) sexual exploitation (to demoralize the slaves) and miscegenation (to reproduce the labor force). The resulting mixed-race population challenged racial stratification and caused the masters to reinforce their hierarchies all the more violently. Williamson notes that the harshest forms of slavery have historically coincided with large mixed-race populations, which acted as intermediaries between white planters and black slaves, and he cites the Caribbean as an example of this dynamic (*New People* 2). These overlapping and mutually opposing forces—mixture and stratification—are both attributed to the Caribbean as a receptacle for American racial tensions and contradictions. Historian Anthony Maingot suggests that "the Caribbean has become a laboratory for the study of race relations" (221). Miscegenation, fluidity, and the harshest conditions of slavery are all frequently studied within the Caribbean context, as if to distance corruption on the islands from a more orderly U.S. race dynamic.

The historiographic opposition between the Caribbean and the United States reflects a desire to push miscegenation south of the border and to eclipse its U.S. manifestations by a comparison with the more thoroughly mixed islands. Significantly, in painting this opposition, Glissant cites William Faulkner as a representative voice of U.S. binary segregation ("Creolization" 272). Alongside the racism captured by Faulkner's texts, however, lies a lack of clarity in racial differentiation. For example, in *Absalom, Absalom!* (1936), characters unknowingly stumble into miscegenation and incest, revealing the uncertainty of racial and familial identity.[6] As Faulkner's narrative suggests, much as in the Caribbean, the boundaries between the races were blurred in the United States, too.

I analyze representations of racial fluidity in the Caribbean with an eye for these shared dynamics, showing how interracial relations have decentered white privilege. Histories of the Caribbean tend to draw out this decentering more than do histories of the United States. In particular, I focus on the former British and Spanish colonies, since they reflect the two dominant racial paradigms I discuss in the United States, mulattoes and mestizos.[7] Despite the many significant historical and cultural differences between the British Caribbean and the Hispanic Caribbean, they share a complex history of colonialism, slavery, and racial mixture that precedes and reflects (with some distortion or magnification) the neighboring Americas, including the United States and Mexico. This history of slavery in the British Caribbean resembles the plantation system of the southeastern United States, while the Hispanic Caribbean bears more affinity to Mexico. The Caribbean island chain thus bridges these regional differences based on British and Spanish colonialism.

English (Post)Colonial Dynamics: Barbados and Jamaica

Barbadian-American novelist Paule Marshall is well known for her exploration of the racial, cultural, and national multiplicity of the English-speaking Caribbean. In one of the most remarked scenes from *Praisesong for the Widow* (1983), Marshall's African-American protagonist, Avey, participates in the nation dance while visiting the Caribbean island of Carriacou. In an annual ritual designed to honor ancestors and to keep African traditions alive, the people gathered for the dance perform their African nationalities, one nation at a time, by dancing in an unmarked circle (237).

Avey watches the Temne, the Banda, the Arada, and the Moko people take turns performing their nation dances. This turn taking separates the islanders by nation, for a moment, before they all return to the Caribbean mix, just as the circle presents an invisible, crossable boundary between peoples. The process of the dance thus reflects the simultaneous national heterogeneity and unity of the Caribbean. The performance culminates in the final Creole dance, dominated by the younger, mixed-blood dancers (238). At this point, Avey takes her turn, performing her own mixed-nation version of the dance, a step that adapts elements of the Carriacou tramp, the South Carolina ring shout, and the Bojangling of Harlem dance halls (248–49). As in the conclusion of Ntozake Shange's *Liliane*, *Praisesong* puts its characters' bodies to work, celebrating their racial and cultural mixtures and representing mixture with dance. Marshall puts this dance at the conclusion to point out that the current generation identifies with mixture. Like Avey, it has no memory of its pure or original African nation. When Avey joins the dancers of this mixed generation, she symbolically links U.S. African-Americans and Afro-Caribbeans based on their shared racial and national mixture.

It is significant that the islanders declare their nationality through dance and that dancing makes Avey one of the Creoles. In this way, public performance establishes one's identity. Avey is previously unclear about her racial affiliations, wavering between *White* Plains society and her African-American heritage. Lebert Joseph, a leader of the nation dances, is unable to determine her African origin from her ambiguous, Americanized appearance. Her economic privilege, her "white" clothes, and her relatively light skin contradict dominant perceptions of Africanist identity, so she must perform her race through dance to make it visible. As a static object, Avey's body fails to signify race, yet once her dance enacts the various cultures of her personal history, her mixture becomes legible.

This multilayered perception of race is based on social and cultural constructions, which are variable and contingent, as much as on biology. I have already discussed how the stability of biological race has been challenged in the United States by miscegenation, passing, and changing definitions of race based on different fractions of black or white blood, but racial categories that are social constructions are even easier to subvert. That is, while skin color can be performed and our perceptions and definitions of it can be altered, it remains attached to the body in an essential way. In contrast, language, religion, dance, and signifiers of class (luxuriant clothing, for example) can be adopted, appropriated, or imitated regardless of one's physical characteristics. In a racial milieu characterized by mixture and multiplicity, it is difficult to pin down any individual to a single, racialized set of manners.

In *Free Enterprise* (1993), Jamaican-American writer Michelle Cliff describes the ways in which the performances of the Caribbean elite cross color lines and draw more attention to purchased accoutrements than to the physical appearance of the individual. At the ball of the *gens inconnu* (unknown people), status is a costly possession: "With a huge cake covered all over by the finest slivers of coconut, like the hairs of an old white man, carried into the ballroom on the shoulders of footmen dressed in white silk, a pearl dangling from an ear. The ladies wore gowns decked with albatross feathers. . . . deadwhite gowns fought the deadwhiteness of a full moon for paleness. . . . A long table, inlaid with squares of Carrara marble, was piled high with hundreds of eggs laid by the masked, red-footed booby, who nested in the black volcanic sands of the beach" (13).[8] Although elite status is still coded here in terms of color, the color is displaced onto artificial objects: silk, gowns, moons, and coconut. The presence of an old white patriarch is replaced by that of a white cake. Genes are less at issue than costume or wealth. The eggs on the table were laid in black sands, reflecting the racial context in which Creoles are produced, but this juxtaposition seems to highlight all the more the whiteness and the rarity of the eggs. The Carrara marble, the elegant footman, and the French doors similarly create the illusion of European aristocracy. The *gens inconnu* have money enough to bring objects from Europe to the Caribbean, and those objects constitute their racial identity. Even the name *gens inconnu* leaves their individual identity unknown, immaterial in comparison to the expensive gowns.[9]

In *The Land of Look Behind* (1985), Cliff talks about the "colored" (or mixed-race) elite of Jamaica, people who are called red or some other shade between white and black. After the decline of British rule, these colored people assumed the roles of the displaced English colonizers, replacing white British authority with colored authority. In Cliff's description, *color*, an infinite variety of shades with more fluid social connotations, replaces *race*, a limited range of officially recognized categories. Postcolonial Jamaica remained trapped in a system of "colorism" in which light skin was privileged and barriers kept dark and light from commingling (*Land* 73). Yet Cliff clarifies parenthetically, "I should say here that I am using the categories light and dark both literally and symbolically. There are dark Jamaicans who have achieved lightness and the 'advantages' which go with it by their successful pursuit of oppressor status" (73). Once again, acting as an oppressor, imitating the Euro-American colonizer, can define one's status regardless of skin color. Like dance, acts of oppression mobilize the body and create relationships that give the body racial meaning. Such acts probably become all the more necessary when mixture befuddles standards for reading one's status based on color alone.[10]

Since the distinction between the elite and the "masses" is often not detectable at the level of skin color, the elite construct elaborate performances of their status to differentiate themselves, buying proof with physical accoutrements, education, and travel. While U.S. anxiety about the unclear foundations of the social hierarchy led to obsessive study of the racial body in literature, science, and law, in search of its essential traits, Caribbean racialization often regarded the body as an unreliable signifier. In her poem, "A History of Costume," Cliff shows how racial concern is displaced from body to costume in a museum display where plaster models' heads are "swathed in varicolored nylon stockings":

> My mother and I meet in public places—and move between
> the swathed heads:
> the faceless heads and covered bodies
> the covered faces, the emblazoned bodies
> the paisley-shawled bodies
> cut off from the undistinguished heads.

(*Land* 35)

In this image, public identity is determined by shawls, since the heads are otherwise "undistinguished." Cliff reveals how this lifting of identity off of the surface of the body denies human individuality, cutting bodies off from heads and judging these "faceless heads" by the veils that obscure them. While the desire to conceal one's body reflects continued perception of status based on appearance, the lack of clarity in the hierarchy of visible traits is further complicated by the layers of costume. In public, the body often does not signify, either because it is concealed or because it carries no clear meaning. In this milieu, the poem's speaker and her mother negotiate identities.

The unreliability of color as a social category has a long history in the English Caribbean. Barbados was the first plantation society in the Caribbean, settled by the English in 1627. Initially, white indentured servants worked the cane fields, but as early as the 1680s rapid importation of African slaves formed a black majority on the island (Rogozinski 68–69). Because of the small percentage of whites, black slaves were trained as managers, bookkeepers, slave drivers, and domestic servants, giving them significant power in the social hierarchy (111). By 1834, when England began to abolish slavery, three-quarters of the whites on Barbados were working-class "Redlegs" who made their living by fishing or farming small plots of land.[11] Many of these Redlegs were indentured servants who had been displaced by African slaves; some married and mixed with the black slaves (112). They were called *red* because of their sunburns, but there is some suggestion that their whiteness was also in question, either because of their low class status or because of their relationship to the blacks in Barbados.

Historian Hilary McD. Beckles discusses the blending of black and white and the inversion of color hierarchies in nineteenth-century Barbados. When the slaves finally achieved complete freedom in 1838, many black and colored Barbadians advanced above whites in the social and economic order (1). While poor whites in the post–Civil War South were similarly disadvantaged, their anxiety about losing their superiority over blacks was to some degree assuaged by the practices of Jim Crow. In the Caribbean, however, there was no such official system of white privilege. A white proletariat developed at the same time as freed slaves entered the skilled occupations and higher positions in the social hierarchy. Beckles argues that property ownership became the determining force in the construction of "racial" hierarchies. In the case of Barbados, wealth or even labor skills founded the social system as much as race did. Perhaps this economic basis freed Barbados from the color foundation of U.S. racism, which associated all psychological, social, and intellectual aspects of identity with color. Indeed, Beckles claims that white Barbadian laborers were considered an "immoral and vicious group": "they were accused . . . of commonly enticing slaves into drinking excessive quantities of alcohol, and sexually abusing female slaves" (5). This characterization inverts the racist stereotypes of the United States, accusing whites of sexual immorality and intemperance, and links stigma to class disadvantage rather than color. Furthermore, poor whites lived in such close proximity to blacks that they became "partly creolized into elements of Afro-Barbadian culture" (6). As they crossed racial lines, "black" and "white" carried less meaning about culture and status.

Despite this fluidity of race and culture, the British Caribbean was nonetheless hierarchical, exclusive, and violent. As long as plantation economies persisted, so would social stratification, whether based on color, class, or social caste. As in the United States, ideal racial stratification clashed with or responded to actual mobility between categories. In his history of race and class in Jamaica, Aggrey Brown claims that the color-based hierarchy was merely "a mask" for social and racial "incoherence" (21), recalling Cliff's veils and costumes. Throughout the nineteenth century, the tension between hierarchy and fluidity continued, creating friction that led to increased resistance, political awakening, and revolutionary sentiment. As abolitionism spread throughout the Americas, Caribbean plantation societies responded to the threatened collapse of their social and economic order. The British colonies were dominated by large plantations and immense slaveholdings, and the white minority was often anxious about its tenuous control over the African-descended majority. Says Knight, "Every slave society struggled to preserve its carefully delineated hierarchical order and only reluctantly accepted the unavoidable breaches of social boundaries" (145).

Part of this struggle to limit "breaches" of boundaries was legal. In most Caribbean countries, laws were enacted to limit the mobility of free colored persons, that threatening middle sector of the population that was not clearly either black or white. These individuals represented the breakdown of color stratification, but they also served as reminders of the light-skinned masters' sexual power over their slaves. Mixed-race individuals were targeted to reinforce unstable color lines. During the nineteenth century, while the United States was reaching a crisis over the issue of miscegenation, Caribbean laws similarly restricted the comportment, dress, residence, occupation, and material inheritance of free coloreds, rendering their difference publicly visible (137). In Jamaica, for example, "free" coloreds experienced only limited freedom: they could not give evidence in criminal court cases, serve on juries, act as overseers, or be elected officers (A. Brown 44). As in the United States, when mulattoes remained "safely" classified as slaves, they were rewarded with higher-status duties in domestic or skilled labor (Knight 128). Without the legal bindings of the slave system, however, Jamaica also worked to impose racial difference on its mixed population.

Violence was another means of reinforcing social hierarchies. Many slaves resisted their imposed subordination, forming maroon colonies that existed outside the plantation system. Throughout the eighteenth and nineteenth centuries, many thousands were killed in slave rebellions in Jamaica. After England abolished slavery, social tensions increased. In the wake of the 1865 Morant Bay Rebellion, more than four hundred blacks were systematically killed for daring to confront the white and colored leadership over unjust treatment. With this mass execution, the government publicly broadcasted its intolerance for resistance (A. Brown 69–70; Knight 282–83; Rogozinski 194–95). As mixture and resistance defied racial stratification, color-based hierarchies were enforced all the more aggressively.

Spanish (Post)Colonial Dynamics: Puerto Rico and Cuba

While all of the Caribbean islands share large mixed-race populations, historical studies often separate the Hispanic Caribbean from the other islands and idealize the former Spanish colonies as models of racial tolerance. A much larger percentage of imported Africans survived under the Spanish system of slavery, as compared to other colonies where they died in great numbers.[12] This difference might be attributed to leniency on the part of the Spanish colonizers, themselves often a "darker" people with a long history of mixture with North Africans. This hypothesis could also explain the openness to *mestizaje* in Mexico under Spanish colonialism. According to Francine Jácome, "el proceso de mestizaje fue mucho más pronunciado en el Caribe hispano, especialmente en República Dominicana y Puerto Rico, que en el resto del Caribe [the process of *mestizaje* was much more pronounced in the Hispanic Caribbean, especially in the Dominican Republic and Puerto Rico, than in the rest of the Caribbean]" (201). Perhaps the greater similarity of skin color among Spanish, indigenous, and African peoples enhanced the illusion of blending into the "brownness" of *mestizaje* and problematized racial segregation, in contrast to the African-British confrontations of Jamaica, Barbados, and the southeastern United States. But the Spaniards were certainly not inherently less racist than the northern Europeans.

The lower death rates for slaves in the Spanish colonies more likely result from the fact that slavery simply did not reach significant proportions in those colonies until long after the heights of slavery in the British, Dutch, and French colonies. Large-scale slave importation coincided with the emergence of large-scale sugar production. The development of large sugar plantations peaked in Cuba in the nineteenth century, and Puerto Rico did not have many large sugar estates until after abolition

(Rogozinski 118). By the time the Spanish colonies became major sugar producers, the conditions of slavery had evolved somewhat beyond the harsh plantation systems of Barbados or Haiti. Gang labor had become less common, nutrition improved, and the colonists had developed new methods for combating the tropical diseases that killed so many slaves in the seventeenth and eighteenth centuries.

Puerto Rico was, ironically, founded under the principles of *insularismo*. In 1508 Spain regarded Puerto Rico as a tropical laboratory for European ideals, an isolated experiment in humanism (Morales-Carrión vii).[13] In 1520 the Carib peoples were cordoned off in segregated *pueblos* to separate the Spaniards and the indigenous people, but after twelve years of intercultural contact, it was already too late to preserve ethnic distinctions. Arturo Morales-Carrión notes that the Caribs had lost their cultural purity through contact with the Spaniards and by mixing with the growing African population (4).[14] The natives certainly were not the only people affected by this mixing. Indeed, Rogozinski claims that after a decline in the sugar industry and early plantation society in 1600, Puerto Rico's population became "predominantly colored" through intermarriage and "more casual contacts" (53). Throughout the seventeenth and eighteenth centuries, with the extinction of the Caribs and the Arawaks, the importation of African slaves, and competition between the European maritime nations for access to Puerto Rico, this island, like the others in the Caribbean, became an "ethnic microcosmos" and a "mosaic" of different peoples (Morales-Carrión 57). In 1815, when the United States entered the competition for trade in Puerto Rico, the island *criollos* convinced Spain to end its policy of exclusivism. Despite Spain's official policy toward monocultural insularism, Puerto Rico became racially, culturally, and nationally mixed. This clash between the European ideal and its implementation in America resembles the impossible illusion of racial segregation in the United States.

The colonial period through the nineteenth century witnessed a "steady blending of races" in Puerto Rico (Rogozinski 208). Luis Martínez-Fernández suggests that Puerto Rican conditions favored miscegenation because, relative to other Caribbean islands that were dominated by sugar plantations, a larger percentage of Puerto Rico's population was "outside the grip of the state and export economy" (112). He attributes racial mixture to activities lying outside the sphere of the official economy: piracy, smuggling, illegal immigration, desertion, and *marronnage* (112). This argument problematically distances miscegenation from the dominant plantation economy and national system (a faulty claim, I would argue) and associates interracial relations with subversive, even illegal, activities. In any case, by 1860, 41 percent of Puerto Rico's population was racially mixed and free (112).

Rogozinski suggests that Puerto Rico's "mixed population encouraged egalitarian sentiment" and favored the abolition of slavery (209). In this assertion, the lessening of racial barriers coincides with a democratic lessening of economic barriers, so the absence of racial hierarchies supposedly leads to an economic leveling as well. Puerto Rican dynamics were less rigidly structured around color and class differences than were relations on other Caribbean islands, which featured large-scale black slavery and economic control in the hands of an elite white minority.[15] This characterization of a relatively egalitarian Puerto Rico, however, should not obscure the racism and classism that still existed there. Rogozinski's insistence on Puerto Rican egalitarianism here might result in part from the tendency to see the Caribbean (especially the Hispanic Caribbean) as a model of fluidity.

In Cuba more than in Puerto Rico, society was stratified according to the plantation system, and there was a close correlation among color, class, and social status (Martínez-Fernández 112).[16] In 1805 Cuban laws were enacted (much like earlier ones in the United States) that outlawed marriage between blacks or mulattoes and people of supposed *limpieza de sangre* (racial purity). Yet as Vera Kutzinski claims, this legislation was difficult to implement in a society where phenotype was ideologically collapsed with social status (19–20). Few interracial couples were denied marriage licenses until 1864, when fear of the potential impact of U.S. slave emancipation increased racial anxiety in Cuba.

In 1840, when blacks officially became the majority in Cuba, the planter class feared for its fragile social equilibrium. Abolitionist sentiment from England and the United States destabilized the foundations of color-based hierarchies (Knight 138). A worried Creole intelligentsia unsuccessfully tried to encourage white immigration to Cuba to counter the racial imbalance. Racial tensions reached their peak in 1844, in an incident called the Conspiracy of La Escalera (the ladder), when Cuban whites, in reaction to an alleged islandwide conspiracy, staged a preemptive massacre that decimated the Afro-Cuban intellectual and economic leadership (143).

Spanish authorities took advantage of this fear of insurrection and threatened to free the slaves when Cuba's Creole elite rebelled against

Spanish trade restrictions. Cuban conflict centered on the clash between *peninsulares* and Creoles, two white groups divided over regional allegiance, and used the black population as a tool for negotiations. Opposition was based on place of birth rather than race. When the revolution for Cuban independence finally broke out in 1895, blacks and whites from rural Cuba joined in defeating the urban, Spanish-born leaders (Knight 205). An independent Cuban culture united black and white based on their shared rejection of Spanish authority. As in Mexico, mixture defined Cuba's national particularity in opposition to Spain.

Cuban culture reflects a strong African influence. African gods and goddesses (for example, Changó) merge with Spanish Catholic religious figures (such as Santa Barbara) in the fused intercultural religion, Santería. This fusion subordinates and decenters Spanish culture, effacing its original features and transforming them through island practices. Cuban mixture reflects the synthesis of Spanish, African, and native beliefs and subverts the myth of a "Spanish" Cuba. The mulatta/o became a dominant cultural symbol to reflect the fusion of black and white. According to Kutzinski, Cuba "encodes its national identity in the iconic figure of a mulata—that of the Virgen de la Caridad del Cobre, the coppery Virgin of Charity who is Cuba's patron saint—not to mention in the countless images of mulatas that have been circulated in the island's literature and popular culture for roughly the past two centuries" (7). Kutzinski claims that the mulatta's cultural visibility contrasts with her social invisibility. As in Mexico, social reality, in which people of mixed race are often marginalized, contradicts the official national discourse of *mestizaje*. In addition, the celebration of mulattas in Cuba often masked continuing racial divisions and racial hierarchies that encouraged the whitening of Cuban racial identity through mixture. As Sara Rosell writes, "La noción de mestizaje . . . tiene su origen en el miedo a la africanización del país y aunque, en cierta forma, es una celebración a la diversidad racial, al mismo tiempo niega las divisions reales que existen en la sociedad [the notion of *mestizaje* . . . has its origin in the fear of the Africanization of the country, and although in a way it is a celebration of racial diversity, at the same time it denies the real divisions that exist in the society]" (16). The place of racial mixture in the national discourse suggests the degree to which Cuban nationality is founded on the incorporation of differences, ultimately defeating Spain's attempt to maintain unilateral political and cultural authority over its Caribbean colonies.

Cecilia Valdés, Cuba's "Tragic Mulatta"

One of Cuba's greatest cultural heroines is Cirilo Villaverde's Cecilia Valdés. *Cecilia Valdés: Novela de Costumbres Cubanas* (1882) has been regarded as one of the most important works of Cuban literature and attributed with authority over the construction of Cuban national identity.[17] This abolitionist novel captures many of the racial and sexual tensions of the nineteenth-century Caribbean. Villaverde describes the degree to which the light-skinned elite of Cuba "se rozaban con la gente de color [rubbed elbows with the people of color]" (18). Cecilia, a mulatta whose color is light enough that she can pass for "pure" Spanish, resembles a "Venus de la raza híbrida etiópica-caucásica [Venus of the hybrid Ethiopian-Caucasian race]" or "la Virgencita de bronce [the little virgin of bronze]," worshiped by the Cuban people (165, 20). In these comparisons, her sexuality is celebrated at the same time as her purity according to both European and mulatta models. Her grandmother, Seña Josefa, also has an ambiguous racial identity. Her relatively high social status—as mistress of her own house rather than servant—complicates her race as much as the shawl that disguises ("*disfrazarla*") her color and makes her appear Indian (2, 128).

Nonetheless, Cuban society in this novel does observe some degree of color hierarchy, and Cecilia aspires to marry a white man to improve her station rather than to lower herself by marrying a fellow mulatto. In-eke Phaf considers Cecilia a stereotypical Cuban mulatta, opportunistic in romance to fulfill her desires for money and status (178). Her reasons for wanting to marry lighter are superficial: she claims that marrying a mulatto would earn her a only silk shawl and marrying a "negro" would give her eyes and hair (Villaverde 24). In this way, race is detached from essential identity and social standing. Cecilia thinks that she might buy her entry into elite society if she were of a higher class. Money purifies the most turbid ("*turbia*") blood and covers physical and moral defects ("*defectos*") such as race (52), as in Cliff's passages quoted earlier. Wealth increases the mobility of other mulattas in Villaverde's novel and allows them to conceal their origins: "Tal vez otras menos linda que [Cecilia] y de sangre más mezclada, se rozaban en aquella época con lo más granado de la sociedad habanera, y aun llevaban títulos de nobleza; pero éstas, o dis-imulaban su oscuro origen o habían nacido y se criado en la abundancia, y ya se sabe que el oro purifica la sangre más turbia [Perhaps others less beautiful than her and of blood that was more mixed had connections in that period with the most select of Havana society and even carried titles of nobility, but these women either dissimulated their obscure/dark origins or were born and raised in plenty, and it is already known that gold purifies the most turbid blood]" (52). Cecilia lacks the money to purify herself without marriage, and her last name points to "lo oscuro de su origen [the obscurity/darkness of her origins]" that wealthier women are able to "dissimulate" (53). It is significant that Villaverde describes these origins as *oscuro*, which indicates simultaneous darkness, ambiguity, and concealment, like the often masked centrality of Africanism in Cuban culture.

Racial boundaries are unstable and frequently crossed, particularly by wealthy men or beautiful mulattas (sexualizing privilege for women). No one in *Cecilia Valdés* is free from racial uncertainty. The wealthy hero, Leonardo Gamboa, has a Creole mother with no guarantees regarding racial purity, and even his Spanish father is not beyond suspicion because of the Arab influence in his native Andalusia (38). To secure a title in Spain, Señor Gamboa has a purified family tree fabricated in which not a drop of Jewish or Moorish blood could be seen ("en que no había de verse ni una gota de sangre de judío ni de moro") (62). This illusory genealogy causes Leonardo no anxiety, and he attributes his love of mixed-race women to his own uncertain parentage (38). Villaverde suggests that most of the supposedly white counts, lawyers, and physicians in Havana have African ancestry (73). Racial mixture problematizes both *black* and *white* as distinct categories of identity, making race an unreliable basis for determining social privilege or exclusion. In the end, it would be difficult for a mixed-race woman such as Cecilia to choose a white husband, since there could be no certainty about his whiteness. Indeed, in a narrative turn that prefigures later U.S. works such as Pauline Hopkins's *Of One Blood*, the white man with whom she falls in love, Leonardo, turns out to be not only racially mixed but also her half-brother, again marking the intersection between interracial sex and incestuous sex and indicating the ways in which mixture crosses taboos erected internal to and between racial groups.

There are several different versions of *Cecilia Valdés*. Although an early version appeared in 1839, the first completed edition of the novel (including the expression of antislavery sentiment) was not published until 1882, after the decline of literary censorship in Cuba following the abolition of slavery (Luis 100; Kutzinski 19). The novel was written over a period of several decades, beginning in the 1830s, when Cuban fears of slave insurrection were high, and Villaverde was forced into exile in the United States in 1849. Therefore, Villaverde worked on the novel while in the United States, and he was probably influenced by that country's racial climate.[18]

Cecilia Valdés resembles U.S. tragic mulatta narratives of the nineteenth century, but the Cuban novel's encoding of mulattas' sexual identity is a bit more complex. According to Kutzinski, "Much like North American writers of the ante- and postbellum periods, Cuban novelists were particularly fascinated by women of ambiguous racial origin. However, whereas the tragic-mulatta stereotype in U.S. fiction conformed to the ideal of the Southern lady and 'possessed none of the lasciviousness associated in the popular imagination with her race,' some Cuban writers, including Villaverde, created a rather different female type" (21–22, quoting Shannon Elfenbein). Unlike the chaste heroines of Elizabeth Livermore or Frances Harper, Cecilia Valdés is often malicious, her strong sexual desires lead her to conceive a bastard child, and she ultimately tries to have Leonardo murdered. She is flesh and blood, strong, and driven. She need not offer any pretensions toward purity, piety, chastity, and domesticity, as literary mulattas in the United States did to address U.S. race and sex conventions. While U.S. tragic mulatta narratives often originate with the rape of a virtuous black woman by a white man, the women in Villaverde's novel are not passive victims but instead choose their white lovers. Yet this choice is less personal than it is structural: Cecilia follows the model of her mother and grandmother, repeatedly playing their assigned roles in a hierarchy that positions dark-skinned women at the mercy of light-skinned men. As Kutzinski notes, three generations of women in *Cecilia Valdés* are locked in a cycle of sexual exploitation (20). This exploitation is enacted through racial boundary crossings, asymmetrical power relations between light-skinned men and dark-skinned women, and the ultimate defeat of the mulatta women, who end up dead, crazy, or imprisoned. Yet Villaverde codes this racialized sexual oppression as one reinforced by the agency of women. Kutzinski suggests that "the iconic mulata . . . is a symbolic container for all the tricky questions about how race, gender, and sexuality inflect the power relations that obtain in colonial and postcolonial Cuba" (7). *Cecilia Valdés* reveals the ways in which the symbolic centrality and apparent agency of mulattas often correspond with violence against them. If, as an iconic character, Cecilia Valdés embodies Cuban race and sex dynamics, then Cuba's history is one of exploitation, boundary crossings, violence, and revenge. Yet how much of this emphasis on corruption is the product of Villaverde's U.S. influence?

Once again, the Caribbean not only is accorded greater subversion and complexity than the United States but also becomes a symbol of the darker side of race dynamics. Significantly, violence in *Cecilia Valdés* corresponds to racial fluidity and punishes those who cross racial boundaries. In this way, fluidity is condemned or contained. As in the nineteenth-century United States, racial barriers and tragedies constitute a reaction against border crossings. Fluidity and tragedy are paired, and both are often projected onto Caribbean culture and in particular the Cuban mulatta, who is situated at the intersection of sexual domination and racial mobility. Villaverde's text helps to perpetuate this damaging association of corruption with mixed-race women. Phaf argues that *Cecilia Valdés* marks the emergence of the mulatta as a Caribbean stereotype and that this novel acts as a defining model for the nineteenth century (176). Contemporary female writers from across the Caribbean also frequently return to and revise this racist and sexist representation, pointing out the fault lines within Villaverde's model and assigning power to the central mixed-race heroines.

Racial Mixture in Contemporary Puerto Rican Literature

As Glissant considers the Caribbean to be more racially fluid than the United States and Jácome considers the Hispanic Caribbean as a model for the greatest *mestizaje* in the Americas, Rogozinski regards Puerto Rico as the most mestizo island within the Hispanic Caribbean. The blending of the Arawak and Carib peoples with the Spaniards, the importation of African slaves, and the inability to create a successful plantation hierarchy led to a high concentration of racial amalgamation on this small island. Puerto Rico is also distinctive because it is the most recent U.S. territorial acquisition. Puerto Rico's 1952 incorporation as a U.S. commonwealth adds additional components to the long American history of *mestizaje*, merging European and U.S. colonialism, "Third World" and "First World" development, and a wealth of racial, cultural, and linguistic differences. This new *mestizaje* forces a radical rethinking of the terms of national identity.[19] Puerto Rico's official status as part of the United States complicates the drawing of national borders because the U.S.–Puerto Rican border is, quite literally, fluid. As a result, Puerto Rican narratives bridge Caribbean and U.S. racial, cultural, and literary influence.

Rosario Ferré's *The House on the Lagoon*

Rosario Ferré's racial representations reflect Puerto Rico's ambiguous national and cultural status, and her mulatto characters are poised between Caribbean and U.S. ideologies. Like many of the writers who investigate the engendering of racial mixture (from Jovita González Mireles to Ntozake Shange), Ferré is of a privileged class: bilingual, economically advantaged, well educated, and able to move freely between racial and cultural realms, the U.S. mainland and Puerto Rico, without being excluded from either. Ferré explores this betweenness in her work, translating and traveling among nations, cultures, races, and languages. Ferré translated her earlier work herself, and her novel *The House on the Lagoon* (1995) was first published in English. Like Sylvia López-Medina and Cirilo Villaverde, Ferré criticizes the obsession with bloodlines and ultimately depicts empowerment founded on the subversion of racial purity. Both López-Medina's *Cantora* (1992) and Ferré's *The House on the Lagoon* begin with sketches of a family tree, but Ferré's tree subverts genealogy with four question marks indicating uncertain paternity and with the mulatto line running parallel to the Spanish line. The Mendizabal bloodline complicates any pretensions to Spanish purity and shares many racial qualities with the Gamboa genealogy in *Cecilia Valdés*.

Ferré also analyzes the ways in which U.S. intervention in 1898 transformed Puerto Rican attitudes toward nationality and race. She writes about the Spanish "Bloodline Books," first instituted by priests during the colonial period to keep Spanish blood free of Jewish or Islamic "taint" (*House* 22). This obsession with purity recalls U.S. antimiscegenation ideology, but the Bloodline Books, as Ferré describes them, true to colonial Spanish racialization, were interested in religious and national exclusivism more than in color. Puerto Rico's shift from Spanish to U.S. domination complicated the matter of bloodlines, shifting attention from Spanish definitions of race to U.S. racial definitions. Yet Puerto Rico's diverse color spectrum did not easily lend itself to black-white discrimination. Ferré exposes the irony of Puerto Rico's adoption of racial prejudices based on U.S. history.

She claims that the Bloodline Books were officially abandoned by 1917, when the Jones Act made all Puerto Ricans U.S. citizens, because U.S. citizenship is supposedly based on equality. At the same time, Puerto Ricans visiting the United States learned about and began to imitate antiblack racism (23–24). Some historians concur with this analysis, claiming that antiblack racism was one of the first products of the U.S. occupation of Puerto Rico.[20] Says Ferré of the discovery of U.S. racism, "The situation caused Puerto Rican visitors [to the United States] considerable distress. Even though they were Caucasians, their skin was never as white as that of the Americans milling around them; it had a light olive tint to it, which made them suspect in the eyes of the conductor when they were about to board the first-class coaches in New Orleans" (25). The hypocrisy of Jim Crow laws in a country founded on legal equality confused Puerto Ricans and made them fearful of their own ambiguous racial status, too light to be black but too dark to be white. Bloodline searches continued in secret, as Puerto Ricans sought to lighten their race further to keep up with North American racial standards (25). Racial traits were even more closely scrutinized after 1917, according to Ferré, because Anglo-Saxons were less lenient about "exotic physical traits" than were the Spaniards, who were less suspicious of olive skin or curly dark hair after having been "colonized by the Moors for seven hundred years" (26).

In this way, like Jácome and Rogozinski, Ferré suggests that racial dynamics are more fluid in Puerto Rico than in the United States. The myth that Puerto Rican racism is a product of the United States blames the new colonizer for social injustice, when in fact Puerto Rico had its own long history of slavery and colorism. Nonetheless, in Puerto Rico, the *mestizaje* originated by Spanish colonization clashed with the overt structures of U.S. racism.

As a result of this culture clash, *The House on the Lagoon* is peopled with racist characters who have European or U.S. pretensions as well as by mixed-race and antiracist characters. Ferré's patriarch, Buenaventura Mendizabal, notes, "Here islanders have kept many African rites alive. It's going to be difficult to teach the Congolese and Yorubas the good manners of the *Mayflower*" (20). Although characters such as Buenaventura and many of his relatives favor spreading Anglo-American, *Mayflower* culture, those characters who are the strongest and who triumph in the end over his dead body are the mulatto descendants of the Avilés line. The mulatta and quadroon women of this family seem to be the most powerful in the novel, and they consistently manipulate and apparently dominate the light-skinned men (23). Unlike the U.S. tragic mulatta model, these women's power is physical, sexual, and African, far removed from white sentimental womanhood.

Petra Avilés, the mulatta whose witchcraft controls the Mendizabal family from generation to generation, stands at the center of the novel and the Mendizabal clan. By the end of his life, Buenaventura trusts no one other than Petra, and he uses her remedies to resolve all of his personal ailments and business problems. The real driving force behind his powerful industry is Petra's African rites and her prayers to Elegguá rather than Buenaventura's Spanish traditions. Indeed, Isabel, the main narrator, concludes that she has developed more faith in Petra's god than in her own Christian deity (388). Chronicling the hypocrisies of the Mendizabal legacy, Isabel exposes the degree to which it is founded on interracial alliance and an underground Africanist influence.

However, this influence remains underground, and Petra's power is revealed to the reader only as a secret, to expose the hidden source of Mendizabal authority. The mulatta characters exercise power only through dark, subversive, secretive measures—witchcraft and sexuality. Both Buenaventura and his grandson, Manuel, have mulatta mistresses, but these relationships remain illegitimate, hidden, and, in the case of Buenaventura and Carmelina, forced. The mulatta characters' subjectivity and power thus correspond to their willingness to act as sexual objects. Repeating the model of *Cecilia Valdés*, mulattas continue to perform a sexual function for light-skinned men, reassuring the men that sexual power ultimately remains in their hands. The public display of power and its material rewards still rest with the Mendizabal men. And the limited power that the mulattas can claim as nurturers, mistresses, and pagans reinforces racist mythology regarding mulatta impurity and illegitimacy.

In one particularly symbolic scene, Buenaventura's daughters, Patria and Libertad, cover the black baby, Carmelina, with white paint because they want to play with a white doll rather than a black one. When Carmelina sees her painted image in the mirror, she believes that she is a ghost and screams. In this incident, Ferré imagines whiteness as an evacuation of life, an artificial substance that induces terror, an unnatural nightmare.[21] Tragically, the lead in the paint almost kills Carmelina, who has to be rushed to the hospital in Buenaventura's Rolls-Royce. In this scenario, whiteness is not only horrific in appearance but also deadly. Blackness is not the tragedy here, as it is for the tragic mulatta convention—whiteness is. Significantly, this episode opens the Mendizabal house (and family) to Carmelina: Buenaventura's wife, Rebecca, feels so guilty about the incident that she keeps Carmelina in the House on the Lagoon (245). I find this scenario emblematic of Ferré's racial attitudes. She exposes pretensions toward racial purity and snobbery about whiteness as not only damaging but as painted on, too. Beneath these artificial racial poses lies the black skin at the foundation of Puerto Rican society and the racially mixed ancestry of its nobility. The strong dark-skinned women claim some power over yet ultimately remain subject to the "white" patriarch. The bias of Ferré's privileged vantage on race is reinforced by the assumption that women such as Petra and even Carmelina (before she is nearly killed) enter the house only as domestic servants.

Many critics suggest that Ferré's race and class privilege render her fiction politically conservative. Judith Grossman links Ferré's privilege with her experimental literary techniques and concludes that the narrative aesthetic of *The House on the Lagoon*, in its "modernist and postmodernist moves," presents a "profoundly conservative" opposition to any progressive agenda (5). While Ferré may be working within a postmodern literary tradition, and while that tradition certainly has its politically conservative adherents, I hesitate either to define Ferré's work as emanating solely from a postmodern tradition or to lump all of postmodernism with political conservatism. In fact, those characteristics of Ferré's work that might be called postmodern—linguistic code switching; self-reflexivity; crossing among different genres and narrators; and a reconfiguration of subjectivity without a singular, essential center—derive from a long tradition of politically radical mestiza and bicultural writing at least as much as from the Euro-American development called postmodernism. In this dual literary inheritance—postmodern and mestiza—Ferré resembles Anzaldúa and others. Regardless of her potential bias, Ferré provides a way to envision social alternatives to the hierarchy that endows her with privilege. She shows how entwined the different races and classes are, and in *The House on the Lagoon*, strength emerges from interracial alliances. However ambivalent some of her characters may be, Ferré decenters the dominant culture of Puerto Rico by exposing its complicity with the margins, a move that is especially radical because it comes from a writer who inhabits that center.

Ana Lydia Vega's *Encancaranublado*

Unlike *The House on the Lagoon*, Ferré's collection of stories, *Papeles de Pandora* (1976), has already received much critical attention. Ferré's short stories are often analyzed in conjunction with those of Ana Lydia Vega, yet the authors' differences are usually emphasized more than any shared traits. Vega, a short-story writer from Santurce, Puerto Rico, explores inter-Caribbean dynamics in stories that are often humorous or satirical. While Ferré is associated with the culture of the colonizer—she analyzes the

upper classes, she is overtly feminist and intellectual, and she often pub-
lishes in English to make her work accessible to U.S. audiences—Vega
writes in Spanish for a more popular audience of Puerto Ricans on the
island, and she dedicates much of her work to describing interracial tensions, the lower classes, and Puerto Rican politics.[22] Vega identifies herself with "todos los puertorriqueños," emphasizing the fact that her father
was an agricultural worker and that her family is "muy de mayoría negra
[very much in the majority black, or mostly black]" (Negron Muntaner
15). Like Moraga and Anzaldúa, Ferré and Vega could perhaps be said
to represent respectively the light and dark sides of Puerto Rican *mestizaje.* Yet their shared concerns complicate this opposition. In *The House
on the Lagoon* and in her stories from *Papeles de Pandora,* Ferré consistently
reveals the similarities and the mutual investments between the upper
and lower classes and between blacks and whites. For example, "When
Women Love Men" depicts the confluence of two opposing identities,
the upper class light-skinned woman and the mulatta prostitute. Also,
those stories that analyze the upper classes—"Sleeping Beauty" and "The
Youngest Doll," for example—consistently criticize the narrow restraints
imposed by class hierarchy. Not until *The House on the Lagoon,* however,
does Ferré address head-on Puerto Rican politics.[23] Vega's work is more
unambiguously rooted in these political issues.

Like Ferré, Vega also demonstrates an interest in *mestizaje* and the mulatto foundation of Puerto Rican culture. Vega symbolically describes
Puerto Rico as a mulatta, explaining that a character's "love for a Creole
mulatta" relates to his "search for Puerto Rican roots" ("Women" 822). As
in Mexico and Cuba, national identity is represented through racial mixture (and through women's bodies). She associates her familiarity with
"the black world" and "our African roots" with the radical politics of the
1970s generation in Puerto Rico, which rebelled against the dominant
class (824). This political foundation emerges in several stories from *Encancaranublado.* "Otra maldad de Pateco," for example, investigates the nature of biraciality and the artificial imposition of racial hierarchies. Pateco
Patadecabro, a sort of trickster figure, dyes the skin of a baby to make it
two-tone. The child presumably belongs to Señora Montero, the owner
of a large sugar plantation, twenty-five slaves, and a white mansion. Much
like the Mendizabal family in *The House on the Lagoon,* the Monteros possess the legendary pretensions of Spanish colonizers, obsessed with racial
purity and their own ancient lineage: "sus jinchísimas carnes . . . y azul
sangre heredada de Castilla la Vieja [their inflated/swollen meats . . . and

blue blood inherited from the Old Castle line]" (*Encancaranublado* 108). When Señora Montero discovers that her baby has a white body but a black head, a "bestia bicolor [bicolor beast]," she abandons him to be raised by the black *curandera*, Mamá Ochú (108). This parody of the half-black, half-white mulatto is suggestive in that the boy's head, the governing, rational faculty, is black, while his body, the locus of carnal functions, is white. In this way, Vega overturns racist stereotypes that imagined ennobling "white blood" to render the mulatto intellectually superior, counteracting the lower physicality of "black blood."

Furthermore, if racial mixture is a product of "tinto chino [dark Indian/mestizo paint]" rather than blood, race becomes artificial and mutable. If it can be painted on, it can be washed off or painted over, as is the case in Vega's story. This image recalls the painted baby Carmelina in *The House on the Lagoon*. In these two characters, Ferré and Vega explore symbolically the role that skin color plays in identity and the possibility that racial identity can be fluid. They question which color one would choose if such a choice were possible. In the process, both authors ultimately revalue blackness and criticize white "superiority." Their shared interest in painting, unpainting, and repainting challenges essentialist concepts of identity based on color.

As he grows up, the bicolor baby, José Clemente, believes that he is purely white because there are no mirrors in the house where he is raised, and he never sees his own head. Mamá Ochú lies to protect him, telling him that his eyes are as blue as the river and his hair as yellow as the sun (109). However, the first time that he escapes from the house, he discovers in the real world his own racial ambiguity. He falls in love with the first woman he sees, a mulatta slave whom he believes to be a princess, but she is scared by his dual coloring and runs away. As he chases her, José comes to a river, where he sees the reflection of his face for the first time. He cries and begs for "his color" to be returned to him ("devuélveme mi color") (110–11). This scenario parodies that of the conventional tragic mulatta, who believes herself to be white but in adulthood discovers the one drop of black blood that forever cuts her off from the white world (and often a white lover or husband). Like this antiquated literary heroine, José lives in absolute ignorance of race until his "biracialism" keeps him from his love.

Like many African-American writers, Vega refuses to privilege whiteness in her subversion of the mulatto narrative. In the end, José resolves his racial uncertainty by choosing to identify as black. When there is a fire on the plantation, he has a choice between saving the slaves or saving the masters. "Una fuerza superior [a superior force]" drives José to liberate the slaves, and he thus allies himself with those who raised him and denies those who denied him in his infancy (112). Significantly, while saving the slaves, the fire burns his body black, rendering his racial status visually certain (or at least singular). This narrative suggests not only that race is a choice for the bicolor subject but also that those who exclude the "half-breed" will have revenge visited on them. The Montero family is burned in the fire. As in *The House on the Lagoon*, the pretensions of the light-skinned family are thwarted, and the darker-skinned peoples emerge as victors.

Vega ultimately leaves José's racial origins uncertain. She hints that perhaps he was not the Monteros' baby but rather the child of slaves and that Pateco lied to Señora Montero "para escarmentar a la familia Montero [to punish/teach a lesson to the Montero family]" (113). To support this interpretation, Vega writes that the fire allows José to "recuperate" (*recuperar*) the original color that Pateco had hidden, implying that he might have been born black (113). Her refusal to provide a single clear explanation indicates the uncertainty of racial status in Puerto Rico and suggests that in certain contexts, biological race does not matter as much as culturally variable assumptions. Moreover, skin color is an unreliable indicator of racial identity, since what appears to be black skin could mask skin of another color. What does matter, in this instance, are moral and political choices: a "superior" force guides José to liberate the slaves and to seek revenge on his racist masters, purifying his body by fire in the process. In any case, if racial identity is so unstable and apparent color is so fluid, social hierarchies based on race or color are not well founded.

Vega explores the symbolic relationship between the races in another humorous story, "Historia de arroz con habichuelas [History/Story of Rice with Beans]," but this story imagines a synthesis between the two halves, transcending the black-white discontinuity from "Otra maldad de Pateco." Vega describes Arroz as *blanquito* and feminine (*Encancaranublado* 133), while Habichuelas are "mulatos," "sabrosón," and "avispao" (133).[24] They share a long history of attraction. Vega describes Arroz trembling, waiting for "una sola gota colorada de la salsa de Habichuelas manchara la castiza blancura de sus granos [one colored/red drop of the beans' sauce to stain the chaste or pure-bred whiteness of her grains]" (133). Using this satirical tone, Vega suggests that the distinction between color and whiteness might be based on a desire for mixture. Rice and beans are served together. Unlike José Clemente, who must choose between the two halves of his identity, the two halves of Arroz y Habichuelas are inseparable in the duality (or multiplicity) of Puerto Rican culture. Significantly, *arroz con habichuelas* in Puerto Rico usually contain red beans, and Vega describes their salsa as *colorada*, a relatively fluid color designation that could mean "red" or simply "color" in general. In this way, she separates race from simple black-white opposition. In the end, "llegaron al consenso sin plebiscito [they arrived at consensus without a plebiscite]" (140). Regardless of public attitudes and social mores, they achieve mutual happiness and harmony, concluding in song: "dos vale más que uno [two are worth more than one]" (140). The blending of colors is empowering. In the tone of a nursery rhyme, Vega depicts an easy peace between colors, taking seriously the model presented by food eaten every day in Puerto Rico. While this allegory is overly idealistic in its simple and happy resolution, Vega does reveal the interdependence of white and nonwhite and the absurdity of interracial antagonism. Aníbal González, too, finds in Vega's work "una visión utópica de la reconciliación de opuestos [a utopian vision of the reconciliation of opposites]" (294). Indeed, both "Otra maldad de Pateco" and "Historia de arroz con habichuelas" employ the naive optimism of children's stories to explore racial binaries, and both reduce color to a matter of trickery or taste, but this genre allows Vega to separate racial dynamics from the limiting forms of reality, to fantasize resolutions to racism, and to reimagine color as a fluid designation. Moreover, the playful tone allows Vega to explore painfully serious topics with humorous distance.

Aurora Levins Morales: California Puerto Rican

Puerto Rican poet and short story writer Aurora Levins Morales prepares a similar mixed-race feast in her kitchen, but unlike Ferré and Vega, Levins Morales lives in the continental United States. Puerto Ricans on the continent must negotiate even more than those on the island with the terms of U.S. culture. Although officially inside their own nation, since there is no national border between the United States and Puerto Rico, U.S. Puerto Ricans' language, culture, and history make them outsiders. On the mainland, they are often lumped into the same category as Chicana/os and other Latin Americans, either as *Hispanics* or *Latinos*. The fragmentation, marginalization, and multiplicity of Puerto Rican identity become more pronounced at this remove from the island. For Levins Morales, mixture is both intercultural and intracultural, international and intranational: she was born in Puerto Rico to a Puerto Rican Jewish mother and a Russian Jewish father and moved to the United States. Like all immigrants, she brings components of her other national and cultural identities with her to the United States, and her identity reflects a complex racial, cultural, and national *mestizaje*.

In her story "Kitchens," Levins Morales describes herself in her California home stirring beans and rice, watching the "ink of the beans" spread to turn the rice brown and the zucchini black (*Getting Home Alive* 37). In addition to her insistence on the power of the blackness in the mixture, there are also suggestions in Levins Morales's kitchen that color (or perhaps just whiteness) is the product of human intervention. While preparing the rice, she watches the water in which she rinses the grains turn milky from the rice polish and talc. Whiteness, in this image, comes from the products that are added to whiten rice artificially, like the white paint in *The House on the Lagoon*. Levins Morales searches through the murky water to find the "blackened tip" and "the brown stain" (37), echoing Vega by choosing those grains of rice that show the mark of *mestizaje*.

Yet unlike Vega's *arroz con habichuelas*, the beans and rice in Levins Morales's California kitchen are transnational: they enact a deliberate recitation of her Puerto Rican island heritage. She uses "kitchens" in the plural, joining hers to the "mountain kitchens of my people" (39), probably referring to the mountains of Indiera Baja, Puerto Rico, where she lived in early childhood. Her kitchen thus originates from outside California, even though she claims that "mine is a California kitchen" (37). It is dual in location, foreign and not foreign. Levins Morales affirms the presence of Puerto Rico within the United States and the presence of U.S. culture in her Puerto Rican culinary processes, using "bottled spring water and yogurt in plastic pints" (37) alongside Puerto Rican ingredients.

I consider this kitchen image significant, not only because the kitchen has been conceived as a traditionally feminine space—the "womb" of a feminine culture based on storytelling, female control, and domesticity— but also because the kitchen is where one brews new concoctions, mixing various ingredients to produce a desirable blend. It is no accident that the metaphor most commonly used to assimilate cultural diversity in the United States is the *melting pot* (or, more recently, the *tossed salad* or *vegetable soup*), reminding us of the human (and often female) labor required to produce both racial and culinary mixture. Levins Morales calls "the dance of the cocinera" (cook) "magic" (38). The metaphor of magical culinary powers, however, is perhaps overly simplistic: resolving racial difference is more than a matter of mixing together different colors. As with Vega's use of fantasy or Shange's use of art, Levins Morales's recourse to magic enables her to imagine resolutions in literature that are more complicated in reality.

Other stories and poems by Levins Morales exemplify this multiple crossing of identities and this juggling of cultures. While her mother, Rosario Morales, emphasizes the African elements of Puerto Rican identity in "The Other Heritage," Levins Morales says that "I am not african" (*Getting Home Alive* 50). Yet she does not deny that "Africa is in me" (50). The distinction between being African and having Africa in her is one of *mestizaje*. In her poem "Child of the Americas," she shows how the Africa in her is part of her American identity, not merely adding an element of Africa to America but radically redefining America itself to include Africa as much as it includes Europe. Levins Morales claims to have "no home" in Europe or Africa; rather, "I am a child of the Americas. . . . I am a U.S. Puerto Rican Jew, a product of the ghettos of New York. . . . I am Caribeña, island grown. . . . I am of Latinoamerica, rooted in the history of my continent" (*Getting Home Alive* 50). The traces of Europe, of Africa, of Taíno in her are part of this American *mestizaje*. They lose their pure, original state and diffuse throughout the whole of American history and American racial mixture, so she cannot "return" to either Europe or Africa as such. Levins Morales is multiracial, with no pretensions to any original African or European identity. Her "first language was Spanglish," indicating that mixture is her origin (50). She does not claim any single identity beyond *American*, and this *American* includes the multiple races and nationalities that have entered the Western Hemisphere. Importantly, she does not see this multiplicity as fragmenting: "I was born at the crossroads and I am whole" (50). For Levins Morales, part of being American means integrating these multiple components into one mestiza whole. In this way, *mestizaje* forms American identity.

In her prose poem "Old Countries," Levins Morales repeats this sense of being cut off from the original homelands that some Americans refer to as the Old Country. But she does not miss these connections or see herself as homeless: "New York is the Old Country to me" (*Getting Home Alive* 89). She thus endows heterogeneous America with its own national integrity. American nationality is characterized as "Northern Black Irish Polish Russian Hillbilly Puerto Rican Ojibwe" (91). Like America, Levins Morales claims to have "inherited all the cities through which my people passed": Kirovograd, Granada, Jerusalem, Cairo, Damascus, Dakar, Lisboa, New

Orleans, New York (90). This composite empowers her with multiple resources, languages, and stories. With this variety, where races meet at America's crossroads, Levins Morales challenges racism, decenters European authority, and affirms the power of America's multiracial heritage, in the tradition of Ferré and Vega. Yet she goes beyond these writers by adding to the mixture the other racial and national elements that define her as a Puerto Rican Jew in the mainland United States.

Michelle Cliff and the Complexities of Color in Jamaica

In "The Laughing Mulatto (Formerly a Statue) Speaks," Michelle Cliff figures identity as sculpture in which color signifies most prominently: "I am writing the story of my life as a statue. . . . I wish they had carved me from the onyx of Elizabeth Catlett. Or molded me from the dark clay of Augusta Savage. Or cut me from mahogany or cast me in bronze. I wish I were dark plaster like Meta Warrick Fuller's *Talking Skull*. But I appear more as Edmonia Lewis's *Hagar*—wringing her hands in the wilderness—white marble figure of no homeland—her striations caught within" (*Land* 85). Onyx, mahogany, bronze, and white reflect the range of color possibilities in the Caribbean, a spectrum that complicates black and white racial categories. Rather than talking of race as such, Cliff refers to color: red, brown, nutmeg. Significantly, Cliff describes these colors as workable materials (bronze, clay, marble), implying that identity can be molded or chiseled. The parenthetical "formerly a statue" in the poem's title suggests that the "mulatto" might no longer be so rigidly cast in stone. Cliff wants to replace the inflexible marble of past depictions—and the classical whiteness of sculpture such as Lewis's—with more malleable "dark clay" (*Land* 85). Cliff's characters are more than biracial, they are multiracial, multinational, multilingual, and multicultural. Much like the *castas* of colonial Mexico, color is imbricated with class, education, and culture in fluid constructions of identity.

The speaker of the poem, like Cliff herself, is racially mixed but white in appearance. Cliff critiques the whiteness within her by linking it to Edmonia Lewis's *Hagar*, the pale tragic model, and emphasizes the "striations caught within," the dark traces in the marble surface. She thus denies both whiteness and marble their privileged status among artistic media. This wish allies Cliff with many writers who address racial mixture, including, among others, Moraga, Ferré, and Shange. These writers have enjoyed privileges based on light skin, education, and class standing, but they emphasize mixed identity not to celebrate those privileges but to challenge racial stability and to decenter whiteness. Although they all live in the United States, these writers also privilege non-U.S. histories (Mexican, Caribbean, Native American, African) in their work. Cliff and Moraga in particular reject the whiteness in their identity, which often distances them from their Caribbean and Chicana contemporaries, and honor instead their darker mothers. Both also address racial and cultural fluidity with equally fluid form, moving among nations, genres, and languages in dialogue with literature and theory from the past and the present.[25]

Critics have celebrated Cliff's attitude toward flexible subject positions as a sign of her postmodernism. Françoise Lionnet, for example, studies Cliff's use of the "double consciousness of the postcolonial, bilingual, and bicultural writer who lives and writes across the margins of different traditions and cultural universes" (324). Cliff's work subverts the boundaries between genres, languages, cultures, and races, a practice Lionnet attributes to Cliff's use of "postmodern fictional techniques" (324). While Cliff's fluidity reflects the spirit of contemporary theories, she also echoes more than a century of African-American artistic expression, including Frances E. W. Harper, William Wells Brown, and other nineteenth-century writers who crossed margins of race and identity in their work. This tradition is just as important a context for her writing as is postmodernism. It is true that Cliff "demonstrates that marks of difference and otherness are ambiguous and shifting" and that she articulates "a form of multivalent subjectivity capable of resisting shifting networks of power" (Lionnet 340–41). Many critics have picked up on the similarity between Cliff's representations of identity and postmodernism, and recent works on the "postmodern" identities in Cliff reflect this sudden interest.[26] Shifting, multivalent subjectivity and fluctuating signs of difference, however, have been around at least since Brown's *Clotel* passed as a white male slave owner. Studies of biracial literature that use only postmodern lenses miss the other traditions out of which these writers write.

Cliff's contemporary work should also be viewed in the context of earlier African-American texts since this blurring of racial boundaries is a well-established African-American condition.[27] Although Cliff is from Jamaica, her travel between different nations and cultures makes it difficult to categorize her as belonging to any single nationality. My intent is not to claim Cliff as a U.S. African-American writer (although she currently works and resides in the United States) but rather to show how her work fits into and goes beyond depictions of race in the U.S. literary tradition. Cliff signals her relationship to this tradition by naming the heroines in her 1984 novel *Abeng* Zoe, the name often given to the stereotypical tragic mulatta in the nineteenth century, and Clare, recalling Nella Larsen's tragic character in *Passing*. In *Free Enterprise* (1993), Cliff's heroine meets Frances Harper face to face and criticizes her privileging of light skin. The racial mixture of Jamaica's "colored" middle class provides a pronounced example of the privileges, ambiguities, and betweenness of racial mixture. Cliff adds to the tradition of Harper, Pauline Hopkins, Larsen, and Jessie Redmon Fauset an enhanced awareness of racial and national complexity that is the product of her Afro-Caribbean experience. Race for Cliff is not black and white but rather a composite of color, class, gender, culture, and education, and her characters cross each of these axes of subjectivity in multiple different ways.

Cliff's position among Afro-Caribbean women writers is somewhat ambiguous because of her U.S. residence, her class advantage, her light skin, and her education. Belinda Edmondson claims that Cliff's attempt to revalue blackness despite her own apparently white skin "is debated by West Indian feminists and intellectuals": "Many . . . feel that even as Cliff is described as a black feminist novelist in America (where she lives and writes) her novels are not truly part of an Afro-centric Caribbean discourse, because her project as a feminist emanates from an American feminist sensibility and perhaps more importantly that her discovery of a black identity is a foreign fashion that she has appropriated" (181–82). According to Edmondson, women such as Cliff who experience the privileges of the dominant culture come to represent "not simply both 'First' and 'Third' World sensibilities but also 'male' (white, Euro-American) colonizing culture and 'female' (black, post-colonial) colonized nature" (182). This depiction implies that Cliff is less black, less "Third World," and less female as a result of her privileges, an extremely problematic suggestion in that it reserves privilege for "First World" white men. Since Cliff's characters (autobiographical and otherwise) embody multiple sides of many identity categories, they challenge such limiting reservations based on race, class, nation, and sex.

Furthermore, Cliff's sexual politics, her lesbian feminism, is often seen as part of her co-optation by Euro-American feminisms.[28] In their introduction to *Her True-True Name* (1989), Pamela Mordecai and Betty Wilson imply that feminism is not authentic to Caribbean women, asserting that in "recent writing by anglophone Caribbean women . . . there is no ritual pursuing of pseudo-feminist agendas" (xvii). Mordecai and Wilson ally Cliff with Jean Rhys (also a feminist) because of their shared "whiteness," alienation from the Caribbean, education, and association with "the metropole" (xvii). According to Mordecai and Wilson, as a result of Cliff's privilege, "one of the prices she has paid is a compromised authenticity" in her renderings of Creoles (xvii). Yet Cliff's feminism also emerges from a powerful nonwhite tradition—Granny Nanny, for example—that de-centers the supposed Euro-American dominance of feminism and situates Cliff in an "authentically" Caribbean history.

So Cliff is already impure, corrupted by foreign influences, as a model of Afro-Caribbean authority or feminist authority. Yet this foreignness supports my argument and adds another dimension to the multiple axes of identification that the mixed-race subject crosses. Cliff's work, while retaining roots in Jamaican culture, also moves fluidly from the Caribbean to Europe to the United States, crossing not only oceans but also borders of identity and belonging. She cannot be simply categorized as black or white, as Jamaican, American, or European. According to Edmondson, Cliff creates a location that is "elsewhere," that emanates from "the geo-political space of memory," that goes beyond existing categories (185). In this interpretation, Cliff maintains geopolitical and historical ties through memory at the same time that she transcends the existing categories of reality. She creates "an alternative 'reality' [that] both extends and en-gages West Indian and European representations" (190). Much like some postmodern literature, Cliff's narrative space combines multiple different histories and places to imagine an alternative space in which different worlds coexist. The multiple components of Cliff's texts, picked up from her travels among nations, races, and cultures, refuse to fit into any single existing nation, race, or culture. One question inevitably arises: Does not fitting into one mean fitting into many or fitting into none? Cliff explores both of these possibilities.

In *The Land of Look Behind*, her 1985 collection of poetry and essays, Cliff describes mulattoes in Jamaica as living proof of interracial sex, usually a light-skinned man's transgressions outside the color line (41). Cliff claims that many fathers have broods of "outside" children who come and go by the back door (26–27). According to Cliff, these darker children are out-side because they are produced in extramarital alliances. This exclusion is based on their illegitimacy and their class status as much as on their color. They remain outside the realm of manners, outside the family, attending different schools, distanced from the light-skinned children to hide the shame of their fathers' border crossings. This going outside is subversive in that it questions the superiority of white lovers, denies racist repulsion on the sexual level, and decenters white-centered power structures by exposing the center's involvement with outsiders. Perhaps the outside is so fundamental to the status quo that the two are interdependent: the status quo is a product of their hidden proximity. In another racial materialization that prefigures the Derridean concept, the inside is constructed by its relations with the outside.[29]

While the darker mixed-race children are positioned outside the "charmed circle" of racial advantage, those mixed-blood children whose lighter skin puts them in a position of potential racial domination among the "hierarchy of shades" are expected to advance the whitening, or the centering, of the darker-skinned Creoles and to encourage assimilation by adopting the colonizer's culture (59). The process of moving up in the racial hierarchy means choosing partners within the lighter-skinned Creole population, looking inside the privileged circle and keeping the darker shades outside, an internal racism earlier exemplified by Charles Chesnutt's "The Wife of His Youth."[30] As a result, the mixed-race individual, who inhabits the margins of a white-centered society, experiences a tension between crossing inside or outside through sex, using reproduction to move the family into the inner circle of whiteness or to reject that center and turn outward through further racial mixture. As with Ntozake Shange's Malveaux family, incest and miscegenation, inbreeding and outbreeding, form two sides of the same coin. Yet both directions of breeding reproduce the same racist hierarchies at different locations. This tension, or often slippage, between inside and outside within the mixed-race family questions the distinctness of the racial inside from the racial outside, undermining the exclusionary principles that such racism tries to reinforce.

As the lines of racial demarcation in Jamaica blur, racial whitening is not always necessary to achieve status. Regardless of color and parentage, culture, education, and even personal connections can move an individual up in the hierarchy.[31] Indeed, since Jamaica received its independence in 1962, light-skinned or "colored" Jamaicans have taken over the role of oppressor from the white British colonizers. In her important essay, "If I Could Write This in Fire, I Would Write This in Fire," Cliff considers what happens when the "house nigger" assumes the position of master (*Land* 62). In this changing of the guard, the biracial Jamaican crosses the traditional lines of correlation between (white) race and leadership,

(European) nationality and conquest. Cliff claims that at this point, "unreality overtook reality": biracial Jamaican "coloreds" constructed an image of the colonizer in themselves, and an artificial simulation of white dominance overtook the authority of the real white colonizer (62). Privileged coloreds, like Cliff's Savage family in *No Telephone to Heaven* (1987), come and go between Jamaica, England, and the United States, replicating the triangular trade and reflecting the triangular patterns of cultural and economic neoimperialism that exist in Jamaica today.

This middle class, which is often but not always light skinned, is endowed with a "double vision" (*Land* 72). This doubleness is much like W. E. B. DuBois's "double consciousness" but more complex in that it includes a view of colonization from both sides of a crumbling racial and national divide. Cliff concludes her essay with an evocation of the multiplicity of identities within Jamaicans: "we/they/I connect and disconnect," blurring like the Rasta "I and I," self with Jah (76). Just as Rastafarians conceive their identity only in relation to Jah, a transcendental or godlike being, the mixed-race subject defines identity in relation to an other: an other race, an other class, an other being. "I and I" is multiple not only in vision but also in location, identification, and the interrelated categories (color, class, culture) that produce it.

The poems in *The Land of Look Behind* imagine identity as a web of possibilities based on these interrelated categories. Yet Cliff's heroines defy the Zoe model and refuse to pass or to imitate the white colonizer. Like Shange's Liliane, they want more color to solidify their racial affiliation. In "Artificial Skin," Cliff's speaker wishes she could purchase melanin, casting racial identity as an artificial colored surface that must be bought rather than born into (98). In this way, economics is once again connected to color, but this time blackness is more expensive. Unlike the eighteenth-century Mexicans who bought legal white status with certificates of racial purity, Cliff's speaker would use money to buy more color. Cliff's poem literalizes and inverts class-based subversions of the hierarchy of color. As "The Laughing Mulatto" renders malleable nineteenth-century rhetoric and representations of mixed race, "Artificial Skin" rewrites this malleability as a twenty-first-century technological innovation that would change the color of skin itself. Cliff parodies recent developments in genetic engineering, imagining melanin transplants that could reshape identity: "elastic and plastic / a dash of color, please" (98). With her tongue in her cheek, she calls this skin-darkening endeavor "Melanin Project," invoking the top-secret rhetoric of government projects and inverting the traditionally conservative, Anglocentric political agendas of such projects. By calling this fluid identity a "sci-fi / space-age fantasy," Cliff reinforces the implausibility of "Melanin Project" and implicitly criticizes governments that do not pursue research that benefits people of color. This poem thus links postmodern theories of fluid identity with a criticism of the material conditions of racist racial hierarchies.

In her novel *Abeng* (1984), Cliff confronts the tragic mulatta narrative head-on and enacts in the realm of fiction those theories she avows in her essays. The Savage family is racially and nationally mixed, with origins scattered throughout the Miskito Indians, the Ashanti, and the British. The family even attends two different churches, Anglican and Baptist. Clare Savage, Cliff's semiautobiographical heroine, is both black and white, pale and deeply colored.[32] While her white friend, Miss Winifred, claims that "coons and buckra people were not meant to mix their blood" and "only sadness comes from mixture," Clare denies this pessimistic outlook. For Clare, everyone is mixed, and Jamaica is founded on "all kinds of mixture," racial, national, and cultural (164). Rather than following the white colonizers' models, as did Hopkins's characters in *Hagar's Daughter* or the white marble of Lewis's *Hagar*, Clare—and Cliff—affirm this mixture as the true and empowering nature of Jamaican people. In reading Dickens's *Great Expectations* from a Jamaican perspective, Clare identifies with both Miss Havisham (white woman) and Magwitch (dark man), positioning herself on both sides of racial and sexual borders (36). She often feels "split into two parts" (119), white and not white, town and country, academic financial aid and privilege, but this novel and its sequel, *No Telephone to Heaven*, trace Clare's eventual reconciliation of these multiple halves. In *No Telephone*, Clare returns to Jamaica after a British education in the classics, claims Jamaica as her home, and converts her grandmother's property into a base for Marxist revolutionaries. Once she determines to direct the fruits of her color- and class-based privilege to the cause of the Jamaican people, Clare joins a band of revolutionaries and sacrifices her life on an American movie set, taking activism far beyond the limits of previous biracial heroines.

In *Abeng*, Clare spends winters in Kingston and summers in rural St. Elizabeth. After having lived in both worlds, she learns to prefer the more fluid cultures of the Jamaican countryside. In St. Elizabeth, funeral processions bring together an amalgamation of nations and cultures with African chants, British hymns, and Red Stripe torch bottles (50). Schools teach the works of Langston Hughes and Claude McKay alongside Wordsworth

and Tennyson (89). Cliff's postcolonial countryside thus thoroughly decenters the culture of the British colonizer. In this multiplex society, Clare
learns to transcend cultural divisions and follow in the path of her uncle Robert, an outcast who defies social laws regarding the superiority
of whiteness. Robert transgresses convention along multiple axes—color,
nation, and sexuality—by loving a dark-skinned U.S. man (125). Clare,
too, crosses lines of color, class, and sexuality in her love for the darker-
skinned Zoe, whom Clare meets in St. Elizabeth. In this relationship,
Clare learns to bridge the multiple components of her identity and to
challenge the idea that difference is insurmountable.[33]

There is little doubt that Cliff is writing in the tradition of the
nineteenth-century Zoe narrative and its early-twentieth-century revisions, but she goes much further in revealing her characters' racial and
sexual transgressions.[34] Her late-twentieth-century theories of identity,
postcoloniality, and sexuality provide Cliff with tools for making her
Clare a far more complex light-skinned heroine than any of her predecessors. In *Abeng*, Cliff rewrites the mulatta tradition by celebrating dark
maternal origins and omitting the element of passing (since whiteness is
not necessary to communicate status). She also interrogates the positive
and negative potential of the biracial narrative by dividing her mulatta
heroine into two, Clare and Zoe. Together Clare and Zoe present different sides of the Zoe/mulatta narrative: light and dark, privileged and
outcast. While mixture represents advantage for some (Clotel and Iola
Leroy, for example), it also represents alienation for others (Hopkins's
Jewel and Boucicault's Zoe). Yet together Clare and Zoe are not alienated
or passive victims of oppression. The depth of the friendship between
the girls, along with their strength and independence, challenges previous visions of the tragic mulatta. The image of the two girls running after
wild pigs, swimming naked in the river, and shooting a bull with a gun
(115–23) subverts Jamaican standards of "women's work" and overturns
the literary tradition in which the mulatta had to assume white standards
of domestic morality to gain literary visibility.

Cliff's Zoe is the fatherless nutmeg-colored daughter of a poor market
woman, Miss Ruthie (91). Significantly, Zoe is not separated from her maternal origins or ignorant of her "black blood," as in the case of previous
Zoes. Yet she is still marginalized, literally cast out to the edges of lighter
society. Clare's grandmother, Miss Mattie, allows them to squat on the
fringes of her property and tells Ruthie to send Zoe to keep Clare enter-
tained during the summers (81, 93).[35] In this role, the parameters of Zoe's

existence expand by association with the more socially mobile Savages. The distinction between the two is not fixed in plain black and white but rather is social, more permeable, constructed by convention: although Zoe's skin is only slightly darker than Clare's mother's skin, Clare belongs to a different class, she attends a different school, and her grandmother has economic power over Zoe's family.

As their identities both meet and diverge, Clare and Zoe's friendship temporarily erases lines of social inequality. Their differences provided the impetus for their friendship, but the original power imbalance that forced Miss Ruthie to send Zoe to Miss Mattie is not reproduced between the girls. Their union pushes social distinctions into the background, behind the foreground of the imaginary landscapes where they play (95). Together Clare and Zoe create pictographic languages and imitate the Aztecs and Mayans (94). The girls' mixed native fantasy world takes them back to the pre-Columbian period and outside European colonization. This non-European world becomes more real for Clare and Zoe than the "real" world outside their imaginations. Indeed, Cliff describes the world of the rest of the island as equally "make-believe" and ignorant of its own history (96).

Cliff restores history to Jamaica in her contextualization of the narrative, in which she depicts many layers of "reality": fiction, history, politics. The layers of representation in *Abeng* resemble the images on the wallpaper in the old Paradise Plantation. The culture of the colonizer presents a repeating backdrop, a "white background" on the wallpaper, covered in a pattern of white women, white children, and red dogs, "in a park in a city somewhere in Europe" (24). This seemingly out of place scene "is repeated again and again across the wall" and throughout the novel, the insistent British background against which the history of Jamaica and the history of the novel are cast. Yet as the paper ages, it darkens and peels, revealing different layers underneath. Cliff gives us glimpses of various levels that lie beneath the present, but the new layers do not replace the old. Instead, they pile up into a thickness that exposes the palimpsest that makes up the whole. Images from the time when the island rose and sank before it was inhabited, through the rise of native societies; the conquest; triangular trade; slavery; maroon societies; the revolts of Granny Nanny, Cuffee, and Cudjoe; Marcus Garvey's United Negro Improvement Association; and even the Nazi takeover of Germany present parallel narratives to the Savage family history (14–21, 80, 88). The constructed fictional trajectory lies alongside the historical chain of events. History informs the novelistic present for Cliff's characters, and their identities are un-knowable, unmoored without a sense of the literary and historical tradi-tions that meet within them: colonizer and colonized, white and black, those who conquer and those who resist. As Cliff intersperses fragments of history with the fictional present of the same locations, she depicts the various lineages and the evolution of the culture that produced families such as the Savages. One can never forget the repeating background of the plantation wallpaper, but Cliff represents this originally white paper as substantially darkened with historical wear and resistance.

The literary style of *Abeng* emphasizes mixture and resistance to hege-mony. Cliff's cultural references retain African origins and beliefs: obeah, one-breasted warriors, Brer Anancy (20, 34). Cliff's vocabulary is patois, constantly reminding the reader of the multiple origins of Jamaican so-ciety. She includes a glossary to help the reader translate such words as *ñam, smaddy,* and *wunna* and to highlight the extent to which Jamaicans have revised the English language. This violation of the rules of English vocabulary and usage counteracts the earlier violation in which English was forced on African and Arawak-speaking peoples, who subsequently lost their original tongues. Patois resists this linguistic takeover and de-constructs the colonizer's tongue.

Like the social background that Clare and Zoe defy with their fan-tasy worlds, the wallpaper's European background is now faded from cen-turies of revolution from Granny Nanny to Clare (24). "The danger to Clare was that the background could slide so easily into the foreground" (25). Cliff keeps the background at bay by emphasizing the foreground of resistance. In "If I Could Write This in Fire," she maintains that the oppressors "like to pretend we didn't fight back," but "we did: obeah, poi-son, revolution" (*Land* 67). Within Jamaica's dual society, Cliff consistently emphasizes transgressions of those conventions imposed to divide peo-ple of different colors and to put whites at the center. In her refusal to privilege light skin, her emphasis on mixing, and her stories of resistance, she deconstructs that center and opposes its history of racism, conquest, and separation. Cliff is able to go beyond the gestures of resistance in Harper and Hopkins by invoking traditions of West Indian rebellion and twentieth-century historical and political developments.

In *Free Enterprise* (1993), Cliff continues to explore the meaning of color, to celebrate the Africanist elements within the mixed-race tradition, to emphasize resistance (Granny Nanny, John Brown), and to criticize the bourgeois *gens inconnu* who deny their black ancestry and efface their own histories. Like Clare Savage before her, light-skinned Annie Christmas rejects the European pretensions of her family and applies Mr. Bones's Liquid Blackener (perhaps a folk version of Cliff's "Artificial Skin") to "her carefully inbred skin" (*Free Enterprise* 9). The rebellions of one daughter can overturn the racial breeding of her ancestors. In this text, too, Cliff directly addresses the mulatta tradition: Annie echoes Brown's Clotel, cross-dressing to help instrument a slave revolt (136). Annie meets Frances Harper face to face and criticizes her privileging of the "light-skinned female Christian octoroon" (*Iola Leroy*) because doing so ignores "the vast majority of our people" (11). While Harper required recourse to the "exceptional" mixed-race character to "wring hearts dry; white ones, at least," Cliff rejects that investment in white sympathy. Annie denies those Iola-esque elements of her identity with skin blackener, "her back turned on *gens inconnu*," and a careful association with rebels and lepers rather than the Talented Tenth (11). Cliff favors those characters who, although "for all intents and purposes, white" (111), seek out blacks and long for darker skin.

She also emphasizes those elements of disguise that empower her characters and enable them to construct fluid identities. And they are fluid in terms of more than just race. For example, Mary Ellen Pleasant passes for Mammy, blacksmith, house servant, jockey, and middle-aged woman of African-American descent (herself). Annie and Mary Ellen use disguise to "pass through the nets," to move from North to South to West, to transport guns and fugitive slaves, to enter different realms without being expelled (194). Their light skin and their protean power to transform themselves enable them to pass as insiders in many different racial, cultural, and class-based milieus. Says Annie, "It was practically my birthright; you know that. Disguise. Masks" (194). She traces this birthright back to tribal storytelling rituals in Africa, but it also closely recalls Cliff's claim that Caribbean aristocracy (from which Annie also descends) is signaled by costume rather than body. In an ironic sense, masks are Annie's "birthright" because, according to Cliff, birth is not enough in the Caribbean: bodies alone do not communicate identity.

Importantly, while on a Confederate chain gang, the discovery of Annie's female body under a blackface male disguise results in her being gang-raped, reflecting the high cost of discovery when one's body conflicts with one's costume and when one's access to a group—even when that group is made up of black prisoners—is exposed to be illegitimate. Annie's response to this tragedy is to remove her identity from her body in a different way: "I detached my nether parts from the rest of me" (207). Her color washes off in the rain, and she becomes "a light-skinned woman on a leash," "like someone with an amputated limb," her body out of context (208). This horrific scene forms the narrative conclusion of the novel but not the chronological endpoint. In this way, we know that Annie moves on but are left with this sense of violation and lost identity. Cliff does not idealize fluidity or elide the physical violence wrought within mixed identities.

Cliff's collection of stories, *Bodies of Water* (1990), also forces a reconceptualization of racial constitution while more clearly invoking the tragedy conventionalized by the Zoe tradition. "Burning Bush" envisions a woman, the Girl from Martinique, who is biracial, black and white, because she paints patches on her body with whitewash to attract a crowd at the circus (*Bodies* 77). Although she tries to pass off her artificial duality as an exotic practice from her native land, it is really a form of self-camouflage, designed to earn a livelihood. The "patchwork" woman considers this means of self-exhibition a way to escape prostitution, a more empowering form of economically motivated self-exploitation. The skin color is a way out for her. This "parti-colored" "checkerboard of a woman" produces a baby whose racial duality also reflects "certain practices of her native land" (76, 78). But these practices seem more real. The baby is born light skinned, and her mother hopes that her skin will darken with age, perhaps to efface the traces of the "native practice" of miscegenation. The circus woman's whitewash mimics earlier genetic whitenings. While centuries of miscegenation have produced mulatto "circus freaks," the Girl from Martinique takes control over that production, constructing her own biracial subjects who simulate, mock, or parody the biological production of half-black, half-white children. Indeed, her whitewash paints right over the previous narrative, turning racial mixture to her own economic advantage and reimagining biracialism as a constructed, self-chosen artifice. Unlike the racial paints in Ferré and Vega, the Girl from Martinique's whitewash turns the mystique of racial subversion into profit.

The "half-breed" in the story "Screen Memory" is taught by her black grandmother to reclaim the "black part" inside of her and learns to play her grandmother's African piano (92–93). But the daughter's narrative comes closer to that of the tragic mulatta. She is described as "half-them" ("them" being white) and "white nigger," the white blood degrading her and alienating her from herself (97, 93). Her narrative blends with that of "the half-breed daughter" kidnapped by "some crazy Apaches": "polysyllabic and clean and calicoed when the Apaches seize her, dirty and monosyl-labic . . . and violated, dear Lord, violated out of her head" after the at-tack (102). In this scenario, the multiply mixed woman is violated and driven crazy, much like the tragic mulatta in nineteenth-century fiction.[36] Cliff's "girl" ultimately has nightmares of drowning in a pond and turning green (103). Since the racial origin that alienates the mulatta in this case is white and she eventually fears turning green, Cliff again subverts the con-ventional narrative in which black is the threatening color or curse. She suggests that the tragic mulatta narrative might be played with, but the historical frequency of interracial rape should not be forgotten. Cliff tem-pers her celebration of racial fluidity, and her readers are unable to forget that racial mixture often began (and begins) with asymmetrical racial and sexual power relations. While the foreground imagines important strate-gies for resistance, conquest lingers in the historical background.

The repeated incidents of rape in these narratives make the story of the tragic mulatta a primary target for feminist analysis. Cliff returns to the tragic mulatta and criticizes the gendered oppressions of miscegena-tion, which targeted women as the objects of sexual desire and as the sources of "bastard" and "mixed-breed" reproduction. To rewrite patterns of white and male domination, Cliff detaches her characters' identities from black-white binaries and conventional gender roles. She alters the historical trajectory of racial and sexual dominance with parody, inver-sion, costume, and fluidity. The complexity of color and identity in the Caribbean provides Cliff with a context for challenging imposed defi-nitions of race and mixture. Color alone does not determine her hero-ines' fates. Education and imagination allow them to conceive alternate worlds. Cliff thus exposes and condemns the tragedy while envisioning feminist alternatives. Her characters take advantage of their multiplicity and play between different realms of identity. Clare, Annie, and Mary Ellen use their advantages to support revolution with economic resources and knowledge from multiple cultures. They chart new territory for shift-ing, multivalent, empowered, resisting, Africanist- and woman-centered feminist subjectivities.

THREE

The Transitive Bi-

In its constructions of race, sex, gender, and nationality, the television show *Designing Women* provides more than a popular feminist message. The main characters of the show are four white southern women and an African-American man (predictably enough, an ex-convict) who works for them. The four women run the gamut of traditionally feminine stereotypes: conceited snob, ditzy blonde, feisty single mom, and seductive southern lady. Yet Anthony, originally the designing women's van driver and odd-job man, complicates traditional assumptions about black masculinity as he learns to participate in "feminine" activities (including decorating, leg waxing, and Girl Scout camp) and "female" conversations (about bra size, PMS, and menopause). The transformation from ex-con to woman's best friend is eased by Anthony's own effeminacy, indicated by his exaggerated gestures and his shrill laugh.[1] This effeminacy guarantees his distance from racist stereotypes of the black male sexual threat to southern white womanhood at the same time that his series of girl-friends comforts viewers that his gender flexibility does not challenge his heterosexuality.

In one particularly revealing episode ("Foreign Affairs"), the wealthiest of the designing women molds Anthony's identity to suit her needs. When Suzanne Sugarbaker's maid, Consuela, a spell-casting Latina immigrant, needs to take the test for U.S. citizenship, Suzanne sends Anthony to take the test in her place because Consuela does not speak English well.

"Consuela" thus meets the immigration officers in the body of the cross-dressed and semi-Spanish-speaking Anthony. This scenario implies that all nonwhites are somehow the same and that race, nation, and sex are transferable among them. A bad wig, a flowered dress, and a few words of mispronounced Spanish seem to be enough to make a Latina woman out of an African-American man. Not only is Anthony accepted as Consuela, but the white male immigration officer develops a crush on him/her.

The interchangeability of Anthony and Consuela reflects the racist character structure of *Designing Women*. Unlike cross-dressing scenes in William Wells Brown and Michelle Cliff, this costume is imposed by the dominant culture and Anthony has nothing to gain personally from passing. The identities of the people of color in this show are eclipsed by their status as the Sugarbakers' Other. Indeed, Consuela herself, the real Latina woman, is never seen. Yet this depersonalization also unsettles essentialist notions of race and sex. Anthony is not just the stereotypical black man, and it is not just Latina women who wear flowered dresses and practice "voodoo." As with the racist studies of racial mixture that I discuss in chapter 1 (Edward Byron Reuter, for example), playing with race and gender can have mixed effects. Racist though the motivations and underlying assumptions behind a particular performance of mixed identity may be, the performance itself may still destabilize racial, sexual, and gendered definition. Although Anthony's Consuela is almost minstrel-like in its performative excess and visible sexual and cultural duality, stereotypes are undermined as Anthony passes and subverts preconceived ideas about his physical identity.

Judith Butler's analysis of the film *Paris Is Burning* reflects this ambivalence of gender parody, its simultaneous subversion and "reconsolidation of hegemonic norms." Butler argues that "drag may well be used in the service of both the denaturalization and reidealization of hyperbolic heterosexual gender norms" (*Bodies* 125). That is, at the same time that gender crossing appropriates sexist stereotypes, it also denaturalizes those stereotypes and the conventions of gender altogether. The same could be said of Anthony's racial parody. While imitating racist assumptions about Latina identity, Anthony reworks those assumptions and couples them with black male sexual identity. His performance, like *Paris Is Burning*, could be read as a critical appropriation of "racist, misogynist, and homophobic norms of oppression" (Butler, *Bodies* 129). In the case of Anthony/Consuela, racial fluidity coincides with sex/gender fluidity, as he/she defies boundaries between races and sexes and enacts unexpected correspondences among race, sex, and gender identities. As Butler argues, "the order of sexual difference is not prior to that of race or class," but the "norms of realness by which the subject is produced are racially informed conceptions of 'sex'" (*Bodies* 130). Sexual signification cannot be separated from racial signification in the performance. Wigs, dresses, body shape, and ways of speaking do not signify race or sex individually: they carry meaning about sexualized race and racialized sex at the same time.

This episode of *Designing Women* reveals the ways in which identity relies on superficial cues such as clothing and language. Anthony and Suzanne manipulate superficial stereotypes in their construction of "Consuela," assuming (perhaps correctly) that a stuffed bra, a head kerchief, and a few Spanish words are enough to suggest Latina identity to a public accustomed to stereotypes. Yet Anthony's malleable appearance, from his medium-toned skin to his supposed bilingualism and his willingness to wear costumes, subverts certainties of identity based on those cues. The ease with which public identity can be transformed calls into question the role of genetics in determining identity. As Butler has noted, the real meaning of cross-dressing lies in the dissonance between gender and sex, surface appearance and "real" body, what the immigration official thinks and what we know. According to Butler, the transvestite reveals that all gender is a matter of performance: "In imitating gender, drag implicitly reveals the imitative structure of gender itself—as well as its contingency" (*Gender* 137). Anthony's Consuela goes beyond the gendered possibilities of performance and reveals that race, nation, and citizenship also are a matter of performance. Moreover, since Suzanne assumes that a black man would better pass for a Latina woman than any of her (white) female friends, Anthony's race somehow qualifies him for the performance. Perhaps race forms part of the "contingency" that Butler mentions. Racial identity might better position some people for certain gender imitations. Indeed, does Anthony's skin color—which enables him to be racially transitive—facilitate his performance of femininity? This chapter will address that question.

The lesson of Anthony's performance is that biological identity—race or sex—does not necessarily correspond to one's public image. Chapters 1 and 2 examined how the significance of skin color varies contextually, and this chapter will analyze how this variance imbricates other variables of public identity, especially sex and gender. Racial mixtures and the fluidity of racial cues such as skin color deconstruct definitions of racial identity and challenge our ability to perceive and to define identity in general.

Our failure to identify an individual's race could lead to a misunderstanding of culturally specific cues about sex and gender: a body in a dress has different sexual meanings in India, Africa, Scotland, Palestine, and Mexico. Bodies that are racially, culturally, and/or nationally mixed then are expected to respond to multiple different standards of what counts as male and female, masculine and feminine. I title this chapter "The Transitive Bi-" because it explores the ways in which race and sex identities are transitive and examines whether or not biracial fluidity can be translated, transferred, or transposed onto bisexual fluidity. I use the model of the *bi*—bisexual, bigendered, biracial, binational—to show how mixed identities cross conventional definitions of sex, gender, sexuality, race, and nation. While not all of the individuals in this chapter are bisexual on the level of sexual orientation, like Anthony they are dual or multiple in their identifications.[2]

Despite the binarism implied in the term, *bi-* challenges either/or dichotomies by adopting multiple identifications simultaneously: heterosexual effeminate black man and masculine Latina woman, for example. According to Marjorie Garber, bisexuality is "a sexuality that undoes sexual orientation as a category, a sexuality that threatens and challenges the easy binarities of straight and gay, queer and 'het,' and even, through its biological and physiological meanings, the gender categories of male and female" (*Vice Versa* 65). *Bi-* indicates nonassimilation to given categories. As Garber describes it, bisexuality is "an identity that is also *not* an identity" (70). I would extend the nonsingular flexibility of bisexuality to all other categories of identification—race, class, nation, culture, age, gender, language, and context—that interact to produce a subject who can be both black ex-convict and Latina maid.

A 1974 *Newsweek* article titled "Bisexual Chic" attempts to divorce bisexual orientation from sex. Instead, the article figures bisexuality as an extension of gender fluidity: "As his-and-her clothes, hair styles and role assignments blurred the line between the sexes until they overlapped, the only thing left to swap was sex itself" (90). This common attitude keeps a subversive sexuality safely on the level of fashion, playful trends, and superficial gender cues. Bisexuality demonstrates the contingency and the variability of sex and gender practices. Yet beyond these social manifestations, *bi-* also suggests something more radical about corporeal identity: it, too, may be multiple.[3]

Returning to Anthony/Consuela, the black man's ability to pass for Latina indicates that his individual racial appearance—a certain skin tone, for example—could potentially correspond to more than one genetic race. His color could appear both Latino and African-American, blurring the distinction between the two racial mixtures. Extending the same analysis to sex, Anthony's ability to pass for a woman suggests that certain "sexed" appearances—his stature, his voice, or his face—could correspond to either male or female identity. The public accepts as signs of femaleness a broad range of expressions, from Anthony's performance to that of the most masculine woman, and the interpretation of what counts as female is shaped by racial, cultural, and national context. When that context is itself mixed, it becomes difficult to attach identity categories to any body.[4]

The possibility for multiple interpretations is demonstrated by the immigration officer, an instrument of the law, who misrecognizes and desires Anthony at the same time. Significantly, crossing race and sex leads to an expression of homoerotic potential, which is always present in Anthony's ambiguous engendering but only revealed when his femininity is embodied as "Consuela" and homoerotic desire thus appears heteroerotic on the surface. While this heterogendering may seem to contain homoeroticism, to allow it to surface only in heterosexual costuming, viewers are well aware of the male body underneath "Consuela's" dress. Although we see Anthony/Consuela officially recorded as a heterosexually desirable woman, we know that he/she is really breaking the law. The "Consuela" costume is unconvincing for viewers, for whom Anthony's illegal crossings are quite visible. This performance can be interpreted as critical of racial and sexual norms in its exposure of the absurdity of laws that cannot contain the multiplicity of Anthony/Consuela's identity. Yet the immigration officer's attraction to the poorly costumed Anthony is presented as a farce, laughable, definitely not sexy, which renders absurd the possibility of cross-racial and same-sexual desire. Despite its unsettling of identity, this scene does not encourage transgression. The canned laughter enforces heterosexist and racist norms; the humor of it all rests on the taboo associated with mixed identifications and anxieties about the misunderstanding of bodies.[5]

The adoption of a bi- identity highlights these vicissitudes of racial and sexual interpretation.[6] In her study of bisexuality, Beth Firestein suggests, "Just as the existence of biracial or multiracial individuals blurs and ultimately eliminates the possibility of generating meaningful hierarchies of distinction between individuals of different racial backgrounds, bisexual people blur distinctions between apparently differing sexual orientations, rendering the hierarchies of value attached to such orientations increasingly meaningless" (283). The recent interest (or vogue) in bisexuality reflects a "paradigm shift" (270, 283), according to Firestein, indicating a move beyond dualistic modes of thinking.[7] The contemporary popularity of hybridity, border theory, and antiessentialism supports Firestein's claim. The celebrations of multiplicity that appear in recent theories of sex and gender reflect the same impulse as the theories of *mestizaje* and heteroglossia that inform many studies of race and postcolonialism.[8] Today, we want to liberate identity from singular affiliations imposed by the dominant culture. This liberation, however, often oversimplifies the difficulty of passing, universalizes fluidity, and deracializes culturally specific inscriptions, thereby obscuring the terms of racial and sexual domination as well as the bodies of the dominated. These new multiplicities should be considered in a historical context, rather than by privileging contemporary Euro-American theories, and with an awareness of the interrelatedness of different categories, rather than falsely isolating race or sex as independent functions. Just as contemporary celebrations of *mestizaje* reflect a belated embrace of an original American reality, the insistence that bisexuality is a new fad eschews sexual fluidities of the past. The affirmation of multiplicity in identity is new only for those who have suppressed and denied such multiplicity for decades.

The laughter following Anthony/Consuela suggests a discomfort with impurity. American literature and ethnography provide culturally specific foundations for the crossing that *Designing Women* makes light of and the racial and sexual boundaries it reflects. The fact that racial and sexual cross-dressing is a mechanism for entertainment in popular culture today reflects a continued intrigue with the ambiguity of American identities. It is important to contextualize this fascination across different genres of American representation and to combat the rhetoric of purity by foregrounding the empowering political accomplishments of some fluid identities. This chapter analyzes contemporary racialized sexual mixtures in the context of similar representations from the nineteenth and early twentieth centuries. Beginning with the example of cross-gendered Native Americans, I suggest that heterosexist models of identity are a product of Anglo-American culture and do not necessarily encompass the range of American sex and gender identities. I then juxtapose two nineteenth-century narratives of escaped slaves, William Wells Brown's *Clotel* and William and Ellen Craft's *Running a Thousand Miles for Freedom*, with contemporary writings by June Jordan, Cherríe Moraga, Gloria Anzaldúa, and Marjorie Garber, analyzing the ways in which the subversion of racial categories is often encoded in terms of sexual subversion. Next, I examine and historicize the resistance to sexual fluidity in some contemporary writers of color and follow with extended readings of four contemporary texts that destabilize race and sex identifications at the same time, Judith Ortiz Cofer's *Silent Dancing,* Audre Lorde's *Zami,* Ruth Behar's *Translated Woman,* and Michelle Cliff's *No Telephone to Heaven.*[9] All of these texts, with their different historical, cultural, and generic frameworks, reflect an understanding that racial mixture challenges sexual essence. At the same time, all of them confront the need to balance fluid identities with political expedience.

This genealogy of representations of racial and sexual fluidity clarifies the belatedness of hybridity as model for identity. Analyzing earlier texts in which mixture and fluidity coincide with overt racist and sexist oppression can serve as a warning for today: celebrations of hybridity often correspond to attempts to enforce "pure" racial and sexual categories. The frequency with which mixed-race identity is coded in terms of both racial and sexual crossing draws attention to the persistent oppressive boundaries that these subjects feel compelled to cross both historically and today. These comparisons reveal similar conceptions of mixed identity in Latina, Caribbean, African-American, and Native American contexts. Despite their divergent histories and definitions of race, the similarities between representations of identity in these different cultural contexts reflect the force of mixture that all of the Americas share.

Gender Fluidity in the Americas: Berdache, Amazon, and Zami

In some American cultures, sex is not assumed to equal gender. Nor does anatomy determine all manifestations of sexuality, sexual preference, desire, or identification. Current "American" attitudes toward sex and gender reflect the imposition of European ideals on Native American and African cultures, and the practices of certain mixed or non-European individuals often indicate remnants of pre-Columbian gender culture. The existence in America of divergent cultural attitudes toward the relationship between sex and gender challenges the primacy, inevitability, and naturalness of Euro-American codes.

In 1901 and 1902, ethnologist Matilda Coxe Stevenson reported to the Bureau of American Ethnology on her research among the Zuni Indians of the southwestern United States. One "remarkable" informant, a close friend of Stevenson and a highly respected member of the tribe, is We'wha. Stevenson writes, "This person was a man wearing woman's dress, and so carefully was his sex concealed that the writer believed him to be a woman. Some declared him to be an hermaphrodite, but the writer gave no credence to the story and continued to regard We'wha as a woman; and as he was always referred to by the tribe as 'she'—it being their custom to speak of men who don woman's dress as if they were women—and as the writer could never think of her faithful and devoted friend in any other light, she will continue to use the feminine gender when referring to We'wha" (310). [10] This account of a cross-gendered Zuni offers several significant points about sex and gender. First, it was accepted among the Zuni and among other tribes that certain individuals assumed a gender role that diverged from their anatomical sex. [11] Unlike many contemporary Americans, these Zuni saw no necessary correlation between sex and gender. Second, Stevenson, an Anglo-American, attempts to keep her recognition of We'wha at the level of gender. Stevenson refuses to acknowledge We'wha's anatomical sex, eschewing her friend's maleness with the same fervor that she denies the possibility that his/her sex might be mixed (or hermaphroditic). Stevenson seems unwilling to acknowledge that We'wha's crossing of genders might bear a message about sex or sexuality.

Third, despite Stevenson's insistence that she used the feminine *she* to refer to We'wha, the author continually, perhaps accidentally, refers to We'wha as "he" and "him," both in the passage quoted here and elsewhere in her report. The ethnologist's inability to maintain a consistency in the gender of her pronouns reflects the ways in which We'wha's identity resists categorization according to Euro-American conventions of gender and language. Native languages had specific terms, such as *nadle* (men living as women) and *hwame* (women living as men), to refer to transgendered individuals outside of masculine-feminine paradigms. Even in Stevenson's confused pronouns, We'wha is both him and her, male and female. Perhaps the most accurate way to describe We'wha using the English language would be with the general category of *person*, with which Stevenson begins her description of We'wha.

Even more interesting is Stevenson's narration of significant events in We'wha's life. We'wha accompanied Stevenson to Washington, D.C., in the 1880s to meet with President Chester A. Arthur. In Stevenson's account, We'wha's already fluid identity changes even further during this trip, as if on contact with U.S. culture. S/he rapidly learns the English language. Most surprisingly, Stevenson also claims that We'wha's skin color changes in the nation's capital. While before s/he was medium toned, "like the Chinese in color, . . . during six months' stay in Washington she became several shades lighter" (310). This information must be significant in Stevenson's perception of We'wha's identity, since it is one of the few details that she relates about the Washington visit. Beyond the provocative suggestion that We'wha somehow became more Anglo in the Anglo context, this color change reveals that We'wha's flexibility goes beyond a subversion of gender to incorporate racial fluidity as well. Even if We'wha's skin tone itself did not change, Stevenson's perception of his/her color changes with context. We'wha is probably racially mixed, since Stevenson emphasizes the lightness of his/her skin and describes his/her color as Chinese rather than Zuni. We'wha's difference thus crosses axes of gender and race (and possibly sex, too, although Stevenson refuses to confront the issue directly), and this fluidity enables We'wha's chameleon-like transformations. Even at his/her death, We'wha's family emphasized his/her mixture by dressing him/her in both trousers—"the first male attire she had worn since she had adopted female dress years ago"—and feminine shawls, necklaces, earrings, and bangles (313). By putting trousers on the dead body, the family adds a visible reminder of We'wha's maleness, which lay concealed beneath layers of feminine shawls and blankets. This final image highlights sex/gender dissonance.

The most common term for Native American men who cross-dress is *berdache*, derived from the Arabic *bardaj*, meaning a boy slave kept for sexual purposes (Blackwood 27n). Since *berdache* carries this negative connotation, and since it assumes a fixed (male) anatomical sex, I prefer terms that emphasize fluid identification. Certainly not all Native American nations embraced fluid sex/gender roles, and there is no uniformity of gender behavior among different Native American tribes (MacKenzie 173n; W. Williams 239). To refer to a diverse range of Native American practices, Evelyn Blackwood uses the term *cross-gender*, and I borrow her term since it is inclusive and neutral and emphasizes the crossing of conventions.[12] As a framework for identity analysis, *cross-gender* highlights the ways in which many original cultures of the Americas embraced the division between sex and gender, tolerated ambivalence of sex and gender, and conflicted with late-coming European attitudes about gender opposition. *Cross-gender* represents friction with English-language terms for sex, gender, and sexuality that are based on binary opposition.

A cross-gendered "man" like We'wha blurs the distinction between masculine and feminine. S/he performs "masculine" religious and judicial functions at the same time that s/he performs "feminine" duties, tending to laundry and the garden. While Walter Williams suggests that cross-gendered Native Americans are mixed in their gender identifications, assuming both masculine and feminine tribal duties, Blackwood argues that gender roles among some Native Americans are so flexible that such crossover does not present a subversion of a singular gender categories (42). We'wha would be considered feminine, based on clothing and assumed identity, despite retaining a few masculine functions. Blackwood insists on the occurrence of a "complete changeover to an opposite role," which Williams denies (W. Williams 242).[13] Blackwood is committed to highlighting the subversion of Euro-American gender binaries, whereas Williams would do away with those terms altogether for analysis of Native American relations. In either interpretation, the position of liminally gendered Native Americans is often revered for its mobility, its ability to encompass two genders, and its exposure of the overlap between the two.

Searching for a correlation between subversion of gender and subversion of sex, some anthropologists claim that cross-gender Native Americans have an ambiguous anatomical sex. Blackwood counters that "despite some reports that cross-gender women in the Southwest had muscular builds, underdeveloped secondary sexual characteristics, and sporadic or absent menstruation, convincing physical evidence is noticeably lacking" (31–32). The ambiguous genderings among Native Americans leave their anatomical sex mysterious, ambiguous, but more importantly, not significant. Both Williams and Blackwood agree that sex did not matter in these instances: gender was the source of meaning (W. Williams 247; Blackwood 41). As cross-gendered individuals eschewed the value of fixed biological sex, they chose their marriage partners according to a heterogender paradigm: any masculine individual could marry any feminine individual, regardless of sex, without violating social codes. In fact, a feminine woman could marry a masculine man, divorce him, and then marry a masculine woman without subverting traditional family patterns. In such a case, the woman would be, according to contemporary Anglo-American standards, bisexual. Yet terms such as *homosexual* and *bisexual* assume a definite or relevant sexual identity—male or female—underlying sexual practice. The fact that some Native American tribes did not regard men married to feminine men or women married to masculine women as sexually transgressive suggests that social roles had the power to over-shadow sex. The meaning of the body was established by appearance—clothing and behavior—without the fixity of sexual destiny that Euro-American culture attempts to enforce. In this sense, sex operates like race for light-skinned individuals: both can be altered or eclipsed by context, costume, and social standing.

Other original cultures in the Americas are also said to have embraced fluid sex and gender roles. In searching for a model for black lesbian feminism, Audre Lorde describes how women in the Caribbean developed intimate friendships while their men were away at sea. She describes these women as "Madavine. Friending. Zami" (*Zami* 14). These culturally specific terms defy Anglo-American roles as women's working together blends with loving together in the absence of men. These exclusively female relations recall the legendary female tribes of Amazons who were supposed to populate pre-Columbian Latin America and the Pacific Islands. Additionally, sodomy was reportedly a common practice between native men in the Caribbean, otherwise "heterosexual" men included. In 1519 Cortés recorded this sexual behavior in letters to Charles V (as well as to Cortés's mother), adding sodomy to his list of "abominable" native "sins" such as human sacrifice (Chávez González 63–64). According to Rodrigo Chávez González's history of the social influence of racial mixture in the Americas, *El mestizaje y su influencia social en América* (1937), "La homosexualidad no es nada nuevo en América. . . . La práctica homosexual . . . no constituía tan 'abominable pecado' como para los conquistadores europeos [Homosexuality is nothing new in America. . . . Homosexual practice did not constitute an "abominable sin" as it did for the European conquerors]" (63–64). Such statements about the sexuality of early Americans support Michel Foucault's argument that prior to the late nineteenth century, same-sex erotics existed alongside heterosexual practices without constituting a discrete or subversive identity category.[14]

In a racist discussion of the link between race and sexuality, Chávez González, like Cortés, attributes this sexual fluidity to the general decadence of native cultures. It is significant that he dedicates an entire chapter of this book on Spanish-American *mestizaje* to homosexuality, and he considers there to be a distinctive relationship between racial and sexual border crossing. His homophobia leads him to distance homosexuality from Euro-American civilization and to develop a "solution" to—or a means of erasing—the threat he perceives in homosexual practices. The already existent (and somewhat popular) arguments about the natural inferiority of nonwhite races and the corruption enacted by racial mixture provide Chávez González with a ready discourse onto which he projects his rejection of sexual fluidity. Just as early-twentieth-century racist arguments tried to naturalize polar separations between black and white, studies of sexuality of the same period were beginning to delineate between heterosexual and homosexual identifications. In both discourses, highlighting "inverts" and "crossovers" was often intended to reinforce the desirability of racial and heterosexual purity.[15]

Prefiguring the sexually ambiguous products of *Time* magazine's 1993 experiment in crossing races with Morph 2.0, Chávez González attributes sexual "subversion" to "unnatural" crossovers between racial groups that were supposedly "naturally" nonassimilable. He suggests that homosexuality is particularly prevalent "en los productos de violentes cruces de razas, que provocan reacciones biológicas desconcertantes [in the products of violent racial crossings, which provoke disconcerting biological reactions]" (62). Examples of "violentes cruces de razas" include "zamboide ["zambos," a mixture between native and African or mulatto and African parentage]" and "cruce de extremos: blanco y negro [crossing of extremes: black and white]," but for Chávez González, the "violence" of these crossings is not the (un)officially sanctioned rapes but the challenge to racial polarization. He claims that crossing black and white races produces offspring who are "intersexualmente complicados . . . bien invertidos, homosexuales, no siendo extraño que sean también bífaces en su sexualidad, hermafrodita en su libido [intersexually complicated . . . inverted, homosexual, and not uncommonly bipolar in their sexuality, hermaphroditic in their libido]" (62). In this hypothesis, the mixture of contrasting racial elements produces a biological conflict on the sexual level as well. A mestiza is thus more likely to be hermaphroditic (bi- on the level of anatomical sex), bisexual (bi- on the level of sexual orientation), inverted (cross-gendered), or homosexual. While this claim seems rather outrageous, it reveals the tendency to attribute sex and gender subversion to identities that subvert racial categories (in addition to highlighting the sexual anxiety often surrounding discussions of racial mixture). Individuals who destabilize biological determinism along one axis of identification challenge biological certainty in general. The deconstruction of one essential category undermines all other categories, too.

Chávez González attributes sexual fluidity to non-European racial elements, claiming that Native Americans exhibit more ambiguous sex and gender identities than do Europeans. He notes the lack of beard and mustache among native men and the (supposed) frequency with which they cry, and he considers these characteristics evidence of failed masculinity (67). Chávez González's argument is of course faulty in that he uses Spanish standards of gender identity as a universal measure, assuming that the beard makes the man. He also attributes a lack of fertility (impotence, even) and a supposedly feminine sadistic cruelty to pre-Columbian indigenous Americans, additional signs of their degenerated masculinity (93–94). In these racist and misogynist claims, Chávez González consistently conflates biological differences (the presence or absence of facial hair and fertility, for example) with socially gendered differences (the tendency to cry and cruelty). He racializes sexual differences, uses gender as proof of biological sex, and insists that Native Americans subverted all of these categories.

In the process of colonization, Native Americans were improved by contact with the Europeans, says Chávez González, and racial mixture in this instance led to more securely masculine mestizos (67). He locates sexual fluidity and gender ambiguity at some point in America's pre-European past, and he assures his readers (naively) that "[ha] desaparecido totalmente en nuestros indios la homosexualidad [homosexuality has disappeared totally among our Indians]" (65).[16] He believes that the lightening of the American mestizos based on mixture with Europeans occurred simultaneously with the masculinization of the native races.[17] Chávez González thus distances "our" Americas of the postcolonial period from what he perceives to be a threat to European gender certainties. This ethnocentric argument naturalizes European identity categories and attempts to deflate native challenges to those categories.

So what happened when the sex and gender cultures of the pre-Columbian period met with European culture? And how did the mixed-race products of the two cultures define sex and gender identities? Does the convergence of different sex/gender cultures lead to conflict or to fluidity? Probably both. The Spanish colonizers regarded the Native American *berdache* culture as a crime against nature and initiated a campaign against sodomy and cross-gender behavior. According to Williams, "the major impact that the Spanish campaign has had on modern mestizo culture is a decline in status of androgynous males" (148). As a result of this conflict of cultures, mestizos might still be bisexual in their private behavior, "yet they manage to avoid defining themselves as such" so as not to jeopardize their public position (149). With the imposition of European ideals, cross-gender behavior was marginalized, veiled, and rendered perverse.

According to Williams's account, Mexican mestizo culture did not tolerate cross-gendered behavior or openly transitive sexual identification (140). Yet these taboos do not prohibit all homosexual activity. The same-sex relations that native culture supported remained, but they became veiled by Euro-American homophobic genderings. Octavio Paz's influential study of Mexican identity, *El laberinto de la soledad* (1950), supports this claim: "el homosexualismo masculino sea considerado con cierta indulgencia, por lo que toca el agente activo. El pasivo, al contrario, es un ser degradado y abyecto [masculine homosexuality is considered with certain indulgence, with regard to the active agent. The passive one, to the contrary, is a degraded and abject being]" (35). In homosexual acts between men, the active partner, the penetrator, is not considered homosexual or abnormal because his behavior does not violate Mexican (hetero)gender paradigms. Again, sexual identity and sexual behavior apparently do not matter as much as gender. Sexual acts do not challenge social norms as long as the participants perform the familiar gender roles associated with their sex. In this way, homosexual practices between men can reinforce (often misogynist) heterogender paradigms, violating masculinity and passive, abject femininity. Male-male sex, according to these Mexican accounts, is thus as much about femininity as it is about masculinity. Hetero- norms operate on the level of gender and rely on mutually opposing masculine and feminine subjects, even if both are men.

Significantly, the valuation of gender over sex throws the sex/gender system into greater uncertainty. In comparison to sex, gender identity is more fluid, bearing no necessary connection to anatomy. Public acts are perceived to line up with and to support familiar gender roles, regardless of the sex of the performer. Stevenson's insistence on using "she" in reference to We'wha is a case in point. These are what Judith Butler calls "gender fables," which masquerade as "the misnomer of natural facts" (*Gender Trouble* xi). Gender often lies about "natural" sexual identity.[18] Since the social codes of masculinity and femininity vary among cultures, trends, and historical moments, gender is even more uncertain in an intercultural context. Roles perceived as abnormal in the United States might be normative elsewhere.

In chapter 1, I discussed how multiple racial and cultural backgrounds can potentially empower biracial or bicultural subjects by providing them with multiple resources and alternative identifications. Perhaps the fusion of different sex and gender cultures similarly increases the options for mixed individuals, allowing them to move between masculine and feminine realms—between prison and Girl Scout camp in the case of Anthony, or between religious rites and laundry in the case of We'wha. Mixture certainly can lead to tragedy: biracialism often condemns Zoe, and sex/gender subversions often elicit homophobic reactions. Yet the mixed writers I discuss in the next section find power based on their linked racial and sexual fluidity.

The Correlation of Race and Sex

Walter Williams compares sex polarity to his perception of race relations in the southern United States: "The Western notion of two opposite sexes is akin to the idea I grew up hearing in the South: that there were only two races and they were opposites. By this view, all the world is divided into black and white, and the only choice for a 'mongrel' is to be assigned to one race or the other, or to try to 'pass' for white" (80). Certain Native Americans' challenge to bipolar sexual identity thus parallels the challenge to racial definition presented by mixed-race individuals. Williams's South did not allow racial mixture to defy either/or definition, repressing mixed or crossover identification. Yet I have demonstrated how mestiza theory transcends this southern reluctance by defying oppositions based on color. One might extrapolate from what is unrealized in Williams's claim that both race and sex can threaten biological dichotomies and that racial fluidity might correlate with cross-gender behavior in its exteriority to dominant paradigms.

Race and sex certainly operate differently: they are produced at different intersections of biology and culture and carry different weight in different contexts. Sometimes race is more easily concealed or subverted. Sometimes sex is. Either sex or race might be affirmed as primary or essential depending on the political circumstances. In any case, both are categories based on a social reaction to multiple, sometimes ambiguous corporeal cues. Both are culturally determined and contested. Together they interact to determine social privileges or exclusions. Some theorists, such as June Jordan, consider race and sex to be parallel.[19] Jordan describes bisexuality as analogous to interracial or multiracial identity (*Technical Difficulties* 192). She also compares the sense of betrayal associated with bisexuality (the refusal to align oneself fully with a single sexual camp) to the sense of betrayal associated with racial passing ("Naming"

27). Yet she rejects such rigid, either/or notions of alliance in favor of a worldview that respects multiplicity in identifications.

Paula Rust similarly claims that "many bisexuals of mixed race or ethnicity feel a comfortable resonance between their mixed heritage and their bisexuality" (69). This resonance is produced by the racial contingency of sexual norms: answering simultaneously to more than one set of racial assumptions, as people of mixed race do, leads to answering simultaneously to different definitions of sex and gender. This mutuality of race and sexuality also surfaces in the work of Chicana lesbian theorists. For Cherríe Moraga, Gloria Anzaldúa, and others, embracing their lesbianism occurred simultaneously with embracing their mestiza racial identities. For example, in *Loving in the War Years* (1983), Moraga discovers her love for women and her love for brown races as a product of her love for her Mexican mother, so "it was the Mexican women [she] had loved first" (115). Her loving is configured in terms of sex and race together. In claiming her sexuality, Moraga also claimed the race and the sex of her mother: "I am a white girl gone brown to the blood color of my mother" (60). This affiliation fuses object and subject: her erotic attraction is for the brown women with whom she chooses to identify. She says, "To be a woman fully necessitated my claiming the race of my mother. My brother's sex was white. Mine, brown" (94). In this radical configuration, sex is racialized, and both race and sex identity are cast as a choice. Her brother inherits their father's whiteness, while Moraga claims their mother's "blood color" and her name (the father's surname is Lawrence). She allies brownness with female sexuality and lesbianism and whiteness with male privilege, suggesting that marginalized racial categories correspond to marginalized sexual categories.

Yet Moraga's *mestizaje* subverts this neat distinction between dominant and marginal identities. In her essay "La Güera," she explores the ambiguities of her identity as a mixed-race, light-skinned, middle-class Anglo-Chicana lesbian. Her rejection of light-skinned (*güera*) privilege occurs when she chooses to identify as both Chicana (despite her ability to pass for white) and lesbian. At this moment she also discovers her "connection" with her mother (*Loving* 52). This connection, however, is not just direct identification. She "enter[s] into the life of [her] mother" like a lover (52). This image inflects the mother-daughter relation with a sense of sexual penetration and allies Moraga with the active masculine agent desiring the brown-skinned woman, the woman she wants and the woman she wants to be.

This interpretation is supported by Moraga's short prose piece, "The Slow Dance," where she describes her own dancing style as the style her mother always wanted from a man: "A *real* man, when he dances with you, you'll know he's a *real* man by how he holds you in the back" (*Loving* 31). The speaker guides her female dance partner with a strong hand on her back, showing that "I can handle these women," conveying a superior knowledge over women's bodies (31). When she assumes this dominant role, leading a submissive partner, she also adopts a hetero- paradigm on the level of gender. She claims, "I am my mother's lover. The partner she's been waiting for. . . . I can provide for you" (32). As she displaces her awkward, timid father, whose "thin fingers never really [got] a hold on" her mother (31), she assumes the role of provider at the same time that she solidifies her dismissal of whiteness, heterosexuality, and the patriarchal grip on women. Since the brown woman is more successfully masculine (a "real man") than the white father, and since this heterogendering is projected onto the homosexual image of two women dancing together, race, gender, and sex do not correspond to conventional patterns of dominance. Moraga's vision assigns the dominating role to a Chicana lesbian. As in Paz's account of male-male sexuality in Mexico, this female-female coupling retains Euro-American heterogender norms at the same time that it subverts those norms on the sexual level. When she replaces her father in the interracial heterosexual dance partnership, the light-skinned and masculine speaker duplicates both the apparent racial difference and the apparent gender difference of her parents. Yet because she identifies herself exclusively with her mother's race and sex, she negates the differences that she visually repeats and undermines the ability to interpret race, sex, and sexuality based on appearance.

In "Gloria Anzaldúa's Queer *Mestisaje*," Ian Barnard suggests that Anzaldúa's mestiza consciousness "functions at all . . . levels of identity . . . and shapes the articulation of a queer race": "The demarcations of race and sexuality are ultimately reinvented to such an extent that they are torn from their conventional meanings and reworked into an inextricable, mutually dependent, mutually informing, yet polysignifying cluster of meanings and associations" (50). *Mestizaje* reflects permeable boundaries of racial, national, and sexual identification because unmooring identity from racial closure opens all other identifications that coincide with the production of racial meaning. Anzaldúa theorizes what she calls *lesberada* identity as choosing to be an outlaw. In this sense, her lesbian sexuality coincides with the subversion of other laws and cultural inscriptions. In a 1993 interview with AnaLouise Keating, Anzaldúa says, "It's almost like once you've transgressed—once you've crossed the line, once you've broken the law—the punishment is the same if you do it for a few things as if you do it for many. . . . If I've already broken one inscription, gone against one law and regulation, then I just have to gather up my courage and go against another one and another one and another one. If I'm gonna be hung for all the things" ("Writing" 125). Anzaldúa's terminology here reveals the connection between sexuality and law, transgression and punishment. Sexuality is regulated by law—juridical law, cultural law, "natural" law—but once individuals decide to be outlaws, they escape these laws, move outside of them, crossing borders everywhere. If sex and race are legal constructs, they are also a matter of choice, the choice to obey or to disobey. The state, the cultural guardians, and the individual together construct identity categories in a push and pull of legislation, resistance, surveillance, punishment, and oppression. This framework allows for individual freedom of self-definition, which, though crossed by law (which subjects deviants to abuse), confounds the law at every turn so that it never fully achieves its dreams of neat sexual and racial polarizations and classifications.

Like Anzaldúa, Garber shows how a challenge to racial definition can lead to a challenge to sexual definition. She describes these challenges as "category crisis": "a failure of definitional distinction, a borderline that becomes permeable, that permits border crossings from one (apparently distinct) category to another: black/white, Jew/Christian, noble/bourgeois" (*Vested Interests* 16). She claims that the appearance of a transvestite figure in literature reflects a displacement from one blurred boundary to another: the transvestite's subversion of the male-female binary indicates that another binary has been subverted elsewhere. Thus, Garber claims that "it is not really surprising to find that there are a remarkable number of transvestite figures in African-American literature" (17). Rather than addressing miscegenation directly, a text might present a comic crossing of genders to displace anxiety about racial mixture. The transvestite, like Anthony/Consuela, presents visible evidence that categorization has failed somewhere.[20]

Americans have been deconstructing identity categories for at least a century. For example, narratives of escaped slaves, by definition, address failed categorization.[21] Most obviously, the runaway defies the distinction between slave and free. Yet in William Wells Brown's *Clotel* (1853) and William and Ellen Craft's *Running a Thousand Miles for Freedom* (1860),

additional categories are crossed to enable an escape from slavery. Significantly, both narratives use the same model, in which racial passing coincides with cross-dressing.[22] Both Clotel and Ellen Craft pass for white
male slaveholders to get themselves and their male companions (both
named William) across the border to the North.[23] To free themselves
from the disempowerment assigned to black women, they assume the
identification of the powerful in terms of race, sex, and status. For Clotel, cross-gendered passing is depicted as an inevitable or logical choice,
since she recently had her hair cut off by a jealous mistress, making Clotel
look more like a man, and since she has "often been told that [she] would
make a better looking man than a woman" (144, 167). In this way, Clotel's
physical appearance is already ambiguously gendered. This flexibility of
gender coincides with the fact that the quadroon is "much fairer than
many of the white women of the South, and can easily pass for a free
white lady" (167). These descriptions reveal more than the power of disguise to transform public identity. They also suggest that disguise reflects
an ambiguity that already exists on the level of the body. The costume
merely adds to preexisting physical traits and renders their fluidity more
visible.[24]

   While Clotel's disguise is only one of many episodes in Brown's novel—
indeed, it fills only three pages—the image of Ellen Craft in men's clothing is central to *Running a Thousand Miles for Freedom*. The text features a
portrait of Ellen dressed as a slaveholder, and her husband, William, says
that he sold engravings of his wife in disguise to earn money to purchase
his sister's freedom (12). In this case, race and gender crossing is not
merely a means for escaping slavery but also a marketable strategy for
economic profit. The Crafts take advantage of the intrigue surrounding
Ellen's subversion of identity categories. They provide a detailed account
of her disguise, include a visual image of the woman in man's clothing, and
emphasize the ironies produced by their deception when people mistake
the black female fugitive slave for a white male slaveholder.[25]

   Like Clotel, Ellen Craft suffers from an identity crisis from the beginning of the narrative. Her father was also her first master, a dual relation
that the Crafts (incorrectly) describe as "anomalous" (17). As a result of
her mixed parentage, Ellen is so white that she is frequently mistaken—
although it is really no mistake—for a child of her mistress's family (2).
In addition to challenging familial and racial status, Ellen's sex identity is
challenged by slavery, as "the laws under which we lived did not recognize her to be a woman, but a mere chattel" (30). Since slavery deprives

her of her womanhood, the only way for her to regain ownership of her sexuality and her identity is, ironically, for her to pass as a white man. Despite the lack of legal recognition for the enslaved Ellen's biological sex, Craft denies that his wife was somehow predisposed to subvert her assigned identity. He spends much time assuring the reader that the only way that he and Ellen could escape from slavery was with her passing for a white man and that "my wife had no ambition whatever to assume this disguise, and would not have done so had it been possible to have obtained our liberty by more simple means" (35). Ellen's temporary cross-gender identity is thus not a matter of desire but of absolute necessity.[26] Craft explains that it is easier for her to pass as a white man than as a white woman, since white women did not travel unaccompanied in the South. In this way, Ellen's subversion of gender facilitates her subversion of race and her physical mobility: for her to be white, free, and traveling, she has to be a man, too.

Ellen's gender crossing seems to create more anxiety for William than her subversion of race, although the racial crossing makes her his master and him her subordinate. Yet this anxiety does not keep him from accepting her masculine role completely during their travels, and readers are thus allowed to see the Crafts together as two men. In fact, William consistently refers to Ellen as "he" and "my master" from the time that she assumes the disguise until they reach freedom in Philadelphia. He provides no reminders that his traveling companion is not really a man. The narrative becomes so invested in Ellen's disguise that her character truly transforms during her temporary crossover (which fills most of the text). Even her behavior changes: immediately before their escape and as soon as the disguise is removed in Philadelphia, Ellen is conventionally feminine. In women's clothing, Ellen is weak and cries "like a child," but in her disguise she is "firm" and strong (41, 79, 71). The disguise magnifies her protean personality.

It is significant that both Brown and the Crafts choose a light-skinned heroine as the most flexible subject position, the locus of identity crossing. Since race was matrilineally inherited during slavery, and since racial mixture is produced in the body of a woman, the light-skinned female body is where racial meaning is historically produced and deconstructed. She symbolizes both the passing on and the breaking down of racial definition. If the racial status of a woman is ambiguous, her children will also be without known race, problematizing the system of differentiation. Both texts allow us to see the heroine in two different identities: black female slave and white male slaveholder. Since her appearance is racially and sexually bi-, her apparent sexuality is also at times homoerotic. And since she is both slave and slave owner, we are allowed to see a complete voiding of the power structure. As she straddles both sides of the race, sex, and legal-status binaries, her ambiguous physical identity (her light skin and her compromised femaleness) embodies both ends of the spectrum or, rather, shows where they overlap. The ease with which she assumes the dual identities brings the two ends together and deconstructs their polarity. Through the use of costume, Clotel and Ellen do not assume identities that are opposite to their corporeal status. Instead, they reveal actual racial and sexual ambiguities that defy binary opposition.

In *Queering the Color Line*, Siobhan Somerville studies the intersection of race and sexuality in late-nineteenth- and early-twentieth-century writings, noting that "it was not merely a historical coincidence that the classification of bodies as either 'homosexual' or 'heterosexual' emerged at the same time that the United States was aggressively constructing and policing the boundary between 'black' and 'white' bodies" (3). Somerville suggests that the pseudoscientific studies of racial difference discussed in chapter 1 reflect the same impulse as the early sexological studies that theorized the origins of homosexual identity, "efforts to shore up and bifurcate categories of race and sexuality" (3). I would argue that racial purists had to position sexuality at the center of their arguments to demonize miscegenation and to explain the rapes by men of European descent that produced so much of the mixture in the Americas. Even before homosexuality emerged as a category of identity in the late nineteenth century, African-American writers such as Brown and the Crafts knew that to overturn the racial definitions that enslaved African-Americans, they also had to overturn the sexual myths of slavery and the sexual binaries that made slave women subject to white men.

The frequency with which sexual and racial crossings coincide reveals the complexity of the processes that produce and define identity. Ellen Craft and Clotel do not fit naturally or easily into any category (nor do We'Wha, Moraga, or Consuela). Traci Carroll claims that essentialism cannot apply to African-American identity because it is fractured by a DuBoisian double consciousness, the simultaneous identification in white and black worlds. The duality within racially marginalized identities defies psychoanalytic studies of singular sexual essence (189–90). Moreover, since sex/gender expectations vary across racial lines, occupying two racial locations at once invokes two different standards of sex/gender.

Perhaps one could extrapolate that multiply racialized individuals, who already inhabit a contested identity and already negotiate different terms of identification, are more apt to assume sexually fluid or multiple identities. Moraga, Anzaldúa, Brown, and the Crafts support this sense of "natural" multiplicity and fluidity. While Brown and the Crafts use costume to contest their characters' identities, Moraga and Anzaldúa redefine identity through sexual practice. None of these bodies are static: their authors put them in motion, depicting processes, practices, and performances that break racial and sexual laws and give new meanings to identity.[27]

Resistance to Sexual Fluidity

Women writers of color often examine their sex and gender identities at the same time that they examine their racial identities, since these categories are intertwined and lead to simultaneous oppressions (or, for some, simultaneous empowerments). Yet many are not willing to affirm sexual fluidity or to risk weakening their racial politics by embracing a marginalized sexual identity. While letting go of racial essence in a racist society may open doors of opportunity or increase mobility (through passing, for example), letting go of heterosexual privilege in a homophobic society usually closes doors, threatens physical security, and limits mobility.

Barbara Smith is well known for her commitment to studying homosexuality as an additional marginal identification that women of color assume. Like Jordan and Anzaldúa, Smith parallels racial experience to sexual experience and compares the attempts of black writers of the civil rights movement to develop realistic self-representations to black lesbians' contemporary attempts to do the same. She then proposes an analogous relation between manifestations of homophobia and manifestations of racism: "Undoubtedly every epithet now hurled at Lesbians and gay men—'sinful,' 'sexually depraved,' 'criminal,' 'emotionally maladjusted,' 'deviant,'—has also been applied to Black People" (697). Smith points out this parallel to expose the hypocrisy of continued homophobia within the African-American community, to convince "those who refuse to see the parallels because they view Blackness as irreproachably normal, but persist in defining same-sex love relationships as unnatural" (697). It is significant that Smith invokes what is "natural" or "unnatural," suggesting that sexuality and race are comparable products of nature. The affirmation of one should lead to the affirmation of the other.

According to Paula Rust's analysis of race and sexuality, "Because homosexuality represents assimilation, it is stigmatized as a 'white disease' or, at least, a 'white phenomenon.' Individuals who claim a bisexual, lesbian, or gay identity are accused of buying into white culture and thereby becoming traitors to their own racial or ethnic group" (65). Moraga finds a similar dynamic in the context of Chicano culture, where she claims lesbianism is construed as "being used by the white man" and being a traitor to Chicanos since "homosexuality is *his* disease with which he sinisterly infects Third World people" (*Loving* 114). Homophobia within the communities of racialized Americans often coincides with a defense of group solidarity. People whose identities challenge heteronormativity are seen as betraying opposite-sex people of their race by rejecting sexual alliances with them. In addition, heterosexuality is often seen as the only cultural center that can be occupied by a marginalized racial minority. Marginalized sexual identities present a threat to attempts to join the mainstream and add an additional margin within groups that cannot afford to compound their already marginalized status.

Despite the wealth of non-Euro-American models of same-sex erotics, homosexuality and bisexuality are still often regarded as white identities, a risk that only whites can afford to take, or a disease with which whites "infect" nonwhites in attempts to divide and conquer the Other. While earlier writings, such as Chávez González's, associate sex/gender subversions with people of color, Rust and Moraga show how that equation has been inverted. Marginal sexual identities have been attributed to people of marginalized races, cultures, and nationalities from the time of Cortés through the McCarthy years. In an effort to escape the social and economic margins, many minority groups rejected the sexual stereotype with such virulence as to turn it back on Euro-Americans. For example, Henry Louis Gates Jr. suggests that homophobia "is an almost obsessive motif that runs through the major authors of the Black Aesthetic and Black Power movements" ("Black Man's Burden" 234). Gates notes that the formulations of black nationalism in the 1960s were founded in part on homophobia. Valuing blackness as a signifier of strength and empowerment occurred simultaneous to the vilification of homosexuality as weak, abject, and white. Defending black masculinity and the black family against structures of racism, much like the valuing of machismo and *la familia* in the Chicano movement, implied a centering of heteronormativity. Similarly, in *Zami*, Audre Lorde describes the ways in which homosexuality was shunned, considered "bourgeois and reactionary," by her communist friends, white and black alike (149, 180). Being gay made one suspicious and subjected the group to scrutiny by the FBI and other arms of the dominant culture.

While Lorde, Moraga, Anzaldúa, Michelle Cliff and others find ways to embrace their lesbianism within the context of their racial and national identities—referring to Caribbean and Mexican models such as Zami, Granny Nanny, and *mita' y mita'*—other Afro-Caribbean and Latina writers are less willing to accept marginalized sexualities on top of their marginalized racial and national identities. Those who feel that it is necessary to deal with one oppression at a time, healing racial wounds before moving on to others, often regard nonheterosexual identifications as compromising the political commitment to race. Paule Marshall, for example, emphasizes racial, cultural, and national duality throughout her work but creates an undercurrent of resistance to sex and gender identities that deviate from the mainstream.

For example, in her first novel, *Brown Girl, Brownstones* (1959), Marshall's protagonist, Selina, criticizes the pretentious "Young Associates" of Brooklyn's Barbadian Homeowners Association by calling them "Queers!" (226). She despises the effeminate Julian Hurley, resists his "sly eye" and "his small viciousness," and calls him a "fairy" (227, 229). By the end of the novel, she develops the courage to confront him with a "contemptuous glance" that "told him that she knew why his eyes darted to each man that passed" (270–71). Selina's statement assumes that homoerotic desire is something shameful. Julian and the Young Associates represent the "clannish" and "provincial" attitudes of the Bajan (Barbadian) group that "feverishly court[s]" the "white world" (227). Marshall opposes the politically and racially aware attitudes of Selina and her boyfriend, Clive, to the pretentious, white-aspiring Bajans, who strive for middle-class security and regret that "We ain't white yet" (221). A sexual opposition lines up with this political opposition, in which the heroes are clearly straight and the Associates' sexuality is in question.

Another despised group in this novel are the bohemians, also described as sexual deviants: "That horde of colored cats in hot pursuit of a few mangy white chicks—desperate for a sponsor and a taste of the forbidden. The few sad colored chicks enacting their historic role with the whites. And those others of confused gender: *be-whores* and *bullers* as the Bajans would aptly call them. All mixed together in one desperate potpourri" (243–44).[28] The suggestions of sexual desperation, disorder, and moneygrubbing in this image signal the supposed perversity of this racial and sexual mixture. Significantly, the criticisms of the Associates and the "pathetic Village scene" (243) focus on their subversion of both sex/gender norms and black integrity. The Young Associates are to be despised because they are effeminate and they worship white America, and the bohemians are to be despised because they observe no racial or sexual distinctions in their erotic lives. Marshall thus parallels sexual crossing with racial betrayal. Clive suggests to Selina that there is no room for deviation within the Barbadian-American community: "there are so few of us," and "it's a long haul," so the group needs full support (263).

In Marshall's second novel, *The Chosen Place, the Timeless People* (1969), the mythic Caribbean society of Bournehills also has no room for same-sex desire. Merle's greatest crime, the hidden secret from her dark past, is that she slept with a woman in England. Merle describes herself as a "kept woman," trapped by a wealthy English lesbian who "collected people the way someone else might paintings or books, the bitch" (328–29).[29] In this instance, lesbianism is a sort of prostitution that traps Merle under the influence of a female pimp.[30] Merle was financially dependent on this "bitch," whose sexual manipulation becomes a symbol of English corruption, imperialism, and domination. Marshall thus provides an image of lesbianism as perverse and exploitative. Merle recalls their lesbian sexual relations with repulsion, and the affair led her to fear that a man would never again "look at [her] twice" (329). Merle's affair with the woman is not so much a sign of her bisexuality as it is a temporary, regrettable deviation from her heterosexuality. The Euro-American ethnographer Saul echoes this dismissal of lesbianism as a viable identification: "I've never been able to take that kind of thing between women very seriously" (327). Merle responds to Saul's interpretation: "Ha! . . . My lady friend . . . took it seriously, I can tell you. Damn seriously. I wasn't to realize how much so until she had done her worst" (327). This response implies that only evil women like her "lady friend" take same-sex relationships seriously, and that seriousness itself presents a dangerous, damaging threat.[31]

In *Daughters* (1992), resistance to homosexuality persists in the attitudes of the protagonist's best friend, Viney, who compares gay men to narcissists and drug addicts (71–72). Viney simultaneously criticizes cross-racial relations ("the little white girls out here eyeing what we eyeing, and the brothers who only have eyes for them") and same-sex relations ("not to mention *pu'leeze* those among the brothers who have eyes only for each other") (71). These deviants not only challenge heterosexual African-American allegiances but also take black men away from black women. These homophobic statements directed at gay men contrast with a quiet acceptance of lesbian partnerships, which do not provide any competition for Marshall's heterosexual black heroines (whose empowerment is the novel's central concern) (326). It is important to note that homophobic sentiment in *Daughters* is distanced from Marshall's main character and occupies little narrative space. Finally, in *The Fisher King* (2000), there is a suggestion that Marshall's heroine, Hattie, has a crush on her girlhood friend, Cherisse, and the two women end up living together (significantly, in bohemian Paris) in a triangulated relationship with Cherisse's husband.

Marshall's work thus reflects a consistent interrogation of the social implications of homosexuality, and her more recent texts reflect less generalized hostility toward homosexuality and a greater willingness to value sexual diversity. The progression of sexual representations in Marshall's work coincides with the historical progression of sexual attitudes in the United States. Marshall's first two novels, written in the 1950s and 1960s, are products of a climate of resistance to homosexuality in the wake of McCarthyism and Cold War panic.[32] These decades also marked a climax in the civil rights movement, when black solidarity and identity politics took precedence over the contemporary attentions to sexual and cultural heterogeneity within African-Americans. In *Brown Girl, Brownstones*, for example, Marshall depicts characters who rate property ownership and education as their highest goals and reach toward these goals without necessarily regarding those within their community—artists, intellectuals, and gays—whose different definitions of success might impede progress. In contrast to her early work, Marshall's later novels reflect a relative acceptance of homosexuality as a social reality. *Daughters*, in particular, contains a greater variety of personalities and a greater diversity of identifications among African-Americans and Afro-Caribbeans. Marshall's representations thus capture the gradual de-essentializing of the black community as a homogeneous and stable ground for identity politics.

In addition to this resistance to homosexuality, a resistance to bisexuality also appears in the writings of some mixed-race lesbians. While homosexuality is sometimes regarded as a threat to racial solidarity, bisexuality is sometimes regarded as a challenge to gay identity politics, a fracture within the foundation of gay alliances. Since bi- identity refuses to choose a single identification, it challenges the idea that sexuality is a singular essence. Many gay-affirmative arguments attempt to secure rights for gays and lesbians by arguing that sexuality, like race, is something with which one is born. They assume (perhaps correctly) that the general public will not have sympathy for a chosen or fluid "lifestyle." In configuring sexuality as a choice rather than an anatomical inevitability, bisexuals are thus often seen as traitors to gay and lesbian political interests. Susie Bright rejects such essentialist notions of sexuality. Her celebration of choice and sexual play announces that same-sex desire is not something she assumed passively at birth. Attempts to gain essential status for sexual orientation also suggest that sexuality is something about which nothing can be done: people have no choice but to assume the sexuality with which they are born. Bright rejects this sense of sexual fatalism and affirms bisexuality and same-sex erotics as something she chooses and desires.

Bright criticizes the "gay family's" resistance to transgressions and its insistence that bisexuality reflects a failure to commit (151–52). Bisexuals are often seen as hanging on to heterosexual privilege and fearing to ally themselves with gay or lesbian identities. Maria Pramaggiore describes bisexuality as "fence-sitting" but criticizes political stances that fear the ambiguous "epistemologies of the fence" and impose "restrictive formulas" on sex and gender (3). In Pramaggiore's argument, gay and lesbian communities join other oppressive cultures that "continually hem in and border our desires" (4). "Biphobia" intersects with racism and sexism in its attempts to limit fluid identifications. And people with already marginalized identities are likely to resist internal differences to shore up those identities as solid foundations for group politics.

Moraga recognizes the deep political connotations of sexual and racial identification and suggests that bi- identification dilutes political signification. For her, bi- identity only goes halfway in its politics: "I have always hated the terms 'biracial' and 'bisexual.' They are passive terms, without political bite. They don't choose. They don't make a decision. They are a declaration not of identity, but of biology, of sexual practice. They say nothing about where one really stands. And as long as injustice prevails, we do not have the luxury of calling ourselves either" (*Last Generation* 126). In this passage, Moraga contrasts identity that one chooses for political reasons to biology that one passively inherits at birth. Yet I would argue that the perceptions and manifestations of biology are not passive: biology itself involves choices of presentation, accommodations, and cultural assumptions. While Moraga emphasizes the multiplicity within racial identities and the shifting cultural foundations of race, her declaration of sexual identity is less fluid.

Unlike many manifestations of homophobia and biphobia that are based on ignorance, Marshall and Moraga's sexual politics are a product of racial and sexual commitment. While Marshall shores up support for the black community and celebrates black heterosexual partnerships, Moraga solidifies the foundations of Chicana lesbian identity.[33] Moraga suggests that nonsingular identification is a "luxury" that cannot be risked in times of political injustice, and she poses even chosen identity as a singular stand or location to which one must commit. The risk of this positioning is the creation of an exclusive foundation and a sense of erotic and political destiny. Moreover, I believe that there is an internal contradiction in any argument that accepts racial fluidity but denies fluidity of sexual identification. Although Marshall and Moraga affirm the multiple heritages that meet within their mixed-race identities, at times they convert that mixture into a singular (almost essential) identification.

When she creates her Codex Xerí to represent the contemporary historical moment, Moraga chooses as a model identity the "*jotería* [gay people], 'two-spirited' people" (*Last Generation* 189). In equating *gay* with *two-spirited*, Moraga misses the ambiguities of the Native American "two-spirited" tradition. Native American cross-gendered culture predated *homosexuality* as a term and disrupts any single sexual identification, including homosexuality, in its fluidity. Anzaldúa's model identity, borrowed from *Tejano* valley tradition, is *mita' y mita.'* This "half and half" comes closer to the fluidity of the two-spirited tradition: "Half and halfs are not suffering from a confusion of sexual identity, or even from a confusion of gender. What we are suffering from is an absolute despot duality that says we are able to be only one or the other" (*Borderlands* 19). *Confusion* implies that there must be one essential self and that all other identifications are deviant aberrations, Other. Anzaldúa defies such absolutism, defining sexuality in a much more fluid way: "You can become a lesbian and be a lesbian for twenty years and then decide that you want to be sexual with a man" ("Writing" 121). She compares the self to a railroad train that hits occasional crossways, points of ambiguity and change, where the individual can go either way, reinterpret the past, become lesbian or heterosexual, without threatening personal integrity as a subject (121). Sexuality is thus an open-ended identification, not always identical to itself. Anzaldúa contrasts her own lesbianism, a choice that she made for political reasons, to Moraga's lesbianism, which was something more essential, emotional, and uncontrollable that she had felt since "a very early age" (119).

In this way, Anzaldúa keeps her lesbian identification flexible, more bisexual, than Moraga's one-track commitments. Anzaldúa extends mestiza consciousness beyond racial fluidity to include sexual subversions and other challenges to identity categories: "the squint-eyed, the perverse, the queer, the troublesome, the mongrel, the mulato, the half-breed, the half-dead; in short, those who cross over, pass over, or go through the confines of the 'normal' " (*Borderlands* 3). She includes sex identity itself, not just sexuality, in these transgressions, suggesting that *mita' y mita'* balances both male and female in one body: "half a month we're a man and have a penis, and half a month we're women and have periods. That's what a lesbian is, that's what a dyke is. But instead of it being split like that I think of it as something that's integral" (*Borderlands* 19; "Writing" 126). This corporeal metaphor of lesbian identity radically fuses sexes—embodied as both male and female, not hermaphroditic—without being split, without losing coherence as an identity. In this configuration, lesbian identity is divorced from sexual singularity and embodies the subversion of categories that I attribute to bi-.

In a recent interview with Ann Reuman, Anzaldúa clarifies her rejection of binary sex identifications: "you're a woman, you're a man, and there's no in between. And so here come the transsexuals and the drag queens and they say, 'Well, identity is enacted, and it's performed.' And then Judith Butler in her book brings that aspect out. But even before she was dealing with it, I was dealing with it about what takes center stage, which identity takes center stage" ("Coming" 12). Mestiza consciousness is thus dynamic and performative (even before postmodern theories of performativity); it resists essence by continually trying on new identifications and breaking down "the unitary aspect of each new paradigm" (Anzaldúa, *Borderlands* 80). Anzaldúa welcomes new possibilities for identification that would cause her to reinterpret her self and to challenge her perception of the world: "nothing is thrust out, the good the bad and the ugly, nothing rejected, nothing abandoned" (79). Exclusion occurs when shoring up these marginalized identities closes them off to new outsiders. Once again, Anzaldúa's mestiza consciousness borders on the idealistic, the utopian, or the unrealistic. Is it possible to have an identity with no outside? The texts I discuss in the next section contain representations that gesture toward ultimate inclusiveness and fluidity in identity, but they discover the impracticability of such inclusion and confront the need to limit identification in some aspect.

Ky-Ky, Bi-Gender, and Bi-Sexuality

As I have already shown, texts by Latina, African-American, and Afro-Caribbean writers often include elaborate performances of race and sex, employing costume, role playing, and hidden identities to challenge racial and sexual hierarchies. Rather than being merely superficial or playful, these performances serve crucial political functions. In her reading of Nella Larsen's *Passing*, Butler suggests that calling race and sex *performative* enables their usage against racist and sexist norms (*Bodies* 248n). Performance releases these categories from predetermined assumptions and allows them to be contested, rearticulated, and reconstructed in new contexts.

In recent texts, Judith Ortiz Cofer, Audre Lorde, Ruth Behar, and Michelle Cliff offer characters who perform multiple races and sexes to counteract racelessness, racism, heterosexism, and misogyny. When Lorde's heroine wears an Afro despite "gay girl" fashion and when Cliff's Clare chooses to identify as black despite her light skin, they draw public attention to racial identification as a matter of political importance. Behar's Chencha takes on feminine attributes to ease identification with the women she wants to help and takes on masculine attributes to give her strength, power, and authority. Cliff's Harry/Harriet performs and exaggerates femininity, attaches it to a male body, and overturns conventional associations of masculinity with violation and femininity with passivity. These subversive identifications carry an implicit critique of limiting stereotypes and force readers to abandon their preconceived ideas about race, sex, and gender.

In the readings that follow, one discovers that sexual fluidity results from, or at least correlates with, mixed-race identities. Butler argues that "sexual regulation operates through the regulation of racial boundaries, and . . . racial distinctions operate to defend against certain socially endangering sexual transgressions" (*Bodies* 20). Although she intends to show that sexual difference is not prior to racial difference, Butler's assertion that sexual norms are "racially articulated" uses race in the service of sex. Indeed, her reading of *Passing* disregards the racial contingency of sexual norms and uses race to signify taboo homoerotic attraction within and across racial lines. In this reading, sex turns out to be more socially endangering, unspeakable, while race becomes the safe code through which sex is regulated. Mestiza writers Ortiz Cofer and Behar ultimately support this association by using race to highlight forbidden sexual desires and sexual ambiguities, but Afro-Caribbean writers Lorde and Cliff suggest that race is not safe and is not merely a means of articulating sexual identity.[34] Racial categories often conflict with the characters' sexual identities. Lorde's semiautobiographical heroine finds it impossible to articulate

her identity through the sexual categories available because her race exceeds the given sexual boundaries. And Cliff's Clare solidifies her racial
commitment by eschewing sexuality. In both instances, race is the more
heavily contested identification and thus requires more dedicated political
support. Race and sex do not contain each other, but the overlap between
them radicalizes our perception of both.

Judith Ortiz Cofer and the Bisexed Lover in *Silent Dancing*

Latina poet and novelist Judith Ortiz Cofer describes the persona in her
semiautobiographical *Silent Dancing* (1990) as biracial, the product of a
marriage of opposites. Her father is "pale," her mother "dark" and "sultry"
(38–39). This racial duality mirrors Ortiz Cofer's cultural and national duality: she was born in Puerto Rico, spent her life shuttling back and forth
between the island and the mainland United States, and currently resides
in Georgia (outside the Puerto Rican barrios she describes in her novels).
In the words of José Piedra, "Ortiz Cofer fancies herself a tightrope walker
never reaching either end of her geographical or existential spectrum.
She inhabits a world of pieces of home, made of a personal archipelago
of experiences in foreign lands(lides)" (90). In this metaphor of tightrope
travel, Ortiz Cofer's identity is always mobile, between lands, with "home"
crumbling beneath her.

Ortiz Cofer navigates these slippery foundations throughout *Silent
Dancing*. Racial and national fluidity multiplies into the greatest complexity in the section titled "Marina," with the added categories of gender
and sexuality. The title "Marina" refers to the legendary origins of racial
mixture in the Americas: Marina is the Spanish name for La Malinche,
the symbolic mother of *mestizaje* in Mexico. Marina/Malinche supposedly
betrayed her native people by translating for the Spaniards, moving between cultures, and sleeping with the enemy. Ortiz Cofer invokes these
issues of betrayal, crossing over, and subversive sexuality. "Marina" begins
with the narrator reflecting on her own "dual existence" and the gap between herself and her mother after her mother "had gone totally 'native,'"
returning to Puerto Rican customs and abandoning U.S. culture (151–
52). While her mother gravitates toward Puerto Rico, the speaker gravitates toward feminism and other progressive U.S. political movements,
betraying Puerto Rican definitions of femininity. In questioning gender
identity, Ortiz Cofer questions cultural identity as well, since the two are
inextricably bound.

As the speaker and her mother part ways over both issues, a primary uncertainty left between them is the definition of *woman*, and the narrative that forges their "new place to begin our search for the meaning of the word *woman*" is the story of Marina/o (152, 160). In their search for *woman*, race, class, and sexuality also come into play. Significantly, their point of departure is bisexed, a man raised as a girl since birth.[35] The child's mother disguised her baby son as the daughter she had wished for, and Marina grew up thinking that she was a girl. Even after discovering the "truth" of his/her ambiguous gender identity, mother and son/daughter continue to fool the town with their sex and gender bending. In a sexual revision of the U.S. laws that defined children's race and status based on maternal authority, Marina's sex identity is assigned by her mother.

The masquerade continues until Marina/o falls in love with Kiki, the sheltered daughter of the town mayor. The mayor has decided to allow his daughter to bathe with the common girls of the town to demonstrate his democratic principles. Kiki and Marina/o then meet in the river where the Black Virgin once appeared, Marina/o with her "thick black Indian hair" and Kiki "a pale fish" in the water (156). This description reveals the racial differences between the two and endows Marina/o's darkness with a sacred quality that echoes the Black Virgin. Moreover, by comparing the black apparition with whom Kiki falls in love to the Virgin, the narrator masks the bisexed adolescent's sexuality, a masking that continues as sex and sexuality are ultimately resolved outside the boundaries of the narrative. Marina/o is probably racially dual as well, since Ortiz Cofer describes her/him as having green eyes, "*café-con-leche* [coffee with milk] skin," and black Indian hair (156). This visible racial contradiction reflects the hidden sexual contradiction that Marina/o embodies, and it causes her/him to stand out as different. Kiki and Marina/o are both outsiders in the group based on their race, sex, and class, and their shared difference fuels the attraction between them. Their romance then crosses boundaries of apparent sex and gender identity, race, and class. An awareness of the forbidden nature of their desire leads Kiki and Marina/o to run away together. The story reinforces the ambiguity of sex/gender and the illicitness of Kiki and Marina/o's mutual desire by never depicting the realization of that desire (157–59).

An alternate reading could, in fact, suggest an essential foundation for identity. Perhaps Marino's gender crossing—his assumption of feminine identity—is halted by his innate heterosexual desire for the white woman: he returns to his original male identity as soon as he meets Kiki. Yet the fact that Ortiz Cofer uses Marina/o as a place to begin the search for the meaning of *woman* suggests that one cannot look at him/her as solely male. Instead, his ability to pass as a woman provides a point of departure for considering what it takes to assume a sexual identity. Like Anthony from *Designing Women*, Marina/o forces us to rethink what counts as female and to accept that femaleness is a construct that can be adopted by men. Marina/o qualifies as a woman because of his/her mother's authority in naming the sex of her child and because his/her presence in the all-female bathing community is taken as proof of his/her sex. Sex thus varies according to personal account and according to context. If Marina/o is not clearly a man, his/her love for Kiki cannot be seen as only heterosexual. The scenes with Kiki and Marina bathing together as women insist on the possibility of a homoerotic reading. Yet the narrator's authority tells us that Marina/o is sexually male, so their relation cannot be read as solely homosexual either. This text thus allows for a double interpretation, both hetero- and homo-. In its refusal to make a clear choice between sexualities and its refusal to pin Marina/o to a single sexual identification, *Silent Dancing* is a bisexual text.

The new origin of *woman* for Ortiz Cofer lacks a stable positioning along the axes of sex, gender, race, and class, allowing her to construct her own *woman* apart from narrow social and biological conventions. Although she uses Marina/o as a model for *woman* (in the singular), the new *woman* is racially and sexually mestiza. The simultaneous exploration of gender and sexuality along with culture, race, and class suggests a relationship between the different categories of identity. Through the figure of Marina/o, Ortiz Cofer imagines a way for her bicultural fluidity to expand her sex/gender identity rather than leaving her trapped in between rigid U.S. and Puerto Rican standards. The confusion of Marina/o's origins leads to mobility and choice: s/he can bathe naked in a "girls only" homosocial ritual, have a romance with the mayor's daughter, and act as a grandfather to a little girl in pink ruffles (as the narrator sees Marino at the beginning of the story) (153). With this narrative, Ortiz Cofer envisions a way to transcend the sex-, race-, and class-based limitations conventionally imposed on women, and she redefines *woman* on a shifting foundation with which both she and her mother identify, on both sides of the U.S.– Puerto Rican divide (and many other divides, too).

Audre Lorde and the Resistance to Identity in *Zami*

Audre Lorde also challenges definitions of *woman* from a perspective that incorporates racial, national, sexual, and gendered differences. As Ortiz

Cofer examines the complexities of identity through Marina/o, Lorde interrogates the internal contradictions that emerge with every identification. Yet Lorde's *Zami* (1982) explores racial and sexual mobility more directly, in the body of her main character, rather than projecting those issues onto a minor character and allowing potential sexual conflicts to take place offstage, as Ortiz Cofer does in *Silent Dancing*. Marina/o and Kiki exist safely in the narrative past, in the realm of storytelling, and Ortiz Cofer does not describe what happens when they discover their sexuality. *Zami*, however, is not so veiled.

In the prologue to this "biomythography," Lorde writes, "I have always wanted to be both man and woman, to incorporate the strongest and richest parts of my mother and father within/into me—to share valleys and mountains upon my body the way the earth does in hills and peaks" (7).[36] Lorde thus translates her desired duality onto a metaphorically hermaphroditic body. Claudine Raynaud interprets this passage as Lorde's resolution of differences within one subject, her unification with both mother and father, and her ultimate integration into wholeness (223). I argue that Lorde does just the opposite, that she refrains from constructing one unified, "whole" subject in favor of a series of divergent identifications. Like Anzaldúa, Lorde breaks down the unifying impulses that would assimilate differences into a single identity, suggesting that the body is merely the "house of difference," the site of partial and contradictory identifications (226).[37]

The mother in *Zami*, Linda, provides one point of origin for Audre's fluid identity.[38] Linda is mixed-race Afro-Caribbean, with skin light enough to pass for Spanish. As a scullery maid in a tea shop, she is not black until her dark-skinned husband appears in the teahouse and alters the owner's perception of Linda's race (9). Lorde describes Linda as a "powerful woman," which "equaled something else quite different from ordinary woman, from simply 'woman.' It certainly did not, on the other hand, equal 'man.' What then?" (15). Like We'wha, Linda is not woman or man according to Euro-American conventions: her sexual identity is "unexpressable in the white american common tongue" (15). Significantly, Linda's nontraditional sex is a product of her racial identity, since the word for it does not exist in white American language "unless it was accompanied by some aberrant explaining adjective like blind, . . . or crazy, or Black" (15). When Lorde describes Linda as "different" seven times in two pages, this emphatic difference is a product of both her nonassimilation to white American sex categories and her racially mixed "red-bone" color (15–16). Lorde compares this difference to that of woman-oriented women, "Black dykes," though Linda would "rather [have] died than use that name" (15). In this way, Lorde sexualizes racial ambiguity. She concludes that Linda must be *"other* than woman" and reiterates "again, she was certainly not man" (16). She is not white or black, woman or man, conventionally straight or dyke. She is Other, somewhere outside and beyond the identifications available to Lorde.

Linda is committed to revising the world around her and its definitions, reinterpreting racist insults, altering perceptions of reality (18).[39] This subversion of perception becomes a key concept in *Zami*, as the narrator (Audre) discovers that identity is produced in display and public perception. Audre, in turn, learns to alter her public persona and to play with the cues—clothing, for example—that people perceive as signs of identification. Like Linda, Audre tries to remain outside identity categories. In so doing, she adopts many different cues and assumes many different identities. While Linda lacks an identity—man, woman, black, white—Audre has many.

While still in high school, Audre's favorite activity with her best friend, Gennie, is creating costumes for role-playing: "Bandits, Gypsies, Foreigners of all degree, Witches, Whores, and Mexican Princesses—there were appropriate costumes for every role, and appropriate places in the city to go to play them all out" (88). One of the most important aspects of this role-playing is the public element, finding the "appropriate places" for each identity: double-decker omnibuses for workers, Fifth and Park Avenues for hussies, the Village for Africans. They find a context that supports each costume, a place in which they might be mistaken for real. They sing and curse loudly to ensure public attention, and they court that attention to reinforce each role, "to match whomever we decided to be" (88). The insistence on trying "to match" something suggests that they are trying to pass for real and to reveal that the real itself is something that can be duplicated by teenagers in costume. As in Butler's analysis of drag queens, Audre and Gennie prove that identity categories are produced in role-play and audience interpretation.

Once she moves out on her own, Audre continues to assume a series of identities, yet these identities have a more real physical impact on her body and her livelihood. Significantly, each identity that Audre assumes has its own location. This series of different apartments and cities highlights the mobility of Audre's identity and circumscribes each new identification in a particular interpretive context. When she first moves out of her parents' home, she is heterosexual and a member of the predominantly white Labor Youth League. A small apartment in Brighton Beach is where the lonely and financially impoverished Audre spends a miserable winter after an affair with a white man leaves her pregnant and her lack of money leaves her with no choice but to obtain a painful illegal abortion (103–10). In Stamford, Connecticut, she is a lesbian and a factory worker. She has her first lesbian relationship with a black woman, and her job in an electronics company exposes her to dangerous X-ray levels and leaves dark marks on her fingers (122–47). In Mexico, she rents a comfortable house and joins a community of upper-middle-class expatriate Anglo-American women (154–76).

In each place, Audre develops new nicknames—"slick kitty from the city" in Stamford, "La Chica" in Mexico—and new groups of friends. She transforms herself to meet the expectations of her surrounding public, and her sexual and racial identities change with each new context. Her mobile sexual orientation redirects her erotic life from white men to white women to women of color. In those relations, her sexual practices also change, from passive object with Peter, to "stone butch" with Ginger (always being the active partner, refusing to be made love to), to a more mutual relationship with Eudora, to a three-way dynamic with Muriel and Lynn (104, 140, 169, 212). In different places her sexuality takes on different meanings: in Mexico the expatriates conceal their lesbianism and bisexuality; among progressives in New York homosexuality was "bourgeois and reactionary"; in the Village gay scene she is disparaged for not fitting into butch-femme gender roles (160, 149, 178). Her race, too, has different significance in different locations. Among her progressive white New York City friends, her race is often effaced and ignored, but in Mexico it makes her an object of desire (154).

Some critics, such as Raynaud, suggest that Audre's series of identifications follows a teleological progression. According to this interpretation, Audre's final affair with Afrekete (chapter 31) performs a resolution of identity, the ultimate discovery of self in the arms of another black woman, the completion of her "forward motion from fragmentation to wholeness" (Raynaud 239). By the end of *Zami*, Audre is unquestionably lesbian and clearly committed to black women in particular. Despite this narrative progression, however, other elements of the text decenter the concluding scenario. Chapter 31 was initially written and published separately as "Tar Beach." In *Zami*, it seems tacked on, a final attempt at closure. It is dreamy, mythic, ideal, utopian. In Afrekete's room there is a "glowing magical tank of exotic fish," the lovers' bodies are "dappled with green sunlight from the plants in Afrekete's high windows," and they make love "under the Midsummer Eve's Moon," "coated in the woman's power" (*Zami* 248). The rest of the text, including its literal center, is written in a more realistic mode and imagines identity much more fluidly. Loving Afrekete occupies fewer than fifteen pages, and the concluding epilogue emphasizes separation and new meetings (255).

In this way, there is a tension between the Afrekete episode, which describes a sensual rediscovery of self, home, racial heritage, and "roots" through lovemaking and the enjoyment of "authentic" Caribbean fruits (249–50), and the remainder of the text, which resists fixing self, home, or authenticity in singular locations. This tension mirrors tensions in feminism during the 1970s, the period during which Lorde wrote *Zami*. Perhaps Lorde resisted letting go completely of essence and "black lesbian identity" as such. *Zami* traces a tension between the desire to hold onto the essentialism that founded much 1970s feminism and the desire to critique the limiting, singular, and often exclusive definitions of *woman* that emerged from such feminism.[40] This tension between political foundations and open-ended identifications is precisely what closes off sexual identity in Marshall and Moraga, too.

As Audre struggles with political allegiance in her process of self-definition, labels present a reoccurring marker of identity politics. Throughout the text, Audre resists labels: "my experience with people who tried to label me was that they usually did it to either dismiss me or use me" (108). In this explanation, the imposition of a label removes her identity from her control: it is either dismissed or manipulated by others. In her attempts to exercise control over her identity, she rejects all of the labels that momentarily describe her. She is and is not a lesbian, a student, a Marxist, or a factory worker. This defiance is most obvious within the lesbian community, where she resists butch-femme conventions and joins "the 'freaky' bunch of lesbians who weren't into role-playing, and who the butches and femmes, Black and white, disparaged with the term Ky-Ky, or AC/DC" (178). Despite her desire to escape labels, the mechanisms through which society "controls" or delimits identity, Audre inevitably encounters new ones. As soon as she rejects butch and femme roles, she is given a new label, "Ky-Ky." Yet Ky-Ky embodies contradictions and is never identical to itself. Although the term is attributed to Audre in a disparaging manner, it becomes positively charged as a signifier of her resistance to familiar social roles, heterogender paradigms, and the dynamics of domination and subordination that are associated with butch-femme identities. Butch-femme pairs resemble the gay male identities in Mexico that Octavio Paz claims uphold Euro-American gender binaries, but Ky-Ky does not fit the normative aggressor-object pattern. As an "identity," Ky-Ky resists preexisting identifications.

In Audre's lesbian community, where the butch-femme paradigm dominates, clothing is invested with great significance and is used to signify more fundamental aspects of each woman's race or sexual identity. Crossover articles, like Bermuda shorts, are rejected by many fashionable "gay-girls" "to keep the signals clear," because "clothes were often the most important way of broadcasting one's chosen sexual role" (241). Yet Audre upsets the system and mixes the signals. To display her fluidly gendered Ky-Ky identity, Audre plays with the cues: her casual clothes (riding pants and sweatshirts) approximate butch identity but diverge from familiar butch signifiers (pressed, creased, and starched pants and shirts). She also adopts ambiguous signifiers that are worn by butch and femme alike, such as the brass-buckled black leather belts that both she and the more feminine Afrekete wear (245). Since clothes are an easy variable to change, sexual codes can be quite fluid. As in her high school days, changing costumes is Audre's way of subverting fashion and playing with identity. Her self-fashioning provides an illusion of control. She changes the image she chooses to portray as she moves between cultures and identities: "When I lived in Stamford, I had worn old dungarees and men's shirts to work. . . . When I lived in Mexico, I wore the full peasant skirts and blouses so readily available in the marketplaces of Cuernavaca. Now I had my straight clothes for working at the library—two interchangeable outfits of skirts, sweaters, and a warm-weather blouse or two. . . . I had very few clothes for my real life, but with the addition of Muriel's quixotic wardrobe, we developed quite a tidy store of what the young gay-girl could be seen in" (208). A flexible wardrobe enables her to adopt different roles at work or in bars, straight or gay.

Through the manipulation of costume, Audre breaks down the process of identification. She rejects butch-femme lesbian fashion to reject heterogendered dynamics: "role-playing reflected all the deprecating attitudes toward women which we loathed in straight society." Her determination to remain outside of this hierarchical power dynamic leads her to what "the majority" calls a " 'confused' life style" (221). Significantly, she attributes her resistance to sexual categories to "our art or our craziness or our color," suggesting that there is a correlation between racial marginalization and the choice to defy the majority categories within the lesbian community (221). Audre's marginality within the gay-girl scene is, in part, a product of her racial difference, which sets her apart. Her subversion of sexual codes thus carries meaning about more than sex: her Afro, which is uncommon for any "gay-girl," "broadcasts" her racial difference from white lesbians, and her outfits from the army-navy surplus and John's Bargain Store communicate her lower class status in opposition to the fashionable "proper Black ladies" at the Bagatelle (178, 209, 242).

Audre's lover, Muriel, describes the social "outsiderhood" of lesbians in terms of racial marginalization when she says, "We're all niggers" (203). Here, she borrows the more established paradigms of American racism and the more familiar pejoratives that go along with it to explain the oppression of lesbians. Audre regards Muriel's comment as both true and false. Audre shares the feeling of being twice a minority only with her black lesbian friend, Felicia. In the end, Audre finds herself in "the very house of difference," where people are brought together by multiple differences rather than by "the security of any one particular difference" (226). Not just sex or race or class define her as different; instead, these overlapping categories deny her the security of a single difference or a single identity to broadcast. While the categories *black lesbian* or *Zami* potentially encompass these differences in a singular, non-Euro-American identity, that identity is divided within itself. Audre is always fighting to include additional categories, such as fat or working class, but she does not find them all in any other individual: even Felicia and Afrekete come up thin.[41]

In the fairly large body of criticism that addresses Lorde's work, relatively little has been said about this manipulation of so many different identity categories. In her analysis of *Zami*, Cheryl Kader describes Lorde's project as "an attempt to redesign gender through the lens of [lesbian] sexuality" that "foreground[s] the discontinuity between sex and gender" (185–86). Kader's analysis presumes that lesbianism ruptures gender conventions, but I think the reverse holds true. I find gender more fluid than sexuality in *Zami*. The most radical aspects of Audre's identity are her subversion of labels and her self-fashioning with costume, both of which radicalize her otherwise singular orientation toward women. Kader suggests that lesbianism dislodges the "reliability" of identity (185). I would suggest, however, that lesbianism alone does not redefine identity; instead, Ky-Ky does the redefining, redesigning, and challenging in *Zami*. *Lesbian* can be limiting in terms of sex, race, and gender roles, so Ky-Ky emerges as an identity that is always different, always outside some category, never even identical to itself. Audre consistently resists identification with singular terms such as *lesbian* because they force her to pin down her identity to a limited paradigm. In fact, she does not even self-identify as Ky-Ky: others attribute the label to her. She distances her own identity from purely sexual categories with constant reminders of her other identifications: race, class, weight, gender. She critiques the communities that expect her to closet other categories and to identify singularly with just one: the gay-girl scene denies her racial identity and her nonconformist gender, just as the progressive political scene denies her sexuality (179, 220). Yet Audre resists. Katie King's analysis of *Zami* reflects this resistance to identity and search for "strategies proliferating non-unified, contingent identities" (54). Audre adopts and subverts cues of different racial and sexual identities, using them to revise herself continually without ever settling down into one unified identity. In the process, as King suggests, Audre destabilizes oppositions such as black-white, butch-femme, Ky-Ky–role-playing (56).

Ruth Behar and the Translation of Sex Roles in *Translated Woman*

Ruth Behar's *Translated Woman* (1993) is an anthropological narrative that explores Latina gender roles. Behar is part of a new generation of anthropologists who are self-reflexively feminist, literary, theoretical, and postmodern in their writing. In her introduction to *Women Writing Culture* (1995), Behar suggests that practices that are just now surfacing in the postmodern works of men are characteristic of the ways in which women wrote about race and identity throughout the twentieth century. When contemporary theorists such as James Clifford and George Marcus call for a "new," self-conscious, literary ethnography, they fail "to take into account that throughout the twentieth century women had crossed the border between anthropology and literature—but usually 'illegally,' as aliens who produced works that tended to be viewed in the profession as 'confessional' and 'popular'" (Behar and Gordon 4). For example, Behar claims that Zora Neale Hurston was "postmodern before its time in enacting an exemplary hybridity that combined engaged scholarship with a nuanced portrait of Hurston's own intellectual process" (18–19). Behar also acknowledges Jovita González Mireles as a precursor "whose paradoxical embrace of male power complicates our image of ethnic-feminist consciousness" (19). All three of these statements could apply as well to Matilda Coxe Stevenson and her personal connections with

We'wha. These early-twentieth-century women, with their nascent feminism, self-consciousness, intergeneric crossings, and subversions of conventional femininity, serve as models for Behar's work and foreshadow the subversions of sex/gender that Behar enacts.

Unlike Lorde, Behar does not directly address race or sexuality; nor does she approach the issue of lesbianism. Instead, race and sex run subtextually throughout her narrative. Behar's goal in *Translated Woman* is to provide an account of indigenous Mexican women's private lives and gender identifications, and her primary focus is the *historias* [histories/stories] of an Indian street peddler, Esperanza. Yet Chencha, a minor character, provides the best entry point for analyzing race, sex, and gender in this text. Chencha is a spiritist medium and the head of a cult dedicated to Pancho Villa. Through the mechanism of spiritism, *Translated Woman* redefines identity—more radically than the passing and costuming in my previous readings—as a series of performances.[42] Chencha embodies multiple personalities and adopts roles that deviate from her assumed sex. This multiplicity makes overt the more subtle gender fluidity of Chencha's followers, who challenge conventions of femininity to adapt to different situations. Behar's commitment to analyzing her subjects through the lens of feminism weighs her interrogation toward the social meanings of gender, but very complex racial and sexual dynamics lie beneath the surface.

As a medium, Chencha takes on the spirits of Villa; one of his wives, Amalia Díaz de Bonilla; and the *angelito* (dead baby/little angel) niño Tomasito. This multiplicity of spirit identities and the sexual border crossing involved in the process of assuming them mirror the multiplicity in Chencha's physical being. Esperanza describes Chencha as "prieta" and "morena," meaning dark-skinned. Chencha's Afro-Mexican heritage makes her stand out from the indigenous peoples of San Luis Potosí, yet her sexual duality makes her even more interesting. On meeting Chencha, Behar, a U.S.-educated feminist academic, claims, "I couldn't figure out whether she was a man cross-dressing as a woman, or indeed, as Esperanza and everyone else who knew her seemed to think, just a very 'manly woman,' *una mujer hombrona* or *macha*. No one described her as a lesbian, a transvestite, or a gay person, categories which seemed nonexistent among the participants of the cult" (205). Chencha's physical appearance leads Behar to conclude, based on her Euro-American interpretive experience, that Chencha is a man cross-dressing. Behar feels almost certain that Chencha has a male body and in fact fears that "at any moment this supposed woman, who clearly shaved her face, would pull off her dress and reveal a man's anatomy and maybe even attack me" (206). While Behar insists on Chencha's anatomical maleness and fears its most violent expression, the participants in Chencha's cult do not think of her as a man. Despite physical evidence that suggests male biology—stubble on her face, for example—the Mexican community accepts her as a woman because she dresses as one and identifies as such.[43] This acceptance of Chencha's public identity renders "irrelevant and simpleminded" the issue of her biological sex (205). Although it is a source of intrigue and anxiety for Behar, perhaps because of U.S. gender expectations, Chencha's anatomy remains hidden. Indeed, Behar's perplexity with regard to Chencha's "real" identity reinforces the insufficiency of the Euro-American categories that "seem nonexistent" among the cult members. Much like Stevenson's account of We'Wha, *Translated Woman* thus leaves sex and sexuality unspoken in the subtext and focuses on the more overt, familiar, and performative assumptions of gender.

Esperanza claims that Chencha has been seen pregnant but that she "lost all her pregnancies because of having to take on so many 'male' qualities to fight evil" (206). Esperanza describes Chencha's manly traits as something that she chose to adopt to empower herself as a healer, but this masculinity overpowers her supposedly female body so that she cannot carry her pregnancies through to birth. This rumor is meant to prove the femaleness of Chencha's sexual body and the performativeness of her masculinity. Yet her supposed decision to sacrifice maternity in exchange for masculine power doubly negates the female embodiment that Behar has questioned from the start. While the truth of her biological sex remains suppressed, her sexual orientation is ambiguous as well. She was married twice but currently prefers "the female world," living with several female assistants and servants (206). Chencha's sexual duality is organized around a heterogender paradigm, and her care for women is an extension of her professional manliness. Her followers do not think of Chencha in terms of lesbianism because her private sexuality is irrelevant to her status in the cult and because her masculine attributes distance her from female sex categories. No one cares what her actual body is or does: what matters are the spirits who occupy that neutral site.

Chencha's visible duality illuminates Esperanza's more subtle gender fluidity. Esperanza, too, admires and imitates the masculine qualities of Pancho Villa. She says of her hard life, "All of those years, I have been both man and woman [to my children], supporting them, helping them grow up" (157). Esperanza moves between the feminine realms of kitchen and

garden and the masculine realm of street commerce. She is both mother
and father to her children, economic provider and nurturer, since their
real fathers are incompetent. After she separates from her husband, Esperanza has the freedom to go wherever she wants, far greater mobility than
most women in her town. As a laborer, she is physically strong, and the
U.S. anthropologist finds it impossible to keep up with Esperanza (237).
She can wield a hoe and a pick or carry two heavy buckets of vegetables
to sell on the streets (158). Like Chencha, Esperanza is *macha*: aggressive,
litigious, and prone to violence. She takes her ex-husband and mother-in-
law to court for cheating her out of property, she kicks her sons out of the
house, and she beats her husband's female lover on the streets until she
is "dripping in blood" (82, 105, 145, 186). Esperanza repeatedly refers to
herself as filled with *coraje*, a word that signifies rage, courage, strength,
and valor. In this way, she challenges conventional definitions of both the
female body and the feminine gender.

In Behar's analysis, "Esperanza has a keen sense of her gender blending"
(293). However, Behar criticizes Esperanza's expressions of masculinity,
claiming that she consciously adopts misogynist values in her desire to
be manly: "That she appropriates culturally male values that oppress her
as well as other women in order to liberate and redeem herself is contradictory. Her violence toward other women, and ultimately toward herself, is problematic. Her fascination with Pancho Villa, in light of her
experience with male domination, is ironic" (296). Villa is legendary for
his exaggerated masculinity, his violence in war, and his mistreatment of
women. In 1916 he had ninety female soldiers of the revolution massacred
and then, rumor has it, rode his horse over their dead bodies (314). Behar suggests that Esperanza subverts expectations for conventional Mexican femininity—suffering, passive, martyred, motherly—by assuming the
opposite, violent, supermacho role (315). As with Chencha, Esperanza's
appropriation of power is manly. Behar measures both women by her
own Euro-American sex/gender standards, and her criticism of Esperanza's
treatment of women reads like a feminist critique of men (296). Yet Esperanza, unlike Chencha, is clearly not a man. Nor is she completely masculine. Instead, her sex and her gender are dual. Esperanza is both a victim
of patriarchal dominance (at the hands of her abusive father and her abusive husband) and a perpetrator of that dominance (in the ways that she
abuses her own children). She mixes her feminine, female identifications
(mother, obedient daughter, conventionally dressed Indian woman) with

male, masculine identifications (aggressor, businessperson, head of household, Villa).

It would be overly simplistic to assume that these women's worshiping of Villa involves direct imitation. As with many of the cross-dressing characters I discuss, there is a potential for critical reworking. Chencha's mostly female followers recognize and play on "the construction of official history by the ruling powers as a triumphantly masculine national epic history" (208). And they revise this epic in Chencha's celebration of Villa's birthday, fusing Catholic and "pagan" rituals, eating birthday cake, drinking soda pop, and offering each other the sign of the peace in addition to marching in place and singing the Mexican national anthem (211–13). They thus counter masculine violence in their celebration of Mexican nationality by adding peace and food to ritualized marching and anthem singing.

Behar also analyzes the relationship between Esperanza and Chencha: "Feeling that she, too, is not fully a woman in the socially conventional ways, Esperanza found in Chencha a powerful interlocutor with whom she could identify, and she found in Chencha's spritism sessions a safe place to act out her ambiguous gender identity" (293). Yet I think that the connection between the two manly women goes beyond this direct identification that Behar proposes. There are two possible interpretations: either Esperanza, while narrating her *historias*, displaces her own sexual subversions onto Chencha (the "safe place"), or Chencha's overt sexual mixture is meant to draw attention to Esperanza's less visible sexual mixture. *Translated Woman* produces both effects. This dual relationship is the result of Behar's literary manipulations. Behar's emphasis on Chencha's and Esperanza's mixed identities and suggestion that Esperanza identifies with Chencha reflect the process of forging a correlation between the two. Perhaps Behar intentionally projects Esperanza's duality onto Chencha to distance the threatening topics of hermaphroditism, transvestism, and bisexuality from her *comadre*. The author's self-reflexive concern over Esperanza's potential reaction to *Translated Woman* would explain any attempt to protect her heroine's identity in this way. As in *Silent Dancing*, the most radical challenges to sexual convention occur offstage, within the bodies of minor characters.

It is not coincidental that the greatest subversion inhabits the darkest bodies in these texts. While the Mexican-Indian Esperanza and the Cuban-American Behar are both racially mixed, Chencha is the only

morena in the text (199). The use of African-derived spiritist culture allows Behar to explore sex and gender mixture in a more literal manner
than Esperanza's *historias* allow. A problematic result of this mechanism,
though, is that every minority identification along the axes of race, sex,
and gender is contained within the body of Chencha and distanced from
the lighter skins in the text. These overlapping identifications invoke the
familiar tendency to associate sexual subversiveness with non-European
subjects, which I discussed earlier with regard to Chávez González. Behar's text repeats the marginalization of sexual "deviancy" by projecting
it onto her darkest character. According to this paradigm, Chencha's race
renders her a more suitable subject for sexual subversion than the lighter-
skinned women.

Behar's insertion of her own autobiography "in the shadow" of *Translated
Woman* also invites a comparison between author and subject (323). Behar,
too, is a mestiza character in this text. She is both gringa (as a middle-
class U.S. academic) and nongringa (as a Cuban-born native Spanish
speaker). As a Cuban-American in Mexico, her identity embodies literal border crossing, and her status as an anthropologist provides access
to multiple cultural contexts in her search for feminist empowerment.
Her most self-conscious crossings are national, and she addresses her literal border-crossing privileges very self-reflexively. While Esperanza's and
Chencha's movements are circumscribed by the limited spaces of San Luis
and Mexquitic, Behar and the text she narrates move back and forth between the United States and Mexico, carrying radios, passports, and multiple frames of reference as they go. More interesting are the unexplored
crossings within *Translated Woman*'s narrator/author. She herself possesses
an ambiguous gender identity as she expresses self-consciousness about
leaving her husband to take care of their child and their home while she is
away conducting interviews (231, 323). In "Writing in My Father's Name:
A Diary of *Translated Woman*'s First Year," Behar emphasizes her status as
head of household, paying her husband's bills, and purchasing their house
and car. And she describes this status as an assumption of male power:
"When I bought our house, I asked to have my name listed first on the title, just like a man." (73). As in her depictions of Esperanza and Chencha,
Behar's power is masculinized, yet she attributes this behavioral cross-
dressing to "feminist honor" (73) rather than sexual fluidity.

In the same essay, Behar quotes Deborah Gordon's analysis of *Translated
Woman* as an allegory of "the end of heterosexuality" (79). Does Gordon
mean that the abusive heterosexual relationships in Behar's work will bring

about an end to heterosexuality, or does Gordon merely mean to suggest that such abuse is the endpoint of heterosexuality? And what does Behar mean by quoting Gordon? Behar writes of the ways in which the bonds between women in her text revolve around men: "It seems odd to me now that my book appears to be about the encounter of two women, meeting and forming a relationship against all odds, against the barriers of race, class, and nationality, but what obsesses us is our relationships with the central men in our lives" (80). Behar adds, "especially our fathers," but Esperanza's abusive husband and Behar's dutiful one take up far more narrative space than either father. Husbands remain central to the female characters' relationships with each other, in triangulated tension, perhaps as an excuse for or a heterosexual legitimization of the bonds between women. Although Behar interprets Esperanza's assertion that she does not need any more men in her life as "a critique of compulsory heterosexuality," the author also insists that Esperanza's relationships with other women are too ambivalent to assume that she feels "totally nurtured by the female bosom, either" (*Translated* 295). Lesbian sexuality is thus pushed to the margins as irrelevant or out of the question, as it was with Chencha.

Behar embodies fluidity in terms of nation, race, sex, and language, but her mixed identity is the most concealed one in the text. Confronting these mixtures, particularly in the person of Chencha, seems to make Behar anxious. She says that she feels "uncomfortable" about Chencha's gender ambiguity and that "she frightened me more than anyone I had ever met" (*Translated* 216). When Behar tries to interview Chencha, the anthropologist is too intimidated to ask questions, and she flees as soon as Chencha releases her from the—significantly—locked room in which the interview was taking place (207). As a result of Behar's inability to uncover information about Chencha, she represents an impenetrable mystery, an unexplored body onto which both Esperanza's and Behar's greatest subversions are projected and a locked room in which fluid sexualities remain hidden.

Michelle Cliff's Revolutionary Identities in *No Telephone to Heaven*

Michelle Cliff's novel *No Telephone to Heaven* (1987) explores the ambiguities of mixed-race Jamaican identity. As in her other work, including *Abeng* (1984) and the essays and poems discussed in chapter 2, Cliff uses racial duality to highlight the complexities of identity, to combat narrow conventions, and to defeat tragic narratives. *No Telephone* forms a sequel to *Abeng*, as Cliff imagines her protagonist, Clare, in adulthood. The racial ambiguities from Clare's childhood remain, and they are compounded by additional sexual ambiguities. Cliff's adult characters are revolutionaries, in both the literal and the figurative sense. Their multiplicity revolutionizes identification, yet their revolutionary commitments force them to choose singular allegiance. Racial and sexual identity are disjointed in *No Telephone* more radically than in any of the texts discussed earlier.

As in *Silent Dancing* and *Translated Woman*, the greatest sexual subversion in *No Telephone* is distanced from the main character. Harry/Harriet, "boy-girl," is Clare's close friend (*No Telephone* 21). The first time we see Harry/Harriet is at a pool party, wearing a "bikini-bra stretched across his hairy, delicately mounded chest, panties cradling his cock and balls" (21). This description, which focuses explicitly on the dissonance between male anatomy and women's garments, is itself mixed. It modifies the bluntly graphic "cock and balls" with effeminate qualities, such as "delicate" and "cradling." This sexualized description is quite unlike the modest bathing scenes in *Silent Dancing*. Moreover, while Ortiz Cofer's dual hero/heroine crosses over completely to one gender at a time, Harry/Harriet's bisexed identity is gendered in two ways at once. Later we see Harry/Harriet at a bar, wearing a "proper" dinner jacket, "for Clare's sake," but with spangled eyelids to retain a subtle signifier of his/her mixed identity (121). From the back, s/he looks like a man, but from the front s/he looks like a woman (125). Harry/Harriet plays on the performativity of his/her identity and lies to a tourist, claiming to be Prince Badnigga of Benin, out with his wife, Princess Cunnilinga (Clare) (125). In this charade, s/he attributes the visibly bigendered elements of his/her attire to a racial and national identity: s/he tells the tourist that according to ancient custom, young warriors in Benin must paint the colors of the national flag on their eyelids to enable people to distinguish between Africans of different nationalities (125). *No Telephone* contains several such denials of the sexual content of Harry/Harriet's duality, and Cliff denaturalizes him/her by describing him/her as "one that nature did not claim" (21). In this way, his/her duality is initially outside the realm of nature.

Instead, Cliff attributes his/her gender subversion to experience. She suggests that Harry/Harriet was not born bi-, but by age twelve, s/he was a "battyman [homosexual]-in-training" (123). The status "in training" implies that his/her sexuality is a product of effort, learning, or choice. Ironically, however, Harry/Harriet is the product of rape rather than choice. Echoing scenarios of the tragic mulatta, Harry/Harriet was conceived when his black mother was violated by the white man for whom she worked as a maid. The employer dismissed the black mother but kept the child. As a result of his position as a mixed-race, illegitimate child in the white family, the boy Harry soon recognized that "I was an odd quantity. . . . outside" (124). At this point, his oddness and outsiderhood are associated with his racial and familial status. His marginalization takes on a sexual quality only when he is raped as a boy by a white officer (128). Although Harry/Harriet claims that the rape did not make him/her what s/he is, that s/he was born "not just sun, but sun and moon," Cliff inserts a parenthetical qualification, questioning, "(Was he not romancing . . . could someone be born that way . . . wasn't damage intrinsic . . . what do you know about it, eh? what in hell do you know about it?)" (128). At the same time that Harry/Harriet "romances" sexuality as something with which one is born, Cliff undermines her character's interpretation by leaving unanswered the question "What in hell do you know about it?" Origins and essences remain questionable (and in question) in this narrative of racial and sexual violation.

Cliff adopts the literary convention of the disempowered black woman's violation by her white master, which I discuss in chapter 1, but rewrites the scenario by having the product of that violation be a sexually ambiguous man rather than the conventionally beautiful tragic heroine. She invokes the tradition and the sense of violation that accompanies it but chooses to represent differently the product of the rape.[44] Cliff's descriptions of Harry/Harriet convey sexual excess and performativity. Unlike Iola Leroy, Clotel, or other tragic mulattas, Harry/Harriet celebrates his/her sexuality. Cliff uses this public display of sexuality to reveal or to magnify the sexual component of racial asymmetry and racial mixture. Harry/Harriet embodies both sides of the racial and sexual border crossing that produced him/her: male and female, black and white. S/he symbolizes a breach in racial and sexual identity, a lack of singular integrity within both. As the breach of racial boundaries is often sexualized, Harry/Harriet's simultaneous challenges to the purity of racial and sexual identity serve as a reminder of the sexualization of race. Since the nineteenth century, racist fears have been coded in terms of sexuality, projecting threatening sexualities onto darker-skinned peoples to feign the innocence of whites. Miscegenation was targeted as the source of racial perversion, and white Americans' obsession with race centered on sexuality. Harry/Harriet recalls this history, presents a visible challenge to dominant conceptions of identity, and reminds the public of the mixed-up racial and sexual dynamics that are his/her origins.

Significantly, while the white and the male traditionally overpower the black and the female, Cliff's character ultimately chooses to identify with the black and the female. Harry/Harriet eventually ends his/her dual identification, claiming that everyone must make "the choice," "cast our lot": "Cyaan [can't] live split. Not in this world" (131). In the end, s/he tells Clare that "Harriet live and Harry be no more" (168). Although s/he cannot afford a sex-change operation, she chooses to live as a woman, abandoning her male identification, saying that "castration ain't de main t'ing" (168).[45] In this claim, sexual identity is divorced from genitals or anatomical sex. Harriet's sexual identity is a political choice rather than a bodily fact. Harry/Harriet becomes Harriet in her public identifications, confining her costume to feminine garments, but readers know that she retains a male body. "None of her people downtown let on if they knew a male organ swung gently under her bleached and starched skirt. Or that white powder on her brown face hid a five o'clock shadow" (171). Her male anatomical sex is a secret that is open to readers, but this description renders Harriet's chosen identity an emphatic display. The concealment of her sex is doubly racialized—white powder and bleached skirts—highlighting the racial and sexual masking that opposes the identity Harriet chooses against the body with which Harry was born. As Nada Elia asserts in her recent study of Harry/Harriet, "the most significant aspect of *No Telephone to Heaven* is that Harry/Harriet never undergoes a physical transformation, remaining ever dual in body, as indeed is the fate of all Creoles, diasporans and biracials for whom transformation is impossible" (353). In this way, Harry/Harriet provides a model for attaching singular identity politics to internally heterogeneous identities. Despite the racial and sexual dissonance between skin and skirt, Harriet suggests that coherent revolutionary politics and personal safety demand the performance of singular identity. (One imagines that if her dissonant body were discovered, Harriet might meet with violence like that of Annie Christmas in Cliff's *Free Enterprise*.)

Cliff writes that Harry/Harriet is tolerated and accepted in the social circles of privileged Jamaicans insofar as the other characters "measur[e] their normalness against his strangeness" (21). S/he reminds them of "their wholeness," and they feel comfort in the belief that s/he is "*only* one, after all" (21). As these characters attempt to distance themselves from the ambiguously sexed Harry/Harriet, however, more similarities than differences appear. S/he is not, after all, the only one. The transgendered Harry/Harriet embraces his/her mixed identity, displays it, expresses it

as a sexual choice, while the mixture embedded within the rest of Jamaica is less overt. As Clare's "naked, green" eyes stare into Harry/Harriet's
"deep brown" ones, Clare determines that her friend is "no stranger" than
she is, "for we are neither one thing nor the other" (131). Clare finds
in Harry/Harriet's sexual betweenness a reflection of her own racial betweenness.

Harry/Harriet's public transvestitism magnifies Clare's less campy racial
and sexual mixture. Cliff invokes Clare's multiple racial, political, and national lineages, writing, "There are many bits and pieces to her, for she
is composed of fragments" (87). Each of her affiliations is incomplete:
she is not totally white or black, Jamaican or American. Clare's mother
and sister are dark skinned, but she and her father are light enough to
pass for white. This difference ultimately divides the family, racially and
nationally, as Kitty and Jennie return to Jamaica and Clare and her father build a life (with frequent passing) in New York City. Cliff provides
many metaphors for Clare's duality and her alienation from Jamaica. In
New York, Clare is an "albino gorilla," who, in the loss of her mother, her
tribe, and her jungle home, has watched her skin become covered in moss
(91). Time has effaced her race and her nation. Her racial identity is in
dispute from the moment that her father attempts to enroll her in high
school as "white . . . of course" (98). Clare's lack of single racial affiliation
leads to exclusion, as the high school principal tells them, "we have no
room for lies in our system. No place for in-betweens" (99). She is "white
chocolate"—white in color but chocolate nonetheless, both white and
black (91, 99). She identifies with both Jane Eyre and Bertha, the white
literary heroine and the crazy nonwhite woman in the attic (116). While
in England studying the classics, Clare is Jane, but her Caribbean Bertha
self remains in the shadows.

This racial and national ambiguity is met with a more subtle sexual
uncertainty. Clare's heroine is Joan of Arc, whom she describes as "the
manly girl," and in childhood games Clare took up a machete and pretended to be (white) boys or men: Pip, Peter Pan, Columbus (156, 173).
Clare's female sexuality is ultimately challenged when a genital infection
renders her sterile. She compares herself to a mule, a hybrid for which genetic manipulation leads to sterility. Significantly, her reproductive status
leads Clare to contemplate her racial mixture, concluding that the genetic "lightening up" that produced her skin, eyes, and nose would be "for
naught," since she, like the mule, cannot reproduce her careful breeding
(169).[46]

Clare's sexual orientation is also ambiguous. When Harry/Harriet asks if she has even been tempted by "pussy . . . loving your own kind," Clare avoids the question. With Harry/Harriet's coaxing, she finally concludes, "no, I don't think I have been tempted. Unless you count my own— pussy, that is, not kind" (122). The double meaning in this "my own" (which Clare quickly qualifies) suggests that before the dash she has been tempted by both her own "pussy" (autoeroticism) and her own "kind" (les-bianism). Even after she takes back the same-sex implication, the fact of her desire for pussy remains spoken. Although we see Clare involved with only male lovers, these partners' maleness is in question. With Harry/Har-riet, she spends an afternoon at a secluded beach where they can "swim as girlfriends." They have a heterosexual but homogender encounter of "touching gently, kissing, tongues entwined, coming to, laughing" (130). In Europe, Clare has an affair with Bobby, who has a war wound on his foot that Cliff describes in vaginal terms: "the place where brown skin split and yellowness dripped from a bright pink gap" (143). Indeed, Clare says that she feels for Bobby only because he is "wounded" (154). Both Bobby and Harry/Harriet are both more wounded, more clearly violated or penetrated, than Clare.

When Harry/Harriet tells Clare that their betweenness is only tempo-rary and that people cannot live "split" in this world, Clare does make a racial, national, political choice. While listening to her friend speak, Clare "thought she could feel the tint of her skin deepening, melanin rising to the occasion" (131). The insistence that she must make a choice and iden-tify with one group makes Clare blacker, and indeed she proceeds to get a sunburn, darkening her "mango-hued, indecisive" skin (132–33). With this racial definition comes a new dedication to the people of her country, which ultimately leads Clare to return to Jamaica, to join a band of revo-lutionaries, to turn over her inheritance (her grandmother's property) to the revolutionary cause, and to sacrifice her life in the end. The revolu-tionaries initially mistrust her because of her mixed identity, grilling her on her commitment to Jamaica and to people of color (189–96). When they ask her if she thinks she is morally superior to darker-skinned people, she replies by telling the dark-skinned interviewer, "You are the color of my grandmother" (190). In this statement, Clare emphasizes the dark skin that is incorporated into her own lineage. Clare's political commitments overcome her corporeal uncertainty and render her pale skin insignifi-cant: through her revolutionary choice, she proves herself to be a black Jamaican.

Despite these resolutions and decisions, Clare's sexuality remains unclear. Her racial uncertainty is easier for her to settle. Her racial choice is entwined with her political and national dedication, but her sexuality remains noncentral, tangential to the novel's overt racial, national, and political concerns. She never clearly declares a sexual orientation. In fact, Clare's racial commitment and her return to Jamaica occur simultaneously with the genital infection that renders her infertile, which suggests that her political commitments occupy the void left by the loss of genital activity and reproductive sexuality. At this transitional moment, while in the hospital, Clare stares at a black moth on the ceiling of her room. She imagines "touching her, the grain of her pattern black on black" (170). The desire to touch the moth can be read as homoerotic, since the moth is described as "her," but Clare does not touch the moth or realize this potentially homoerotic desire. She wonders "what would make her stir" (170). Clare's contemplation of the moth prefigures her own destiny. She identifies with the moth, which hides on the ceiling rather than "swoop[ing], wildly" and knocking the doctor's glasses "askew" (170). Clare, too, has never directly challenged patriarchal or colonial authority up to this point in the novel. What eventually makes Clare "stir" is her decision to do precisely that, to upset the dominant order through revolutionary activity. She adopts the moth's "black on black" pattern (the solid racial identity), she takes the plunge to knock down authority, and she never again speaks of sexual desire. The relationship between sex and identity in *No Telephone* thus differs from that in Lorde, Anzaldúa, Moraga, and others, for whom sexuality plays a central role in political, racial, and national identity. Cliff emphasizes the sacrifices involved in revolution by replacing sex with race and nation and eclipsing sexual activity with the taking up of arms against white neocolonialism.

In her ultimate sexual uncertainty, Clare is unique. In the other three texts examined in this section, the main characters develop singular sexual orientations or identifications by the conclusion. In *Silent Dancing*, Marina/o's sexual identity is ultimately clarified when we see the older man, Marino, with his granddaughter (153). Even Lorde's "house of difference" corresponds to an author who elsewhere identifies as a black lesbian, and Anzaldúa's *lesberada* corresponds to a self-described Chicana lesbian. Sexual fluidity often functions as a temporary, private exploration rather than a political declaration. Like Harry/Harriet, these writers seem to suggest that ultimately, "cyaan live split." While identities defy categorization throughout all of the texts I analyze here, there is an attempt to resolve ambiguity on some level—race, sex, or nation—as part of the texts' closure. The singular identifications these writers adopt, however, are self-conscious and chosen rather than essential or passive. They are deployed for political effect, overtly self-constructed to clarify their resistance to racism, sexism, and homophobia. The key is to keep these identities open to difference and redefinition, redeployable, provisional.

Ultimate fluidity in border crossing may seem to present the ideal foundation for inclusive feminist and mestiza politics, but the sexy appeal of these crossings—the thrill as well as the political import of outlaw transgressions—signals the taboo and danger that haunts the borders being crossed. Racial and sexual borders, after all, demarcate inequalities of power. Moraga reminds us in "Ni for El Salvador" that "the dissolution of self, the dissolution of borders / . . . is not safe" (*Last Generation* 41). The image of the body/nation in jeopardy shows where theoretical ideal conflicts with physical reality. Since the racial and sexual boundary crossing that historically produced mixture was rape, one must be wary about celebrating the erotics of such fluidity. *Mestizaje* itself encompasses this dynamism, the process of incorporating and prioritizing the multiplicity of categories with which one's identity intersects, evaluating the historical lessons and the political potential of each possibility to determine, as Anzaldúa put it, "which identity takes center stage" ("Coming" 12).

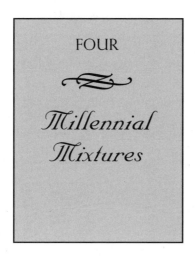

FOUR

Millennial Mixtures

African-American feminist science fiction writer Octavia Butler explores the limits of fluid identities. In *Wild Seed* (1980), her African heroine Anyanwu is a "shape-shifter": she can change the shape, color, or species of her body at will. We see her as an old woman, a young woman, a black man, a white man, a dolphin, a dog, and an eagle. She transforms her malleable identity to escape from dangerous situations: "I took animal shapes to frighten my people when they wanted to kill me. . . . I became a leopard and spat at them. . . . I became a sacred python, and no one dared harm me" (15). The most important effect of Anyanwu's malleability is her ability to defy master-slave relations. In Africa, she was enslaved twice "and had escaped only by changing her identity completely" (9). For this reason, Butler calls her a "survivor," a "fortunate little hybrid" (14). Anyanwu's ability to escape limiting identity categories—including *slave*, *black*, and even *human*—makes her the ultimate survivor.

What interests me most in this book is Butler's fusion of science fiction, usually associated with futuristic cyborgs and space travel, and American slave narrative. As an African, but appearing to be a man so that her extraordinary strength does not elicit suspicion, Anyanwu joins the immortal Doro in his negotiations with slavers on the African coast. Carrying a cargo of new slaves, they travel to America, with the horrors of the Middle Passage somewhat mitigated by Anyanwu's healing and shape-shifting powers. In the last section of the novel, Butler inserts Anyanwu into nineteenth-century Louisiana, where she lives as a white man, married to a white woman, pretending that her black children are her slaves (210–15). By linking familiar scenarios from African-American fiction, including the master's impregnation of female slaves, passing, and escape attempts, with science fiction, Butler highlights similarities between the nineteenth century and the end of the millennium.[1] Both periods share a fascination with mixture and the blurring of racial differences, and both periods have produced female characters in popular literature—such as Clotel and Anyanwu—whose heroism lies in subverting racial and sexual singularity and in passing between freedom and servitude. Yet that which was melodrama for William Wells Brown has shifted to science fiction. Is the accepted truth of race dynamics in the nineteenth century too fantastic to be captured by contemporary realism? Why is Anyanwu's fluidity assigned to the genre of fantasy and futurism? Amanda Boulter suggests that Butler's "narrative invocations of African American history present a potentially homeopathic reworking that imbibes the violent structures of the past to create something new [by] reinterpreting them within a future context" (181). What does the future (or the vision of the future available in the present) have to add to 150 years of literary investigations to make works such as Butler's more "homeopathic" than *Clotel* or *Iola Leroy?* Or is Butler responding to current American anxieties by projecting the white-black-man-woman-animal away from the American present?

That present, the turn of the millennium, is witness to a mass-media-driven drama about shifts in American racial definition. In truth, today's racial shifts are no greater than the shifts of the 1960s—or of the 1860s, for that matter. But the end of the millennium creates a sense that America as we know it, or as we thought we knew it, has come to an end. At this millennial moment, we look forward and back to see how far we have come and to speculate about where we are going. Recent popular writings imply that with the changing of the millennium, America is being forced to adapt to new racial frontiers in which our familiar racial definitions are being undermined, support for civil rights is fragmenting, affirmative action quotas are changing the business world, genes are being manipulated, and technology is uncovering old racial secrets. The faces of the future, computer-generated hybrids, Tiger Woods, and the "new" Thomas Jefferson descendants people the pages of *Time* and *Newsweek.*

This chapter will focus on two aspects of this millennial drama, the role that mixture plays and the telescoping of history. Anxiety about the breakdown of racial categories has led to an increased interest in mixture. The rhetoric surrounding this new obsession often recalls that of an earlier American race drama, the anxiety surrounding racial definition that came with the abolition of slavery. Today, as in the nineteenth century, Americans are unsure about how race will matter in the future distribution of power. People of mixed race are targeted—studied, celebrated, or maligned—for challenging the terms of the debate. The media are feeding a fascination with mixture, and near-white women of color have taken center stage in fashion magazines, films, and popular literature. This chapter will analyze American culture's current obsession with this "new face," the multiracial movement, and light-skinned supermodels and show how this trend recalls the "muleologies," amalgamationists, and tragic mulattas of the nineteenth century. Both in the nineteenth century and in the 1990s, a rhetoric of confusion, tragedy, groundlessness, and futurism inflects popular representations of mixture. In both periods, fear and celebration work in tandem: the fascination with mixture corresponds to (and potentially masks) racist efforts to contain fluidity and to reinstitute categories. I study four prominent literary texts from the end of the millennium—Danzy Senna's *Caucasia* (1998), Shirlee Taylor Haizlip's *The Sweeter the Juice* (1994), Cristina García's *The Agüero Sisters* (1997), and Alice Walker's *By the Light of My Father's Smile* (1998)—that invoke the same conflicted and sensationalist responses to mixture that appear in contemporary popular culture. I then juxtapose these images with representations from a century ago, revealing just how much this millennial anxiety, like Butler's science fiction, is taking America straight into the past.

The Intrigue of White Women of Color: *Caucasia* and *The Sweeter the Juice*

Readers of such popular fiction as Senna's best-seller, *Caucasia*, and Haizlip's memoir, *The Sweeter the Juice*, are drawn to the mystique of mixture and passing. As in Jessie Redmon Fauset's *Plum Bun* or Nella Larsen's *Passing*, both late-twentieth-century texts explore the complexities of living with skin that could seem either black or white. In *Caucasia*, Senna attributes shape-shifting powers and insights much like Anyanwu's to her young heroine, Birdie Lee, the daughter of a black father and a white mother. When the white-looking Birdie is sent to Nkrumah, a Black Power elementary school in Boston, she perfects "the art of changing," a skill she had enjoyed from childhood games of make-believe and dress up. Following in the nineteenth- and twentieth-century traditions of mixed-race literature, passing and disguise are central to Birdie's mobility and the formation of her identity. To fit in at Nkrumah, Birdie has "to become someone else, . . . to erase the person [she] was before" (62). She learns at an early age that racial identity is fluid, can be voided and resignified based on the performance of certain racially specific cues. In another reversal of tragic mulatta convention, Birdie is alienated from her peers at Nkrumah because of her whiteness, so she passes to enjoy the benefits of black society. She braids her hair to mask its fine texture and practices "how to say 'nigger' the way the kids in school did it, dropping the 'er' so that it became not a slur, but a term of endearment" (63). She becomes "conscious of [her] body as a toy, and of the ways [she] could use it to disappear into the world around [her]" (65). Because of her racially mixed appearance, Birdie is able—indeed, forced—to play with her body to adapt to her surroundings. She is led by necessity into an early awareness of performativity.

When Birdie's mother is accused of storing illegal weapons, mother and daughter flee Boston and go into hiding. As she and her mother assume false identities, Birdie must pass as white, like a chameleon, to camouflage her subversively raced body alongside her white mother. The mixed self of her childhood has become criminal in that it would draw attention to her mother's past involvement with the revolution. She erases her Nkrumah performance of blackness to blend into New Hampshire whiteness. Racialized femininity is elaborately constructed in two parallel scenes in the novel. In Boston, Birdie's friend, Maria, helps Birdie simulate the appearance of black girlhood by cutting and restyling her "not black" hair. Maria "heated up the curling iron and sprayed my newly shorn hair with Queen Helene hairspray. . . . When she was finished, my straight hair was curly" (69). Later, in New Hampshire, Birdie's new model, Mona, teaches Birdie the art of white girlhood so that she will fit in there: "I was playing catch-up with Mona, learning how to be a girl . . . how to apply lipstick properly, how to stick in a tampon, how to stuff your bra" (227). Birdie's identity fluctuates yet again as she returns to Boston in search of her father's black family. She is keenly aware of her appearance as white and as performed: "I went and looked at myself in the mirror. I looked country. A girl Nicholas might like, but not Ali. Ali might be embarrassed to be seen with me. . . . I had only a few minutes to prepare. I brushed my hair and pulled it into a tight ponytail so that it masked the New Hampshire feathers. I changed into some of Dot's jeans and a long blue cardigan" (325). Years on the run with her mother teach Birdie how to effect these quick changes, to deal with the need to become someone else within seconds. These defensive shifts void any sense of a core identity. Instead, Birdie views the self as a state of possibility—a "blank slate," she calls it when choosing which ethnicity to assume (130).

As in the works of Michelle Cliff and others, this racial fluidity carries over to the realm of sexuality, too. In the "novel" that Birdie writes as a child, "it wasn't clear to [her] which one of [her characters] [she] was supposed to be identifying with—the burly, macho Richie, who lay on top, or his soft, ultrafeminine girlfriend with the pink lipstick and matching toenails, who lay on the bottom" (172). She finds herself identifying with both. Her sexual attachments follow a bisexual pattern into adolescence. Birdie's first love is Alexis, a girl Birdie meets while she and her mother are hiding out at a women's commune in Aurora. Later, when Birdie has an encounter with a boy in New Hampshire, Nicholas merges with Alexis, as Senna overlays two different sexual experiences and the narrative alternates between Aurora and New Hampshire, girl lover and boy lover. Birdie thinks about Alexis as she kisses Nicholas and measures the feel of his body against Alexis's (202–4): "With Alexis I had always been the one on top, the one doing the groping and the grinding, the one doing what Nicholas was doing. I wasn't sure how to act now that I was on the bottom" (203). Like Anyanwu, Birdie's shape-shifting involves learning to act from different identities, not just black and white but also male and female, dominant and submissive.

It is not just the racially mixed identities that fluctuate in *Caucasia*. On the run, Birdie begins to realize that identity in general is a matter of invention: "The people we encountered seemed—like us—to be in a perpetual state of reinvention. We all were fictive imaginings of our former selves, a fact that somehow neutralized the lies, made it all a game of make-believe. In those years, I felt myself to be incomplete—a gray blur, a body in motion, forever galloping toward completion—half a girl, half caste, half-mast, and half-baked, not quite ready for consumption. And for me, there was comfort in that state of incompletion, a sense that as long as we kept moving, we could go back to what we had left behind" (136–37). Although Birdie might have thought she was uniquely fragmented because of her mixed identity and enforced separation from her African-American heritage, she comes to feel security in perpetual incompletion. This halfness keeps identity fluid, in motion, "not quite ready for consumption," suggesting that stagnation and annihilation of self might occur with any illusion of wholeness or finality. Identity is thus a process, a (de)constructive deferral of identity, an escape from endings, a fiction perpetually in progress. Birdie's academic father echoes this logic in his antiessentialist theory of race. Deck Lee comforts Birdie when she expresses feelings of guilt about passing for white in New Hampshire: "There's no such thing as passing. We're all just pretending. Race is a complete illusion, make-believe. It's a costume. We all wear one. You just switched yours at some point. That's just the absurdity of the whole race game" (391). There is "no such thing" as passing because there is no true or ultimate race from which to deviate or toward which to strive.

As a child, Birdie regarded herself as monstrous: "I had a thick blue vein like a subway line etched in my forehead, which stuck out when I turned upside down. At Aurora, Alexis had told me once that it made me look like Frankenstein. I had liked that image of myself as a monster, an unfinished creation turned against its maker, and had terrorized a shrieking, giggling Alexis, walking toward her with my arms out in front of me, my legs stiff as wooden planks" (297). In playing Frankenstein, Birdie makes a game of identity and gleefully appropriates the concept of artificial and incomplete selfhood.[2] She realizes the power that "unfinished creations" enjoy, the ability to escape and to pass. At the same time, Birdie's fluidity is compelled by dehumanizing racism, which keeps her running, and deconstructed identity, which forces her to build and rebuild her race on a perpetually blank slate. Like Frankenstein's monster, she is alienated by her difference and denied any illusion of essential selfhood. It is never clear if she is the victim of science or philosophy gone awry or a victor in her struggle for identity among competing cultural paradigms.[3] Indeed, until her brief final reunion with her sister, Birdie's narrative is dominated by forced departures and transformations in reaction to color prejudice. Her life is ultimately built on fragments of identity, racism, and the gulf between herself and the black and white communities between which she travels. Is it empowering to be monstrous? Readers who celebrate her fluidity are aware of the tragedies that underlie it.

An important part of the marketing of *Caucasia* is the appearance of the light-skinned Senna, whose photo accompanies some reviews of the best-seller.[4] A promotional article by Senna in *Glamour* magazine, "A Black Spy in White America," begins with a picture of Senna and the words, "Though I'm black, my straight hair and pale complexion conceal my identity—and make me privy to comments I'd never otherwise hear" (102). In a contemporary revision of James Weldon Johnson's central mechanism in *The Autobiography of an Ex-Coloured Man*, the article emphasizes the ways in which Senna's racial invisibility makes her a spy in the "white world." She writes, "Once, at a dinner party where the guests began telling racist jokes, I announced that I was black and said I was doing an anthropological study on what white people say when they think they're alone" (102). She appeals to the current sensationalism and intrigue surrounding ambiguous identities, implying that one never knows when such a spy is in one's midst.

Shirlee Taylor Haizlip's memoir, *The Sweeter the Juice,* creates the same sense of racial intrigue, complete with a family tree that uncovers the secrets of passing and a section of photographs that allows readers to gaze at the spectacle of white-looking African-Americans. Both the family tree and the visual display of ambiguous identities have become central to mixed-race literary convention, allowing readers to participate voyeuristically in the (mis)interpretation of race and the uncovering of secret genealogies. Haizlip begins by analyzing faces in a crowd to discover people who might be passing. She draws the reader in with a conspiratorial second person, "I am a black woman, but many of you would never know it. . . . My skin is as light as that of the average white person" (13). In reading *The Sweeter the Juice,* one gets the sense of solving mysteries, becoming privy to secrets, and undermining an established system of race trickery. In a 1995 article entitled "Passing," Haizlip writes that during her book tour, "hundreds of people volunteered stories about gaps in their identity" (49). She tells of a "flood of letters and phone calls" from people who began to question their own whiteness after reading *The Sweeter the Juice* (48–49). The book creates a stir that unmoors racial classification from its origins and opens up gaps in American identity.

Like *Caucasia, The Sweeter the Juice* contains moments in which fluidity is tempered by alienation and grief. In yet another inversion of the tragic mulatta scenario, the whiteness in Haizlip's memoir is the source of tragedy. Her mother is abandoned in childhood by her father and siblings, who pass for white, leaving young Margaret to grow up orphaned in African-American society. As a mother, Margaret still experiences deep melancholy over having grown up without family. Haizlip "began to absorb [her mother's] sadness" and to realize that "big chunks of my life were missing" (31–32). The whiteness of her relatives marks a void in her black life, "devoid of faces and feelings, places of whiteness, places of pain" (77). And Haizlip renders the whiteness of her relatives as pathetic. When she finally discovers her mother's sister, she is surprised to find that the elderly "white woman" is very poor and lives in a trailer park in Anaheim, "the world of make-believe" (242–46). The successful Haizlip, who arrives in a limousine, barely masks her initial distaste for the "teal indoor-outdoor carpeting" outside her aunt's trailer and the white powder with which "she covered her entire face" (243–44, 249). This experience reinforces Haizlip's claim that "there are no 'real white Americans'" (15). Whiteness here is powder, an unfulfilled promise of success for those who pass, a sad ruse, something of which to be ashamed. In contrast, the dark-skinned Taylor family members emerge as heroes, educated, proud, valuing blackness.

Haizlip ascribes dramatic power to catching people who are passing: "Our experience suggests that America is not what it presents itself to be" (15). She also ascribes a sense of "newness" and an aura of the avant-garde to her mixed identity, suggesting that "I am the new American" (15). In so doing, Haizlip invokes the popular rhetoric about the new face of America, which is supposedly invading our present and threatening white Americans' secure possession of "true" Americanness. Her conclusion that racial definition is a ruse also reflects apocalyptic *Time* and *Newsweek* writings that declare the end of our familiar sense of race: "What is white? What is black? What is race?" (34). Such rhetoric often comes from conservative, sometimes racist, white writers bemoaning the browning of America and the disintegration of the racial differentiation on which their privilege rests, yet Haizlip pairs this rhetoric with a commitment to the black community and to civil rights. Both white supremacists and black advocates often perceive mixture as a threat to their integrity. Haizlip's ultimate conclusion is ambivalent, both in phrasing and in content: "All in all, I have grown a great deal less certain about the vagaries of race and know that I am ambivalent about its implications. But I am comfortable with that ambivalence, for it keeps my doors and windows open" (267).

Unlike the heroic endings of Frances Harper or William and Ellen Craft, tragedy results from mixture as much as fluidity does in Senna's and Haizlip's narratives. Does American society today still shun those who challenge its instituted racial demarcations? If so, how do we explain the celebrations of mixture in the texts discussed in previous chapters— Ntozake Shange's *Liliane*, Judith Ortiz Cofer's *Silent Dancing*, and Gloria Anzaldúa's *Borderlands/La Frontera*? Perhaps the optimism of Shange, Ortiz Cofer, and Anzaldúa is enabled by their affinity with the postmodern, postcolonial, transnational, and mestiza theories that currently enjoy academic vogue. And Senna and Haizlip, whose rhetoric lines up with more popular publications such as *Time* and *Newsweek*, reflect the American public's current ambivalence about mixture. Idealistic theories often do not translate into material practice. Just as the crisis of American self-definition in the nineteenth century produced a wave of racist litigation, propaganda, and literature debating the impact of mixture, Americans at the end of the millennium experienced similar anxieties about ethnic self-definition. Just as many nineteenth-century Americans obsessively studied mixed-race physiology, late-twentieth-century popular media inundated Americans with debates about Tiger Woods, the Hemings family, and the new face of America. And just as nineteenth-century writings on mixture were split between racist fear and enthusiasm for a new amalgamated America, the contemporary fascination with mulattoes, mestizos, and Creoles reflects both optimism and anxiety. Popular mixed-race confessions, supermodels, and sports heroes make public the interrelationship between racist panic and multiracial fervor, and the role of popular culture in redefining American ethnicity for the twenty-first century is perhaps more crucial than that of literature, theory, or academic debate.

Foreseeing the Past: Popular Culture and Hybridity Fashion

Note the similarity between the following two articles. The first argues that the current increased "acceptance of interracial marriage" indicates that "black-white antagonism seems increasingly out of date" and "tolerance has never been higher." These trends, coupled with "accelerating immigration" from increasingly "disparate" nations, lead the author to conclude, "All of this portends an era of increasing multiethnic and multiracial confusion. . . . The idea of race itself is now coming under attack." The second article asserts that "the most impressive sight to be seen in America is the stream of immigrants" coming from around the world: "No waterfall or mountain holds such awesome mystery; no river or harbor, embracing the navies of the world, expresses such power." This power will force America to accept that "fusion is a law of progress" and that "racial amalgamation is the heroic problem of the present, with all it implies in purification and revision of old social, religious, and political ideals, with all it demands in new sympathy outside of blood and race, and in a willingness to forego old-time privileges." In this transformed, assimilated nation, "it is the keeping up of difference" that destroys.

Both articles suggest that America's changing demographics are leading to interracial fusion and the dissolution of old group divisions. Both promise harmony based on acceptance at the same time that they warn of the awesome power of these shifts to transform race as we know it. The qualities being undermined here are race and difference itself, suggesting that harmony can only be based on amalgamation and assimilation. Words such as *portends* and *attack* in the former carry a similar dramatic weight to the *awesome mystery, naval power,* and *heroic problems* of the latter. The first article was by Tom Morganthau and appeared in *Newsweek* in 1995; the second article was written by Percy Stickney Grant and appeared in *North American Review* in 1912. And while one might expect the earlier article to exhibit more alarm over these shifts in demographics, Grant describes as "impressive" that which Morganthau regards more negatively as "confusion." The contemporary essay not only echoes but magnifies the anxious rhetoric of the past.

An even more apocalyptic article is *Time* magazine's 1990 "Beyond the Melting Pot," in which William A. Henry III warns that "the 'browning of America' will alter everything in society, from politics and education to industry, values, and culture" (28). Henry announces that "someday soon . . . white Americans will become a minority group" and "a traditional America . . . will be only the vestiges of an earlier nation."[5] Henry locates this "harder to govern" multiracial society in the "faces of the future," the upcoming generations who "are coming to realize, the new world is here. It is now. And it is irreversibly the America to come" (29, 31). The collision of future with present in this depiction elides America's multiracial history and wrongly points the finger at the new generation as the source of an impending racial showdown.[6]

Similarly, a 1996 *New York Times Magazine* article by Stanley Crouch features photographs of the faces of twenty mixed-race children, captioned, "What will we look like?" He describes the pictures as "previews" of the new "sweep of body types, hair textures, eye colors and skin tones" that Americans can expect in "the future" (171). "Americans of the future will find themselves surrounded in every direction by people who are part Asian, part Latin, part African, part European, part American Indian. What such people will look like is beyond my imagination" (170). Given the proliferation of the new faces of American racial mixture, one wonders why such an image is beyond Crouch's imagination. Crouch's vision of the future is one where there is no search "for something ethnically 'authentic,'" where racial imbalance will "melt away" with "superficial distinctions" as Americans join and assimilate on a common quest for "upward mobility" (171). Again, mixture eases racial difference and erases ethnic authenticity (along with race-based identity politics, one can assume) as all are assimilated into one "upwardly mobile" group of capitalists, "getting as many international customers for their wares as they can" (171). Such a development would do away with racial identification, affirmative action, ethnic pride, and the foundations of progressive racial politics today at the same time that it overcomes racial segregation.

As Patricia Williams warns in a 1997 article in *The Nation*, in response to the growing popularity of interracialism, "I wonder at the sudden and voluble optimism of analysts who opine that intermarriage is *the* political solution to our racial worries. . . . Isn't it a touch premature to hail it as our path to salvation—particularly as we do away with affirmative action and other measures that increased integration in the schools and workplaces?" (9). She worries that celebrating mixture is another way to submerge blackness and that "we will end up only with something like what plagues parts of Latin America: whole skyscrapers of racial differentiation, with 'white' still living in the penthouse, the 'one drops' just below and those with buckets of black blood in the basement or out on the street. . . . Let us hope we are not revisiting the days of quadroons and octoroons and tragic mulattas in the guise of claiming our various parts" (9). Although cloaked in liberal-sounding rhetoric, contemporary celebrations of mixture might be bringing us back to nineteenth-century-style racial hierarchies of light over dark in which only "white blood" is valorized. Perhaps such celebrations are designed to mask persistent racism, to avoid the issues of identity politics and affirmative action in the same way that "postfeminism" justifies a halt to mobilization for women's rights. Perhaps Americans are being persuaded to believe the rhetoric that says we have finally realized our ideals of equality so that we will stop questioning and contesting current balances of power.

These contemporary writings offer striking resemblances to popular essays from the nineteenth century. In an 1886 article from *Popular Science Monthly*, John Reade regards amalgamation as a way "to blanch the negro's skin" (351). He quotes "The Rev. Bishop Dudley," who sees mixture as a way of eradicating "the great races, into which humanity is divided . . . with their race-marks of color and form": "Centuries hence, the red man, the yellow, the white, and the black may all have ceased to exist as such" (342). Too often, those who favored amalgamation as a solution to "the negro problem" did so because they believed that mixture would eliminate the source of the problem: those with dark skin and racial difference itself. This line of reasoning also resembles early writings on *mestizaje* in Mexico, when mixture was advocated as a way to blend away the natives, to acquire their land, and to unify the nation. In 1937, Rodrigo Chávez González celebrated *mestizaje* in Mexico as a means of "improving" Indian races by mixture with Spanish blood: "El mestizaje es la terapeútica para la patalogía indolatina [*Mestizaje* is the therapy for Indian-Latin pathology]" (121). This memory renders even more chilling those contemporary articles that herald an end to race.

The nineteenth-century writing that most resembles 1990s mixture rhetoric is David Goodman Croly's 1864 pamphlet, *Miscegenation*, which offers the first recorded usage of that term. Croly's premise is that "the miscegenetic or mixed races are much superior, mentally, physically, and morally, to those pure or unmixed" (8–9). Despite his supposedly antiracist intentions, he reduces people of color to a vehicle for strengthening white races via mixture: "Providence has kindly placed on the American soil for his own wise purposes, four millions of colored people. By mingling with them we become powerful, prosperous, and progressive" (16). He regards whites as physically weak though intellectually superior and feeds racist stereotypes by locating virility and corporeality in tropical peoples: "The white people of America are dying for want of flesh and blood . . . dry and shriveled for lack of the healthful juices of life" (25, 34). The emphasis on the healthy effects of mixture reappears in many later "scientific" accounts, including the seminal Mexican treatise on *mestizaje*, José Vasconcelos's *La raza cósmica* (1925): "the original mixture of bloods [in Latin America], has served to keep us from the Anglo-Saxon limitation of constituting castes of pure races. History shows that these prolonged and rigorous selections produce types of physical refinement, interesting, but lacking in vigor. . . . Never have they been seen to surpass other men, neither in talent, in goodness, or in strength" (21). Vasconcelos regards Latin American mestizos as the race of the future because of their supposed freedom from the prejudices and purities that trouble U.S. race relations. In opposition to muleologist theories that proposed the sterility and the gradual demise of mixed races, many theories of racial formation reached the opposite conclusion, attributing such weakness to pure races, but often did so in support of racist ideologies, hierarchies, and exclusions.

Croly discusses the benefits of mixture for white Americans in explicitly sexual terms. He suggests that bodies of unmixed white men are "gaunt and cadaverous" and "telling of sterility," their "intercourse . . . formal, ascetic, unemotional," because they are suffering from a "lack of healthful association with their opposites of the other sex" (34, 35). In contrast to such asexual weakness, "the fierceness and fiery wildness of the negro" (42) thrills and attracts white Americans: whites "need contact with healthy, loving, warm-blooded natures to fill up the lean interstices of their anatomy. Looking purely to physical benefits for themselves and their posterity, they might well form the resolve expressed in Tennyson's lines: 'I will take some savage woman; she shall rear my dusky race'" (35). In this way, Croly implies that people of color provide the body, the sexuality, to sustain whites. Once again, sex is at the center of mixture, and sexuality itself is distanced from presumably more cerebral and dispassionate white Americans and attributed to people of color. Such logic was used to justify racial hierarchies and the rape of Native American women and slaves. While much of the mixed population of Croly's time was produced in the rape of women of color, he problematically reframes this violent history as one of desire and mutual benefit. This tactic potentially absolves white men from guilt by coding rape as beneficial.

In creating a sense of the allure that people of color must hold for white Americans to enable this miscegenation, Croly creates his own new face of America. In a section entitled "The Miscegenetic Ideal of Beauty in Woman," he argues that those physical traits most valued by Americans are embodied by mixed-race women: "rounded cheeks" with "a tint of the sun," "pouting" lips, hair that "descend[s] in crinkling waves. . . . The author may state—and the same experience can be witnessed to by thousands—that the most beautiful girl in form, feature, and every attribute of feminine loveliness he ever saw, was a mulatto. . . . This was a ripe and complete woman, possessing the best elements of two sources of parentage. Her complexion was warm and dark, and golden with the heat of tropical suns" (36). There is but a small gap between this description, which Croly intends as the highest praise, and those that describe African-American women as savage and overly sexual.[7] Croly's mulatta, like *Time* magazine's "new face of America," uses an image of feminine beauty to assure readers that mixture produces nothing threatening. She is different, though, from her chaste contemporary, the tragic mulatta, in her overt sexuality. As in the rest of Croly's argument, peoples of color become mere objects to satisfy the needs and desires of white Americans.

In another uncanny prefiguration of contemporary rhetoric, Croly writes of "The Future," in which there will be "No White, No Black": "distinction of color . . . shall measurably cease, by a general absorption of the black race by the white" (59–60, 65). Again, "the negro" rather than the problem "will disappear by absorption in America" to eliminate "the negro problem." Croly supports this prediction with testimony from Theodore Tilton: "the black race in this country is losing its typical

blackness. . . . Men who, by-and-by, shall ask for the negroes, will be
told, 'There they go, clad in white men's skin' " (68). This racist costuming
provides security for white supremacists by promising that future people
of color will be white men (or will at least look and act like them), not
the reverse. And as in the writings in *Time, Newsweek,* and the *New York
Times Magazine,* Croly describes this wave of the future as millennial: "in
the millennial future, the most perfect and highest type of manhood will
not be white or black, but brown, or colored" (65). The "new" or "future"
face of the 1990s thus has its precursor in the 1860s, born alongside racist
stereotypes and white supremacy.

Eerily, Croly's description of the "miscegenetic" ideal of beauty in women could equally describe some of today's most popular icons in fashion
magazines and on television. African-American supermodel Tyra Banks,
one of *People* magazine's "most beautiful people," conforms to white standards of beauty, with golden skin and long, straight golden hair, at the
same time that she fulfills interviewers' ideas of exoticism. For example,
in a 1996 GQ article, Andrew Corsello describes Banks as if she emerged
from a painting by Paul Gauguin or from Croly's allusion to Tennyson:
"Before now, if someone had told me he'd met a woman with great big
beaming brown-yellow eyes, I'd have chalked it up to a tropical illness.
But there's nothing even remotely sickly or waiflike about Tyra Banks.
That brown-yellow, a color I've never seen before in nature, is strangely
radiant, imparting an unearthly, moonlit clarity to her features. . . . Her
face has an aura of detail and stillness that normally only exists in paintings. One can't help but envision her riding a stallion bareback across a
beach, playing Paganini on a violin and wearing nothing but a—er . . .
sorry" (128). Corsello emphasizes Banks's robust physicality and sexuality and suggests that before meeting Banks, he could imagine such a body
only as a "tropical" hallucination. Corsello's image of Banks is not of this
world. It is the stuff of fantasy, emerging from a remote exotic dreamland.

The seemingly unnatural eye color and the "unearthly, moonlit" quality
that make Corsello's Banks so artificial coincide with the rhetoric of James
Ryan's 1995 interview, also in GQ, titled "Tyra Banks Is the Real Thing."
This title emphasizes Banks's defense of her own reality, which seems to be
in question. In response to the question "What makes you really angry?"
Banks replies, "When people say things on my body are fake. That really
hurts. I want to prove everything's real" (176). She tells how drag queens
admire her because, "*Oooh,* honey, you look real!" The solidity of her identity is challenged as people assume that she is a cross-dressing man or that

her breasts are fake, so she must prove her identity at every turn. "You'd best duck if you claim anything about her is fake," Ryan writes (176). Although her appearance lends itself to ambiguity, Banks's propaganda counters this fluidity with assertions of her black, female reality. Yet the fact that there is a debate means that even the real Banks, like Birdie Lee's racial selves and Haizlip's black identification, is constructed in reaction against drag queens and the like. The assertion of her own naturalness is a product of trends in corporeal artificiality. It is not clear whether her popularity rests on this pose of authenticity, which reassures fans interested in identity politics, or on the contemporary appeal of ambiguity.

Despite her exotic sexual appeal, another significant quality in the rhetoric used to describe Banks is the emphasis on her sexual innocence and virtue, which recalls nineteenth-century models of the idealized tragic mulatta. Corsello describes her as having a "hesitant" gait: "tiny steps, with the insoles of her Nikes kissing each other in between—to conjure a newborn calf, wobbly and wide-eyed" (127–28). This innocence is reaffirmed in Banks's own assertions, in which her modesty does not allow her even to name body parts: "No nudes or anything real sheer where you can see the . . . dot-dots. And I won't pose drinking alcohol or smoking a cigarette" (128). Banks defends her role of sexual innocent in refusing to answer Ryan's question about her first sexual experience: "I can't talk about that. I'm a sweet 'Cover Girl'" (176). And this virtue takes on religious overtones when she suggests that her female ideal is the gospel singer Vanity, "a born-again Christian" (176). Interestingly, Banks seems aware that this innocence is a role she must play, designated by her status as Cover Girl model. To fulfill her assigned type, she defends herself against sexualized descriptions such as Corsello's and appeals to Americans' sympathy for innocence, morality, and modesty. On the Internet, an unofficial Tyra Banks biography adds nurture to her virtues, emphasizing "her abiding love for children, animals and the environment." According to Supermodel.com, "Tyra currently is promoting a line of greeting cards for Children + Families, an organization dedicated to helping abused and neglected kids. [And] she's demonstrated her love for nature by journeying to the Costa Rican rainforest to bring the plight of that endangered ecosystem to the world's attention." These charitable endeavors endow Banks with the maternal and domestic qualities that her status as a Victoria's Secret lingerie model defies. As with Clotel and Iola Leroy, Banks's carefully constructed innocence and good works distance her from negative stereotypes of the savage woman of color.

Another one of *People* magazine's "most beautiful" and a Miss U.S.A. first runner-up is Halle Berry, an actress whose mother is white and whose father is black. Lonnae O'Neal Parker's 1999 *Washington Post* article features a picture of the light-skinned Berry with her straight hair dyed blonde. Although Berry "thinks she's just a regular sister from Cleveland," her face is so flawless that she appears to be "an airbrush of herself" (C1, C8). Like Banks, she seems unreal, inspiring in "regular sisters" "the kind of fantasies you remember from when you were a little girl. . . . *Lord, please let me look like her so my life will be sweet*" (C1). Everything about her is an illusion, including the myth that your life is sweet if your skin is light. The film Berry was promoting at the time, *Introducing Dorothy Dandridge*, tells the story of the beautiful light-skinned black actress from the 1950s whose life ended in probable suicide "after a string of career disappointments and broken love affairs" (C1). Parker parallels Berry's life to that of Dandridge, even trying Berry's name out in the film title, "Introducing Halle Berry" (C8). In noting the many similarities between the two light-skinned black actresses, Parker twice tells of how the "vulnerable" Berry nearly attempted suicide after her divorce from baseball star David Justice. And Berry could be "speaking in character as Dorothy Dandridge in 1955" when she discusses her struggles trying to fit in today's Hollywood, where the roles assigned to black women are still very limited: "Crack ho, Ghetto Goddess, Black American princess"—and, I would add, tragic mulatta, the Dandridge role. It is significant that in 1999 a biracial star is described as reliving a 1950s-style tragedy: "Everybody is waiting to see whether this actress will reprise her character role as a tragic beauty, or take her turn at star" (C8).

The biggest names among African-American film stars, according to Carla Hall's 1995 *Glamour* article, are Banks, Berry, Naomi Campbell, and Angela Bassett—all light skinned. During the 1990s, there were at least two mixed-race Miss Americas, Vanessa Williams and Chelsi Smith. Similarly, there has been a recent surge in the popularity of blonde, light-skinned "Latina" models and actresses, such as Cameron Diaz, Jennifer Lopez, and Daisy Fuentes. These icons bear relevance to the American political scene, too, in that they reflect an assimilationist aesthetic rather than the Black Beauty and *raza* pride celebrated in the 1960s. Interestingly, many articles on the multiracial movement invoke Tiger Woods as evidence of a current move away from racial identity politics. For example, in "Blurred Vision," Nick Gillespie describes the convergence of Woods's PGA Masters victory with the proposed *multiracial* census category as "a provocative coincidence," uses Woods's Caucasian/black/American Indian/Asian mixture as evidence of the impracticability of racial identification, and concludes that individuals should not be identified by race, "even for 'enlightened' purposes" (7). Gillespie's two primary examples in support of his conservative agenda are Tiger Woods and Hector St. Jean de Crèvecoeur's 1782 *Letters from an American Farmer.* Are Americans finally "melting"—to borrow Crèvecoeur's two-hundred-year-old model— or does this emphasis on the "blurring" of the races merely reflect the wishful thinking of a nation tired of resolving racial conflicts and redressing minority oppression? Are popular magazines representing an actual shift in American faces, or are they featuring light-skinned people of color as an alternative to Other looks and minority issues? Are the images of Woods, Banks, and Lopez being exploited by media unwilling to take the risk of representing difference? Is mixture currently popular because it reflects a step back from civil rights, affirmative action, *raza* pride, and Black Power? Do the images of Woods, Banks, and Lopez satisfy nostalgia for the days of normative, white American identity? Perhaps unintentionally so.

In her analysis of "modern mulattas" on daytime television," Caroline Streeter also finds "a regressive streak in the way racial boundaries are being discussed," even as "multiracial issues have seemingly acquired 'a place at the table' in public discourse" (314). Similarly, Cynthia Nakashima points out that Morganthau's 1995 *Newsweek* article appears alongside an article calling for the end of affirmative action, linking racial mixture with regressive politics by "featuring a large photo of an interracial couple asking to be judged by the quality of their work" rather than by racial identity (80). In pointing out these overlapping trends, I do not mean to suggest that multiracial individuals or the multiracial movement as a whole support the conservative shift in American politics. Rather, I believe that multiracialism is receiving increased attention in part as a result of this conservative trend. The current erosion of progressive racial politics coincides—temporally and rhetorically—with increased interest in mixed-race identity, and this convergence recalls the racist invocations of mixture from more than a century ago. The millennial rhetoric celebrating mixture felicitously masks this affinity to racially stratifying impulses.

The Official Response: Containing Mixed Bodies

Donna Haraway describes the intersection between biology and technology in the formation of identity, along with the "grammars of purity and mixing, compounding and differentiating," that structure American discussions about race (213). Racial classification has always been built on its own impossibility. Racial labels organize differences around skin color, creating the illusion that color signifies knowable distinctions between races. Yet if difference sorted itself naturally into a few color-based categories, there would be no need for struggle over racial definition, no need for biologists to study racial "compounding and differentiating." Since the real foundation of racial identity is genetically mixed, socially filtered, and culturally contingent, legal, literary, and scientific discourses have obsessively fought this fluidity and sought to fix race into "pure" categories. The image I find most resonant in Haraway's chapter on race is that of "racialized faces, which are taut membranes stretched across the scaffolding of accounts of conjoined biological and technological evolution" (232). Skins are stretched painfully as individuals are defined through officially sanctioned racial frameworks. The obsession with racial identity in both the sciences and popular culture, today as well as in the nineteenth century, subjects corporeality to rigid scrutiny and structures that reflect dominant cultural interests. Visible appearance and biology clash with legal definition. Identities must be contorted to fit assigned classifications. Haraway's study demonstrates the ways in which current technologies continue the torture begun by muleologies, eugenics, and other pseudosciences that manufactured identities to suit social hierarchies, and she exposes the impossibility of neutrality in state- or corporate-run inquiry into identity issues. As current genetic research revives racial/racist obsessions of the past, the intersections among scientific study, government sanction, and public racialization reawaken fears of institutionalized racism.

The Census: (Dis)Counting Mixture

As perceptions of race in the nineteenth-century Americas were ordered into categories to ensure racial stratification, mixed-race identity became an ontological fascination. To reinforce racial hierarchies and to apply legal codes, various methods of racial classification were proposed, ranging from Mexico's elaborate, multitiered *casta* system and Creole Louisiana's complex color gradations—mulatto, quadroon, octoroon, métis, *meamelouc*—to the binary oppositions created by the one-drop rule (Spickard 243). Still today, in an effort to control racial definition, legal discourses manufacture fixed identities. Census categories constrict the actual fluidity of skin tones as they force the knowability of race into five or six categories. In his analysis of the juridical function of census forms, David Theo Goldberg writes, "Rather form(al) identity necessarily presupposes the static nature, the unchangingness, of identity as such, and so freezes what is historically in process, in trans*form*ation. So form(al) identity—and this is especially true for identity fabricated through census forms—always lags behind the more transitory nature of lived identity. The form is always already too late. For by the time the form appears, lived identity has altered; or it captures only a partial (a limited and biased) aspect of that lived identity while silencing all other aspects" (32). The "form" that identity must assume in the census erases all history of identifications outside the boxes of the five or six racial categories offered. Actual fluidity and subversion are effaced within the boundaries of available categories, and those categories themselves become fetishized as *the* salient qualities of identity.

Even the proposed *multiracial* category itself offers another containment and effaces the difference between mixed individuals of Asian, African, Hispanic, or Native American descent. Romesh Ratnesar argues that despite their claim to be eroding America's "ossified categories of race," multiracialists are really just instituting another category, "devising another illusory racial home, . . . inventing some spurious experience, some artificial epistemology that all multiracial people inherit, as if a child born to one black and one white parent holds some inviolable connection with a child born to yellow and white parents" (43). Any potential for radicalizing given boundaries of race is nullified when mixture itself becomes a racial category. As Goldberg writes, "Thus the challenge to the project of racial purity in the celebration of mixed-race identities is at best ambiguous, (re)fixing the premises of the racializing project in place as it challenges that project's very terms of articulation" (63). Goldberg continues, "'Mixed race' may seem to offer exciting proof positive that a deep social taboo has been transgressed, that racial discipline and order have been violated, that liberty's lure once again has undermined the condition of homogeneity by delimiting the constraints of the hegemonic" (65), but a mixed category would merely redraw those constraints rather than challenging the boundedness of race. An example can be found in the term *Hispanic*, which takes a racially mixed, culturally heterogeneous, and geographically dispersed identity and renders it singularly racial, or even officially *white*. Goldberg implicitly links this category with right-wing resistance to the "browning of America": "At the moment of dissolving whiteness in America, a category [Hispanic] is fashioned to extend

America's tie to Europe." *Hispanic* thus serves "to extend the project of purity, even as it is a product of mixture" (68). Perhaps *Hispanic* was created to oppose the rise of *raza* consciousness among Chicana/os and Latina/os: *Hispanic* whitens, while *raza* invokes indigenous ancestry and brown skin. The use of the Spanish word for race is oppositional, indicating nonconformity to U.S. racial categories, while *Hispanic* circumscribes American mixtures with the English language and a European referent (Spain).

Jerelyn Eddings describes the political tensions surrounding the proposed *multiracial* category in 1997: "This issue is . . .'a hot potato.' On the one hand, the concept of multiracialism fits [President Clinton's] goal of creating a country that transcends racial division. Clinton has told friends that trends toward multiethnicity might force Americans to rethink their views on race. But a multiracial category could reduce the numbers and possibly the power of African-Americans and Hispanics" by counting them as multiracial (23). Interestingly, the multiracial movement has won more support from conservative politicians, including Newt Gingrich (who would do away with affirmative action and antiracist legislation), and is opposed by the NAACP and the National Council of La Raza (23). As in the nineteenth century, promixture rhetoric often lines up with (covertly) racist political agendas. Lynn Norment writes in *Ebony* magazine, "It also has been charged that right-wing conservatives and other civil rights opponents are pushing the move [for a *multiracial* classification] in a deliberate effort to divide and dilute Black political power" (108). Norment's choice of the word *dilute* suggests that the multiracial movement is trying to thin the blood of African-Americans and to weaken their racial impact, lightening the Other yet again.

Norment also cites Alvin Poussaint's claim that "there would be much confusion" if a separate *multiracial* category were approved, echoing the dramatic writings of *Time* and *Newsweek* in targeting mixture as a source of confusion, a muddying of American race dynamics.[8] In a 1997 article aptly titled "And Just Who Do You Think You Aren't?" sociologists Ivan Light and Cathie Lee point out that multiracialists' refusal to check one of the preexisting boxes "threaten[s] to expose the ideological nature of ethnoracial claims to biological realism" (30). The mixed-race census debate takes us directly to the meaning of race itself and undermines racial essentialism. Lawrence Wright writes in the *New Yorker* of how Tom Sawyer, chair of the House Subcommittee on Census, Statistics, and Postal Personnel, who is accustomed to mundane tasks such as "overseeing federal statistical measurements" and "safety concerns of postal workers," was surprised to find himself at the center of an inquiry into the nature and significance of race (46). The debate over whether to count multiracials at the turn of the millennium reflects several overlapping trends: the increasing awareness that race is constructed (even popular magazines make this claim), postmodern approaches to defining identity, fragmentation within group identities, and governmental attempts to contain threats to the categories on which its institutions rest. And the resulting debates over what degrees of mixture should and should not be counted recall the same debates that occurred more than a century ago in the United States, Mexico, and the Caribbean.

Perhaps this contemporary tendency to manipulate racial identity is more insidious, though, given our current technological capabilities (the scaffolding in Haraway's depiction of racial definition is partially formed by technological "evolution"). To justify the nineteenth-century segregationist legal system, Americans amassed supposedly scientific data to reinforce their binary definitions of race. While the pseudosciences and muleologies of a century ago could only scratch the surface of apparent racial difference (based on skull shape, skin tone, and other superficial traits), the sciences of today can capture chromosomal mappings and the genetic foundations of identity. There is every indication that genetic manipulation will follow (and perhaps render antiquated) the more superficial corporeal manipulations—cosmetics, plastic surgery—that have been popular for decades. According to Haraway, governmental agencies in Europe, the United States, and Japan already manufacture racial genotypes in genetic databases (244). Such efforts can alter racialized bodies not merely in legal or social terms but also in terms of actual corporeal manifestations. Science fiction or realism?

Surgical Race in *The Agüero Sisters* and *By the Light of My Father's Smile*

Haraway's model of "racialized faces . . . stretched across the scaffolding" of official rhetoric arises in recent literary depictions of mixture. Cristina García and Alice Walker capture this fear that our perceptions of race are being manipulated by technology, bio-industry, government categories, and popular-culture stereotypes. Through painful physical contortions, publicly imposed racial types haunt the skins of mixed-race characters in García's *The Agüero Sisters* (1997) and Walker's *By the Light of My Father's Smile* (1998). While Senna and Haizlip describe the tragedies produced by mixture as social manifestations of racism, García and Walker depict these manifestations assuming corporeally invasive forms. In both of these recent novels, battles for racial definition are mapped out on the bodies of mixed-race characters. Reina (*The Agüero Sisters*) and Manuelito (*By the Light of My Father's Smile*), both working in the service of the government, experience accidents that necessitate strikingly similar surgical procedures in which their skin must be restitched together like a gruesome patchwork quilt. As with Haraway's genome databases, the postaccident skins of Reina and Manuelito are literally fabricated at the hands of the government but with outcomes far more visible than genes are. The natural, pre-accident identities of Reina and Manuelito threaten conventional racial systems, and the surgery following their accidents perhaps reflects an institutional containment of these threats. In opposition to this containment, both novels also narrate the experiences of characters who attempt to self-fashion their racialized appearances, manipulating their own bodies and resisting imposed labels in an inversion of Reina and Manuelito's tragedies. Two opposing narratives of contemporary "miscegenation" emerge, public attacks on the integrity of mixed bodies versus individualized counteroffensives against the eugenic nightmares of a society that fears its own multiracialism. Each body fuses identities, skins, and colors in a manner that resembles the technoscience that Haraway critiques.

García's Reina Agüero is the mixed-race bastard daughter of Blanca ("white") and an unknown father, who turns out to be mulatto (265). The surname *Agüero* recalls the derogatory label *güero* (whitey), so Reina's darker skin conflicts with Agüero sensibility. Her illicit parentage and her color are taboo subjects in the Agüero family, which pretends that Blanca's husband, Ignacio, is the girl's father despite the fact that Blanca became pregnant while away from him. And the secret is not exposed until after Reina's identity is radically altered in an accident.

As a government electrician in the service of *la revolución* in Cuba, Reina is electrocuted at the El Cobre mine. Following the accident, Reina loses her skin as well as the racial uncertainty and sexual taboo that it signified. Her subversively racialized skin is burned gray from electrocution and then removed by doctors, who "scraped acres of cinereous flesh from her back, charred a foreign gray. . . . For weeks, her pores oozed water and blood, until Reina thought it might be better to die" (35). The doctors save her by taking experimental skin grafts from friends, family, and strangers, whose collective skins end up forming Reina's new racial topography. In the end, "Most of Reina's nutmeg color is gone, replaced by a confusion of shades and textures. A few patches of her skin are so pink and elastic, so perfectly hairless, they look like a newborn pig's."

Her skin is a "discordant new landscape," mismatched, itchy, and smelly (66). Reina's color is replaced with confusion and discord. The procedure makes her skin animal, monstrous. Most importantly, her body is redefined without her consent. Her lover and daughter stare possessively at the patches of Reina's body that once were their own rumps and thighs. As she loses ownership over her own body, she also loses her "hot, black scent" (66). Not even her lover, Pepín, "whose hands erase all borders" (66), can reconstitute Reina's former sensual pleasure. The implication of García's description is that some essential aspect of Reina's identity has been violated with the reconstruction of her skin.

In a sense, Reina becomes like *Time* magazine's new face or even the *multiracial* census category, an artificial creation designed to fit official specifications. She is still mixed in that her skin is multichromatic, but the mixture is not her own. The "black" and "nutmeg" racial appearance with which she was born and which once caused the neighbors to stare and whisper (246) is replaced by the hospital's ministrations. In losing her own skin and taking on that of others, she loses privacy and literally embodies the Cuban populace. Her body has been nationalized. If this corporeal procedure reflects the communist government's takeover of private property, García implicitly critiques the revolution by rendering the procedure grotesque. It is significant that the mine where the accident occurs is named for the mixed-race patron saint of Cuba, La Virgen de la Caridad del Cobre. Echoing deployments of *mestizaje* in Mexican nationalism, Fidel Castro embraced racial mixture as the official Cuban nationalist identity. So Reina's new body fits the scaffolding of government-sanctioned mixture. As with the *multiracial* category, officially endorsed *mestizaje*, or racist celebrations of amalgamation, Reina's new skin signifies mixture at the same time that it satisfies official efforts to contain or to suppress resistance.

In a similarly gruesome surgical nightmare, Reina's half-sister Constancia, the legitimate daughter who is wealthy and lives in Florida in exile from the revolution, dreams that her own face is being restructured: "There is a faint whirring that Constancia cannot identify in the slow, surrounding white. It sounds just below the surface, enameled, perhaps, and slightly metallic. Her eyes are closed, but she can hear the surgeon's breathing, muffled and near. His crimson scissors sing neatly through her skin. He pulls and relayers the delicate flaps, so flimsily rooted, dips and loops his special dissolving thread, a bloody pointillist. . . . The surgeon severs roots and useless nerves, reinvests the architecture of her face. Oh, the noise the tight crown makes, newly slotted to her skull!" (104). In this painful description, Constancia's face is a work of art in the process of renovation. The surgeon is a pointillist, creating an image with the placement of tiny homogeneous dots of pure color. The dots of this pointillism create a new, artificial appearance. Constancia wakes in the morning to find her face first "in disarray, moving all at once like a primitive creature," but then it "settle[s] down" into the image of her mother (105). With the younger, creamier visage of the deceased Blanca Agüero ("white whitey"), Constancia makes new strides in her cosmetics career (131–32).

She markets a line of products to the community of Cuban exiles in Florida. Cuerpo de Cuba face and body products promise a fabrication of Cuban corporeality, and the image of Blanca's face on the label appeals to the Florida Cubanas' nostalgia for their lost youth and lost Cubanness. Just as Constancia resurrects her long-dead mother on her own skin, her little blue bottles of "Cuello de Cuba, Senos de Cuba, Codos de Cuba, Muslos de Cuba" re-create on the bodies of the exiled women an exalted ideal of Cuban necks, breasts, elbows, and thighs. "Each item in her Cuerpo de Cuba line will embody the exalted image Cuban women have of themselves. . . . Her ads (glossy, soft-focus affairs with antique mirrors and tropical foliage) appeal to her clients' memories, to the remembered splendors of their Cuban youth" (131–32). Constancia becomes rich as her customers consume these artifacts. Applying Constancia's lotions creates a second skin that refers symbolically to exotic fantasies and blurry memories of the past. Customers find in Constancia/Blanca's "long, unguarded throat" a mirror of the "pink roots of their sadness" (132).[9] In this way, Constancia makes a business of skin, creating illusions of past innocence, whiteness, and authentic Cuban identity with creams and emollients just as the dreamed surgeon creates the illusion of Blanca on Constancia's face.

The difference between Reina and Constancia lies in their relationship to the Cuban Revolution. Both are transformed against their will, Reina in the service of the government, Constancia in the pale image of Blanca Agüero. The sisters' racialized identities straddle a political and historical divide. Reina's mixture recalls the official celebration of mixed racial heritage associated with the Cuban Revolution, while Constancia's satisfies nostalgia for prerevolutionary purity, beauty, nobility, and Eurocentrism. Reina's mismatched skin alienates her from her own identity, but Constancia experiences definite advantages from her new whiteness. She turns her racial identity into a moneymaking enterprise, in true capitalist fashion.

While Reina's surgical experience reflects the ultimate loss of control over the terrain of her own body, Constancia's transformation empowers her and motivates the cosmetic self-fashioning of an entire exile community. Since Constancia's transformation occurs after Reina's in the chronology of the novel, her dream face could be a response to Reina's tragedy, an inversion, in which epidermal surgery leads to self-fashioning and empowerment. Constancia rejects her officially assigned identity and the changes brought about by the revolution by staging a protest on the level of her own skin (and spreading the protest by marketing it to other women). The lesson that Constancia suggests is that governmental attempts to define race or identity are unsuccessful, as individuals control their own appearances with makeup or plastic surgery.

Yet the tools for resistance that Constancia offers are not particularly empowering, as they reinforce sexist stereotypes of women as pure surface and objectified beauty. She becomes wealthy by making other women feel insufficient in their natural skins. Moreover, Constancia's marketing image buys into a nostalgia for racial purity that equates beauty with youth and white skin. I can hardly imagine that García wants to endorse these strategies. Perhaps Constancia is a spoof, a parody of power, used to highlight these women's actual lack of power over determining their own identities. Indeed, in her resemblance to the notorious Avon Lady, Constancia inspires more laughter than respect. And Reina's tragedy certainly reveals that the government's tools are larger and more powerful than the cosmetics saleswoman: no amount of makeup could cover the skin grafted onto Reina or recover her stolen identity. Constancia's efforts seem feeble and trite in comparison to Reina's loss. Constancia is successful because she buys into U.S. mythologies of whiteness and capitalism. Reina's subversive mixture, however, is contained, punished, and torn from her.

Skin battles are also an issue in Walker's *By the Light of My Father's Smile* (1998). Manuelito belongs to a mixed-race, migratory people called the Mundo who live temporarily in Mexico to be apart from dominant American society.[10] After moving to the United States as an adult, Manuelito is blown apart in the Vietnam War, stitched back together, and reassembled with wire. "His face had been so destroyed that even his eyelids had been stitched together unevenly. And yet, oddly, passersby would not necessarily have noticed anything wrong. Of course, no one really looks at anyone anymore, and of course no one any longer looks like themselves. They all have the same perms, the same bleached sidelocks, the same bland skin. Big noses have mostly been left in the surgeon's rubbish bin"

(82). In this description, Walker moves directly from Manuelito's accident to ethnic conformity. She compares Manuelito's stitched-together
appearance to plastic surgeons' removal of un-WASP-like noses. Also in
this passage, Walker emphasizes eyes and visibility. Manuelito's eyelids
are uneven after the surgery, altering not just his perspective but his appearance in public, where he now blends in with others (nobody would
"have noticed anything"). The statement that "no one any longer looks
like themselves" implies that people have lost their personal identities.
Any original selfhood is invisible as they are perceived through cultural
norms and given labels.

To borrow Judith Butler's philosophy of bodies, individual identity is
constituted by the cultural categories through which it is seen: bodies are
"orchestrated through regulatory schemas that produce intelligible morphological possibilities. These regulatory schemas are not timeless structures, but historically revisable criteria of intelligibility which produce
and vanquish bodies that matter" (*Bodies* 14). Census categories, gender
roles, and racial stereotypes such as the tragic mulatta are all "criteria of
intelligibility." For Butler, identity is produced in the relationship between
individual appearance and public expectations, which derive from these
familiar criteria. Agency lies in the subversion of familiar "criteria of intelligibility." Yet in Walker's description, Manuelito's postaccident, fabricated appearance does not subvert expectations about what bodies should
look like: it assimilates easily into American crowds. The new body as-
sembled for him by military surgeons effaces Manuelito's private identity,
his Mundo mixture, and conforms to military specifications, "a regulatory schema." His skin is stretched across the scaffolding of official criteria. Unlike Butler's vision of agency and empowerment, Manuelito has
no control over the performance of his own bodily matter: "This fuck-
ing country had blown all of that up" (Walker, *Light* 122). In contrast to
Butler's drag queens, there is no critical reworking of racial criteria. The
surgeons remove that conflict. Like Reina and *Time's* new face, Manuelito's
Mundo identity, which would have threatened U.S. racial definition, is
erased by ethnic cleansing, mandatory plastic surgery. I find this fictitious
procedure to resonate disturbingly with the ways in which officially recognized identities do violence to racial fluidity, migration, and personal
choice. Manuelito does not choose to present himself through the performance of familiar categories (à la Butler); rather, the familiar is forced
on his body with government tools.

Manuelito's childhood sweetheart, Magdalena, also goes through a period of corporeal transformation during her separation from Manuelito. Her father exiles her from her lover and requires that she change her name to appear more "American" as they move from Mexico to the United States. As an adult, "June" rebels against this assigned identity and stages a protest on her own body: she eats her way into obesity, dyes her hair green and sculpts it, and gets multiple body piercings (79). She compares her body to food, jelly rolls and sausages (69, 77). Walker makes it clear that June's new body is the result of self-fashioning, sculpting, choice. It is a work of art. "The suffering of her body [is] a suffering she so carefully, through compulsive piercing (her nipples had small chains dangling from them, her labia a crucifix) and deliberate overeating, inflicted" (73).[11] June attempts to render herself grotesque, according to popular standards of American femininity (including her namesake, June Cleaver). She subverts expectations for the female body to create a more powerful exterior. Yet this attempt to define herself is unsuccessful. She uses preexisting images that are read by others as signs of depression rather than of political protest. Despite her corporeal revolution, her appearance fits expectations for what a discontent "Punk Dyke" academic should look like (85). And her tragic suicide is rendered no less predictable and disappointing by the fact that she dies while eating chocolate cake. Her effort to resist dominant categorization is ultimately contained, and her attempt to be different is preempted by her conformity to "alternative" stereotypes and "criteria of intelligibility." She, too, never escapes the scaffolding of Haraway's image. This tragic conformity resembles Constancia's sellout to stereotype in the makeup industry.

In the case of Reina and Manuelito, officially imposed epidermal mixture blows up actual, original fluidity and replaces it with a nonthreatening facade. These new fabricated bodies preempt the challenges posed by mixed identities. Ultimately, neither *The Agüero Sisters* nor *By the Light of My Father's Smile* envisions effective individual power in resisting officially enforced identifications. Instead, tactical resistance is often unrecognized, contained by stereotype as dominant categories shape public perception. We are left without much hope for individual self-definition given the government's structural power and macrocosmic tools, which today shape the meanings of race in fundamentally invasive, painful ways.

To come full circle, even Anyanwu's sci-fi shape shifting is ultimately co-opted, indeed prostituted, by the godlike Doro. Anyanwu's fluidity makes her an appealing commodity in the eyes of Doro, who exerts his stronger power to force her to breed with his descendants, giving him possession of Anyanwu's shape-shifting genes. Since Doro cannot be a shape-shifter himself, he appropriates Anyanwu for his own purposes. As the leader of his experimental breeding ground, the community of Wheatley, he collects valuable specimens like Anyanwu, "mix[es] and stir[s]," and relishes in his power to do so (O. Butler, *Wild Seed* 102). Once again, this futuristic vision of genetics echoes American slavery, when white plantation owners raped their female slaves and forced them to produce mulatto children, who would follow their mother's status and increase the master's slaveholdings. Those with power desire and fear those whose identities might elude their grasp. And sexual violation is often the manner by which the powerful circumscribe fluidity and appropriate mixed offspring.

This is not to say that the future really is hopeless and that we can expect millennial shifts only into the racist past. Octavia Butler, Senna, García, Walker, and others write to guard against this possibility. Perhaps we are witnessing new forms of identification and racialization, but after centuries of obsessive race hierarchies, Americans are anxious about the dissolution of the old, familiar forms and criteria. And the media are buying into this anxiety, highlighting racial transgressions, marketing the illusion of a social institution under siege. Just as antimiscegenation taboos reacted against actual mixture and just as Jim Crow reacted against actual social fluidity, this popular obsession reflects a reaction to fundamental changes in the ways Americans view race.

Epilogue

The mulatta/mestiza has held the attention of American media for more than a century. Her influence is significant enough to unleash a tremendous body of representations on the popular, the literary, the governmental, and the academic fronts, as all try to claim her with their rhetoric and their ideals. Perhaps this loud (and often racist or misogynist) rhetoric is designed to eclipse her own voice, to protect the myths of U.S. racial history. Even if she is not directly listened to—as the dominant culture mediates her voice and her image—she has exerted symbolic agency over the terms of American race ideology. Indeed, she is more than an object of study, the focus of an anxious American gaze. While there is a contradiction inherent in the simultaneous disempowerment of and obsession with mulattas and mestizas, there is no question that mixed-race women have been central to the formation of American identity. And this centrality decenters whiteness in America and exposes the violations on which American racialization rests.

So, in keeping with the tensions and dualities that abound in this book, I end on a note of simultaneous celebration and caution. It is important to keep in mind the ways in which celebrations of mixture sometimes mask reactionary attempts to contain race within the terms of white supremacy. At the same time, the literature I analyze in this book testifies to the ways in which mulattas and mestizas escape these violent containments. Writers such as Danzy Senna and Cristina García, or even William Wells Brown and Pauline Hopkins, imagine characters who continually redefine their race in resistance to external incursions. Their multiple and fluid identifications enable powerful stories of survival. This conclusion is not utopian or dystopian, harmonious or tragic. Either adjective alone would be ahistorical, unrealistic, and overly simplistic. I want readers to depart with a sense of the empowering ways that mixture can (and often does) redefine identity, even though racial fluidity has always occurred in the face of violent resistance. What remains is that which exceeds official containment, that which survives rape and tragedy: the excess writing in the margins of census forms, the personal narratives on the lines marked "other," and the friction between conflicting perceptions of mixed identities.

Notes

Introduction

1. Says managing editor James R. Gaines, "As onlookers watched the image of our new Eve begin to appear on the computer screen, several staff members promptly fell in love. Said one: 'It really breaks my heart that she doesn't exist'" (2).

2. This chart bears a disturbing resemblance to those created in nineteenth-century Mexico and the Caribbean to delineate the various categories of racial mixture that founded elaborate caste systems.

3. Shawn Michelle Smith studies *Time's* "new face" as a "symbol of a historically codified imagination": "The image is not simply the product of the new visual technology of morphing but also the result of a long legacy of racial science and visual typology, of the discourses and images that have defined racial inscription in the United States" (222). The image's multiracial combination is calculated to match racial census statistics in the United States. Smith suggests that this "mathematically divided racial and ethnic composition signals a renewed interest in separating racial 'types,' even as it envisions them mixing" (224).

4. The problem with comparing statistics from different historical eras is that interracial mixture was more often secret, illegitimate, and uncounted (especially when the mothers were slaves) in earlier periods than it is today, when more such unions are supported by marriage. It would also be difficult to compare the tabulating of mixed-race Americans in the 1992 census (which Root uses to support her claims) with the procedure used in, for example, 1900, when the "one-drop rule" defined mulattoes as legally black.

5. Although the proposed "multiracial" category was rejected for the 2000 census, mixed-race individuals were allowed to check more than one racial box to record their multiplicity.

[213]

6. Many proponents of the "multiracial" census category thank Tiger Woods for helping to gain publicity for their movement. According to Jerelyn Eddings, "the multiracial movement got a big boost . . . when Tiger Woods called himself a 'Cablinasian'" (22).

7. Chicana/o theorists in the United States have drawn attention to Anglo-American additions to the Chicana/o racial and cultural mixture but often elide the African presence in Mexican-American *mestizaje.* Gloria Anzaldúa at least once mentions the African components of her *mestizaje,* calling for Chicana/os to know not only their Indian ancestry but also their *"afro-mestizaje"* heritage (*Borderlands* 86). In this rhetoric, though, the African component is separable from *mestizaje,* an additive to it, while I would argue that it is inseparable, always present in American *mestizaje.*

8. I thank one of my anonymous readers for highlighting how the intermingling presence of indigenous nationalities as well as diasporic nationalities, such as Judaism, further complicates any simple racialization of mixture and distances mixture from binary categories.

9. Earlier in the twentieth century, diversity was suppressed and American identity was represented as a homogeneous category. Henry Nash Smith's *Virgin Land* (1950) works from the assumption that American culture has been "shaped by the pull of a vacant continent drawing the population westward" (3). For this argument to work, however, the actual something that already existed out West—Native American civilization and Spanish/mestizo colonial outposts—had to be effaced. Anyone other than Euro-Americans was excluded from early definitions of *American.* Critics such as Henry Steele Commager (1950) claimed that despite the diversity of American races and environments, "the general triumphed over the particular": "That people, which displayed the most diverse racial stocks and the most variegated climates and soils, achieved a distinctive and stable national character" (5). In this way, Commager does away with difference and replaces the diversity of American identities with a single national entity. He invokes racial difference only to discount it. In *The American Adam* (1955), R. W. B. Lewis finds in America a similarly heroic "archetypal man," lacking in race or history and "untouched and undefiled by the usual inheritances of family and race" (5). As Cecelia Tichi has noted, this sense of a universal American type and a singular evolution of American culture was decentered by theoretical and political movements of the 1960s (209–10). This decentering, however, is not a new phenomenon but a rediscovery. The imposition of a universal artifice, such as the American Adam, was a construction designed to lend coherence to American literature as a national entity and as a viable field of academic study. Yet this unifying moment was temporary, untenable, and easily challenged by the heterogeneity of cultures that have existed in America since its inception.

10. Henry Louis Gates Jr. and Houston Baker Jr. are both often criticized for their deconstructions of race, since their acceptance of poststructuralism is seen

as an apolitical, ahistorical forgetting of their specific racial context. In *Blues, Ideology, and Afro-American Literature,* Baker criticizes those "New Black Middle Class" "reconstructionist" critics who, betraying their own vernacular tradition, adopt the standards, postures, and vocabularies of white theorists (88–89). He includes Gates with this group. Although praising Gates's emphasis on signifyin(g), Baker accuses Gates of apolitical careerism and allegiance to white or "high cultural" models for theory (111). Later, in a three-way dialogue published by *New Literary History,* Joyce A. Joyce criticizes both Baker and Gates for their use of the "pseudoscientific," "distant and sterile" poststructural language, which bears no relationship to "Black lives," "Black realities," and "Black literature" (338–39).

11. Other critics also note that marginalized peoples in the Americas experienced conditions similar to postmodernism even before the rise of modernism. Michele Wallace claims that African-Americans have experienced something like postmodernism throughout their history in the United States because of their marginal status and their experience with unreliable signifiers such as "freedom" (78–79). Similarly, Guillermo Gómez Peña says that Latinos have "always had postmodern, only ours was involuntary" (quoted in Yarbro-Bejarano, "Multiple Subject" 66).

12. Sánchez also emphasizes the history of resistance that this decentered identity invokes: "despite parody, fragmentation of time and space, and decentering of subjectivity, Chicano literature continues to be characterized by counter practices that are contestatory and critical of dominant ideologies and practices" (12). Rather than being invested in dominant ideologies like postmodernism, Chicano decentering is based on political resistance to the dominant.

13. In *The Empire Writes Back* (1989), Bill Ashcroft, Gareth Griffiths, and Helen Tiffin point out a similar dialogue between postcolonialism and postmodernism: "The concern of postmodernist writers and post-structuralist critics to dismantle assumptions about language and textuality and to stress the importance of ideological construction in social-textual relations finds echoes in post-colonial texts. The concerns of these discourses are therefore increasingly interactive and mutually influential" (165). Dialogues between the discourses, however, often occur only as they "fit" into Euro-American paradigms. For example, Inderpal Grewal and Caren Kaplan's outstanding collection of essays, *Scattered Hegemonies: Postmodernity and Transnational Feminist Practices,* is limited as an international, interracial dialogue insofar as it gathers material around issues that have emerged in the Euro-American academy: postmodernism, feminism, and postcolonialism (1–4). As an effort to redefine feminism and postmodernism as heterogeneous, culturally specific practices, Grewal and Kaplan's work is remarkable, but their organizing principles remain committed to "-isms" that are established and fashionable in the dominant culture.

14. Much work has already been done on the subversion of language and genre by contemporary Latina, African-American, and Afro-Caribbean women

writers (see, for example, Alarcón; Sidonie Smith; Grewal; Davies; and Henderson). Teresa de Lauretis suggests that there is a connection between the problematic of "lesbian (self-)representation" (particularly by women of color) and the subversion of conventional forms of writing. She draws attention to the use of "fiction/theory" in Anzaldúa, Cliff, and Moraga, among others: "a formally experimental, critical and lyrical, autobiographical and theoretically conscious, practice of writing-in-the-feminine that crosses boundaries (poetry and prose, verbal and visual modes, narrative and cultural criticism), and instates new correlations between signs and meanings" ("Sexual Indifference" 165). These new genres are part of the "struggle with language to rewrite the body beyond its precoded, conventional representations" (167). Most of the contemporary writers I discuss—Anzaldúa, Cliff, Lorde, Moraga, Shange, Behar, Ortiz Cofer—utilize this intergeneric crossing of literature and theory to redefine identity beyond limiting Anglo-American, heterosexist norms.

15. Mexican-American literature of this period provides a (temporary) exception to this critical prominence only because texts by Mexican-American writers prior to 1950 have only recently been "recovered" through efforts such as the Recovering the U.S. Hispanic Literary Heritage Project. As these older texts are made available, they do receive critical attention, and *mestizaje* is a central focus of critical study, just as mixture is a central focus of nineteenth- and early-twentieth-century African-American and Caribbean literary study.

1. Mulattas and Mestizas

1. As mixture deconstructs racial categories, the effects can be politically or socially empowering. Of course, deconstruction itself is often apolitical or reactionary. It can merely signify the undoing of language, identity, or agency. Yet certain applications of deconstruction can undo exclusionary or oppressive ideologies. As Jay Clayton argues, "The important work being done with deconstruction by critics engaged in a range of political projects . . . postcolonial studies, feminism, lesbian and gay studies, Critical Race Theory, and other oppositional criticisms . . . illustrates the way this theoretical movement has been put to the service of social action" (58). Defying its conservative philosophical and literary origins, deconstruction can be employed in certain contexts to enable political resistance. Similarly, the deconstruction of racial purity can be tragic, produced in violation and leading to alienation, and it has been used in the service of dominant, racist cultures. Yet the effects of mixture—light skin, interracial dependencies, unsettled hierarchies—can also be enabling, can be employed tactically to increase an individual's mobility. This book highlights instances of the latter practice, and I deconstruct identity categories with the goal of decentering oppressive hegemonic paradigms. It is in this spirit that bell hooks proposes a "radical postmodernism" using the deconstruction of essentialism to "open up

new possibilities for the construction of self and the assertion of agency," to challenge "one-dimensional" "colonial imperialistic paradigms of black identity," and to reconfigure identity as the product of multiple and varied racial experiences (27–28). At the same time, it is important to remember that decentered identities do not always transcend racist hierarchies or asymmetrical power dynamics.

2. Vera Kutzinski describes the erasures that occur when *mestizaje* is tied to nationalist interests and ideologies: it "acknowledges, indeed celebrates, racial diversity while at the same time disavowing divisive social realities" (5). In this interpretation, *mestizaje* unifies the nation at the cost of obscuring its heterogeneity.

3. Many Chicana writers, Moraga included, mourn their loss of the Spanish language. Moraga even recounts calling the Berlitz language school for information on learning Spanish (*Loving* 141). Language provides a tool for empowerment, an assertion of mestiza identity, and a means of gaining entry into different cultural realms.

4. See chapter 3 for an analysis of the ways in which Chávez González genders the Native Americans and sexualizes the supposedly beneficent processes of *mestizaje*.

5. Many of the Spaniards already had wives in Spain or in the Caribbean, so some risked trial for bigamy in marrying their concubines in Mexico (Meyer and Sherman 209).

6. La Malinche is the Mexican/mestiza name for Malintzin, an "Indian princess" sold as a slave to the Aztecs, supposedly to secure the inheritance of her mother's son by a second marriage. The Spaniards referred to her as a Spanish lady, Doña Marina. I use the mestiza name to emphasize her role in bridging the two cultures. Cortés also symbolically co-opted the blood of the Amerindian nobility by conceiving a child with a daughter of the emperor Moctezuma. Both women's exceptional status led them to become (perhaps forced) intermediaries between the natives and the colonizers.

7. According to Carey McWilliams, many of the European elite refused to mix with Mexico's darker classes once the settlements had populations large enough to sustain racially selective marriage choices (89). Meyer and Sherman claim that by the seventeenth century, many Spaniards preferred to marry mestiza and criolla (Mexican-born, sometimes mixed-race) women, some of whom possessed estates (210).

8. William Byrd argues in "The History of the Dividing Line" (1728) that the Virginia colonists should have intermarried with Native Americans to avoid violent intercultural clashes and to populate the country. He criticizes the English colonists for "disdaining" these "prudent alliances," which he argues would not have any lasting "reproach" for the "shade of the skin," "for if a Moor may be washed white in three generations, surely an Indian might have been blanched in two" (160–61).

9. One such *cimarrón*, Yanga, held out against the Spaniards for thirty years in the seventeenth century. The government eventually was forced to free him and his followers, who founded the independent black town of San Lorenzo de los Negros. Meyer and Sherman regard this episode as "one of the most successful instances of black resistance in the New World" (217).

10. In the nineteenth and early twentieth centuries, some social scientists endorsed miscegenation to effect the "disappearance of blacks and Amerindians as separate groups." Conniff and Davis (270) locate such rhetoric in Spanish America, but similar rhetoric emerged in the United States during the same period (see Croly or Reuter for examples of U.S. rhetoric).

11. Woodrow Borah's "Race and Class in Mexico" (1954) analyzes the difficulty of determining who counts as Indian in Mexico, given the extent of interracial mixture. The 1940 Mexican census used cultural traits to define racial identity. As a result, any individual who ate corn tortillas, slept on the ground, and went barefoot or in sandals was legally Indian (332). Borah notes that these characteristics are as much economic as anything, and that *Indian* could be replaced with *peasant*, according to the 1940 standards. Moreover, the term *mestizo* came to signify "in rural usage not a mixed blood but a shopkeeper or person of middle class economic position" (337). In effect, racial categories, which were often indeterminable, were replaced by economic ones. In chapter 2, I discuss a similar conflation of race and class in the Caribbean.

12. In *The Limits of Racial Domination*, R. Douglas Cope describes how middle-class Mexicans in the seventeenth and eighteenth centuries often declared a racial identity contrary to the one on their birth certificates, particularly when getting married or when being tried for a crime. In this way, the *castas* contested the labels and hierarchies imposed by the Spanish colonizers.

13. In this configuration, class appears as the bottom line of identity: with purchasing power, an individual can buy social status. While the identities I discuss here break down other categories such as race, sex, and gender, class often remains the material foundation. If class is the one category that cannot be collapsed, the conclusion might be that only the wealthy can afford fluid identities. Yet the frequency with which slaves, for example, successfully defied classifications of race and status contradicts this conclusion. Although economics retains the power to influence hierarchies, the intersecting influences of color, nationality, race, class, sex, gender, age, education, and so on complicate any rigid class-based theory.

14. Forbes says that such certificates could be bought for 500 *reales* in 1795. Anthony Maingot suggests that such practices in Spanish colonial society were a means of raising revenue without "doing violence" to the fundamental racial order or the distinction between whites and nonwhites. Darker-skinned peoples could purchase at best mulatto or *quinterón* status (the equivalent of octoroon in the United States) (227–28).

15. Conniff and Davis suggest that the official rhetoric that hailed *mestizaje* as the "backbone" of Mexico solidified during the 1910 Mexican Revolution (272).

16. In the 1530s, one of the first Spanish explorers in New Mexico was Estevan (or Estéban), an "Arab Negro from Azemur, who . . . had acquired a knowledge of six Indian dialects" (McWilliams 32). Before Coronado's famous journey, Estevan was one of four survivors of a small expedition led by Pánfilo de Narváez to present-day Texas and New Mexico. Estevan initially was welcomed by the Native Americans and was often respected as a medicine man (Meyer and Sherman 145; McWilliams 32). Thus, according to McWilliams, the first "European" to discover the fabled seven cities of gold was actually born in Africa.

17. The racial diversity of Spanish immigrants suggests that the term *Spanish* applies to a set of cultural practices and beliefs more than to any racial or genetic factors. As a result, "Spanish" nationality seems to be flexible and inclusive, something one can develop or deny regardless of birth.

18. Martha Cotera's feminist history of Chicana heritage also characterizes the racial identity of Mexican settlers in the United States as mixed. Cotera claims that women played a primary role in constructing a multiracial American population in the seventeenth and eighteenth centuries. Most of the first twenty-two female settlers in Los Angeles were not of European descent, and many "Spanish" settlers thus sought non-Spanish wives (Cotera 49–50).

19. See chapter 2 for a discussion of similar tendencies in representations of Caribbean racial fluidity.

20. As evidence of the supposed lack of anti-Indian sentiment in Mexico, Jiménez Moreno cites the centrality of the brown virgin in Mexican Catholicism. La Virgen de Guadalupe (who appeared before the Indian Juan Diego in 1531) celebrates an indigenous legacy. Since La Virgen was used as a banner for Mexican independence, *mestizaje* was publicized as a symbol of Mexican nationalism.

21. Similarly, Clotel's daughter later passes as a man to liberate her imprisoned lover (Brown 226). The novel is full of other near-white women who are tragically returned to slavery, each of whom chooses death or imprisonment to avoid having sex with her owner (206–7).

22. Woodward claims that as a result of having lived together for so long, an intimacy existed between blacks and whites in the South that transcended their "formal relations" and "master and slave" divisions (6). Woodward's statement implies that formal public separation did not always correspond to personal experience, in which relations were more fluid.

23. In his essay, "Racism," Kwame Anthony Appiah analyzes the ways in which social scientists searched for essential racial differences based on a belief that extrinsic morphological properties prove intrinsic qualitative differences and justify racist biases. In *In My Father's House*, Appiah notes that as a result of genetic exchange, any classification based on simple racial traits is fallacious. Gross morphological differences, such as skin color or face shape, do not necessarily have a

common biological foundation (37–38). Indeed, Appiah claims that the genetic differences within races are almost as great as genetic differences between races. While color influences experiences, it is impossible to establish correlations between the properties of reflecting surfaces and those of human individuals (39). According to Appiah, as early as W. E. B. DuBois, black American intellectuals have denied any connection between cultural or social capacity and gross morphology (34).

24. In *Of One Blood* (1902–3), Pauline Hopkins reveals the ways in which racial mixture challenges racist hierarchies: "The slogan of the hour is 'Keep the Negro down!' but who is clear enough in *vision* to decide who hath black blood and who hath it not? Can any one tell? No, not one" (*Magazine Novels* 607, emphasis added). The inability to see racial difference was a source of intrigue for many writers, who then concluded, as did Hopkins, that "no man can draw the dividing line between the races" because of this lack of differentiation (607).

25. Much of the attention given to mulattoes results from the mystique surrounding the products of miscegenation. Though (or perhaps because) the derivation from *mule* reflects an attempt to deny reproductive capacity (and thus future identity) to mulattoes, literary depictions of mulattoes often emphasize sexual attractiveness. An example of this intrigue appears in Pauline Hopkins's *Of One Blood.* As a group of (supposedly white) young men surveys the different shades of pretty girls at a performance of the Fisk Jubilee singers, one comments suggestively, "The results of amalgamation are worthy of the careful attention of all medical experts" (*Magazine Novels* 451).

26. Perhaps the greatest drawback of this study is Williamson's definition of America as a biracial society. By *biracial,* he means derived from two races, black and white. While this paradigm highlights the subversiveness of racial mixture, he excludes all other races and thinks of America only in terms of black and white (meaning African ancestry versus European ancestry). A consideration of the many races that do exist in America, along with the many variations and hybridities within them, would free his project from the binarism that eventually renders all mulattoes black.

27. Significantly, Williamson compares racial leniency in the Lower South to that in the Caribbean and Latin America, claiming that the "Latin-like tolerance of mulattoes" declined after 1850 (*New People* 65).

28. According to Williamson, when whites expelled mulattoes from white society during the Civil War, Reconstruction, and the Harlem Renaissance, mulattoes allied themselves with blacks for social and political reasons (75, 80, 151–52, 163, 178–79).

29. See Toni Morrison's *Playing in the Dark* for a discussion of how white American identity was built on opposition to an Africanist presence.

30. Reuter's holding up of the United States to the Latin American model resembles Conniff and Davis's contemporary comparisons; however, Conniff and

Davis are less celebratory of the Latin-style race dynamic and maintain that it "cannot yet be determined" whether Spanish American racial blending "will prove to be more successful or satisfying than the U.S. approach" (291). The tendency to idealize Latin America as a region of racial fluidity elides the actual race- or class-based barriers that persist there. For this reason, Conniff and Davis are more tentative, and they temper their U.S.–Latin American differentiation with a sense of realism about the continued inequities that the two regions share.

31. I am wary about agreeing with anything in this racist study, but some of Reuter's statements, racist though they are, could deconstruct racial opposition. Yet any interpretation of his argument must be qualified by a recognition of its racist bias. He goes so far as to claim that "the Negro woman never has objected to, and has generally courted" "the relationship" with white men (162–63), reinforcing misogynist, racist stereotypes and eliding the element of force involved in so many of those relations.

32. See, for example, Croly, (the first recorded usage of the term *miscegenation*); and Stone.

33. In his introduction to González's novel, *Dew on the Thorn*, José Limón suggests that Dobie influenced González to write folklore for the purpose of charming readers with visions of exotic cultures.

34. González studied *Tejanos* as a student of the Anglo-American Dobie and as the first Mexican-American president of the Texas Folklore Society. Her affiliations with the university and with predominantly Anglo organizations positioned her partially outside the culture she was studying.

35. Another recurring motif in the novel is the veiling of women to enable their masquerades as other characters (226, 261, 279, 282–83).

36. Velásquez Treviño calls *Mexican Village* an anthology of novelettes (120), but I prefer to call it a novel to emphasize the cohesion of its narratives, which together construct a cultural history of the Mexican village. Niggli borrows such formulaic conventions as the marriage plot, mistaken identities, and doomed love affairs that transgress race and/or village allegiance, which allow for a comparison with the romantic novel tradition.

37. Although her protagonist is male, Niggli's description of Bob's racial mixture resembles literary depictions of biracial women: Bob's father is light, wealthy, and powerful, and his mother is dark. Bob ultimately chooses to identify with his maternal legacy.

38. This progression resembles the tragic mulatta narratives that appear in much turn-of-the-century African-American literature. Frances Harper's *Iola Leroy* (1893), for example, narrates the ways in which the discovery of mixed blood evolves from tragedy to empowerment.

39. For example, Judith Raiskin claims that Cliff and Anzaldúa "offer complex postmodern challenges to modern identity categories of sexuality, race, and nationhood" (156). In her 1996 anthology, *Feminist Literary Theory*, Mary Eagleton

locates Anzaldúa's work in her final section, "Locating the Subject," alongside essays by Judith Butler, Seyla Benhabib, Linda Alcoff, Diana Fuss, and Donna Haraway about feminism, postmodernism, and deconstructing subjectivity.

40. Moraga begins her poem "It Got Her Over" with an epigraph from Michelle Cliff's "Claiming an Identity They Taught Me to Despise." In this poem, Moraga is critical of her light skin, which "turned on her" and made her complicit with "the crime" since it gained her favor when confronted by police, when behind on paying bills, or when entering coffee shops crowded with white patrons. Her "guilt by association" with white racial exclusiveness makes her want to blush and bring more blood to her face (*Loving* 69–71). Her greater respect for dark skin leads her to renounce those "anglocized" traits that allow her to "pass in the white world." She claims to have "gone brown to the blood color of my mother" because "the survivor" is "born out of what is dark and female" (51, 59–60).

41. In chapter 2, I discuss a similar dedication to non-European foremothers' resistance in Michelle Cliff's writing.

42. Martha Cotera analyzes the power of Indian goddesses from the pre-Columbian period as evidence of the centrality of women in Mexican and Mexican-American traditions. She claims that goddesses ruled over the gods, that feminine traits were valued over masculine ones, and that this gender dynamic among the deities carried over to power for women on earth (13–23). Cotera returns to this tradition as the foundation of Chicana feminisms and political resistance.

43. Michelle Cliff also sees the greatest tragedy of her identity to be her light skin. For examples of Moraga's identification with her mother's brownness, her rejection of her father's whiteness (a symbol of patriarchal and colonial oppression), and her association of her lesbianism with love for her mother, see her best-known poems, "For the Color of My Mother" and "La dulce culpa" (*Loving*). I discuss the sexual element further in chapter 3.

44. Indeed, *Bridge* presents their last collaborative effort, and Anzaldúa includes only one poem by Moraga in *Making Face, Making Soul* (which otherwise appears much like a sequel to *Bridge*).

45. *Cantora*'s emphasis on bloodlines returns in Puerto Rican writer Rosario Ferré's novel, *The House on the Lagoon* (1995), which I discuss in chapter 2.

46. This maternal identification recalls Bob Webster's choice in *Mexican Village.* Assuming racial identity based solely on maternal inheritance was legal in the United States, where mixed-race children were assigned their mother's race and status during slavery. I discuss this practice in the next section.

47. While I agree with Silvio Sirias and Richard McGarry's recent article on *Cantora* in their assessment of López-Medina's honoring of tradition, I disagree with their claim that her characters "subscribe to the codes of patriarchy" (92). As Amparo recovers her family's tradition, she ultimately revises lineage as woman centered and rejects patriarchy.

48. Mexico had a similar system. Although the mixed offspring of Spaniards and blacks had a chance to move up in society if they adopted Spanish culture, those who remained with their black mothers inherited the mothers' legal status (Meyer and Sherman 215).

49. Thus, in literary texts from Livermore and Niggli through Cliff and Moraga, identification with the mother parallels identification with a darker race.

50. According to Judith Berzon, "nothing supposedly inspires sympathy more than the plight of a beautiful woman whose touch of 'impurity' makes her all the more attractive." Since the character is often raised as a white woman and discovers her Negro blood only as an adult, this literary device facilitated identification for white readers (99–100).

51. Berzon claims that "few male mixed-blood characters are tragic mulattoes in the traditional sense" (74). She contrasts the lovesick female mulatto to evil male mulatto characters in Hughes and Chesnutt.

52. This conclusion disproves Olney's assertion, which Herndl questions (264), that near-white heroines are enslaved to conventional racial forms.

53. See chapter 2 for a discussion of the ways in which Cliff rewrites the Zoe narrative in her 1984 novel, *Abeng*.

54. Similarly, Mary Denison's 1858 novel *Old Hepsy* decries the enslavement of mulatto women, whose destiny should be the same as that of white women. A Quaker character mourns the tragedy that the mulatta Lucinda will never "weave garlands of undying beauty around the dear hearthstone" or "know no altar of domestic beauty" and will have "no hope, no recognition of human nature, no resistance" (117). The only role Denison envisions for Lucinda is the restraining domestic "altar" of the (white) cult of domesticity. When that identity is denied, all that remains for the mulatto is hopelessness, lack of resistance, and unnaturalness (if that is the opposite of human nature). The singularity of identity in these works sharply contrasts with Clotel's form-changing abilities.

55. This association of mixed African heritage with the Caribbean also appears in historical texts. In chapter 2, I provide several examples of historians who attribute interracial fluidity to the Caribbean and distance such fluidity from the United States.

56. Much of this analysis could apply to Chesnutt as well. Chesnutt's story "Her Virginia Mammy" (1899) and his novel *The House behind the Cedars* (1900) invoke the most familiar racial and sexual conventions of tragic mulatta narratives. In "Her Virginia Mammy," lost mothers are linked to lost racial origins, and in *The House behind the Cedars*, the discovery of her unknown mixed ancestry causes Rena to become ill and to die just before her white lover comes to claim her. Both this story and the novel depict passing, cross-racial romance, and an eclipsing of black identity through the adoption of cultural constructions such as fashion plates, middle-class mannerisms, and jousting tournaments. Chesnutt's work seems just as interested as Harper's and Hopkins's in the marriage plot, domestic

or sentimental situations, and strong women who hold the key to racial identity. Moreover, just as Hopkins and Harper have been read for potential feminist
messages, a similar analysis could apply to Chesnutt. For example, in *The Conjure
Woman*, the title character is an empowered, culturally wise Africanist heroine
who works obeah on duped (predominantly white) men.

57. In *The Signifying Monkey* and *Race, Writing, and Difference*, Gates bridges the
black vernacular tradition with academic, poststructural theories, emphasizing
the importance for African-Americans since Phillis Wheatley of achieving liter-
acy and gaining recognition according to the standards of the dominant culture.
Baker also compares black vernacular traditions to poststructuralism, in the figure of the railroad and the black hole in *Blues, Ideology, and Afro-American Literature*.
In *Workings of the Spirit*, Baker criticizes black feminist commentators for refusing
to adopt theory. Barbara Christian would say that African-Americans have been
doing theory all along through signifyin(g) and language games (like the dozens)
("Race").

58. See, in particular, Elder.

59. Deborah McDowell captures this critical conflict in *"The Changing Same"*:
"Critics have long been locked in a fierce struggle over just how to read the
representation of the middle-class mulatta in turn-of-the century fiction by black
women, over just how to resolve the range of cultural tensions around race and
gender/race and class attached to this figure. Their debates have been fueled by
a fundamental question: 'Does the mulatta figure serve or subvert the dominant
ideologies of race and gender?'" (54).

60. W. E. B. DuBois invokes this sexual history in *The Souls of Black Folk* (1903),
the same text in which he delineates the virtues of the "Talented Tenth" and classical education: "The red stain of bastardy, which two centuries of systematic legal
defilement of Negro women has stamped upon his race, meant not only the loss
of ancient African chastity, but also the hereditary weight of a mass of corruption
from white adulterers, threatening almost the obliteration of the Negro home"
(50). In this description, DuBois opposes sexuality and domestic virtue, loathing
the corporeal red stamp of illegitimacy and adultery (euphemisms for rape) to
defend chastity and the home.

61. These duplicated scenes in Brown, Harper, and Hopkins are based on actual accounts. This repetition continues in contemporary literature. Toni Morrison's *Beloved* (1987), a novel often called postmodern for its nonlinear, fragmented
form, invokes this tradition when she retells the story of a slave woman who
crossed the Ohio River to freedom, killed one of her children, and attempted to
take the lives of her two other children. In this way, literature passes on historical
narratives, adding to and revising them.

62. Though she is often discussed in conjunction with Harlem Renaissance
literature, Hurston's relationship to the Harlem Renaissance is ambiguous, given
her unique style of writing, her southern and Caribbean objects of study, and the

later time period for most of her publications. But the evolution of Janie's identity closely resembles the mixed-race heroines of Larsen and Fauset.

63. It is significant that this interracial crossover elicits the same kind of resistance, according to Parnell's 1950s–60s standards of valuing blackness, that African-American critics leveled at mulatta narratives for their supposed whitening of black identity. (See my previous discussion of Baker.) *Liliane* critiques this sense that celebrations of blackness must be racially singular.

64. Contemporary Chicana feminists often return to La Malinche, examining the tremendous power and the overdetermined stereotypes surrounding the mother of *mestizaje*. The women who have given birth to interracial mixing are often regarded as passive victims or betrayers of their culture rather than visionary strategists. Carmen Tafolla's poem "La Malinche" (1985) confronts the stereotype of the raped, victimized Malinche and recasts the mother of *mestizaje* as an empowered woman whose choices and agency facilitated the creation of a new race. According to Tafolla, Malinche chose to be an agent in the conquest:

> I became Interpreter, Advisor, and lover.
> They could not imagine me dealing on a level
> with you—so they said I was raped, used,
> chingada.
>
> (Rebolledo and Rivero 198)

Tafolla claims that legends told of a raped, *chingada* Malinche, manipulated between two cultures, only because "they" could not envision an empowered woman.

> But Chingada I was not
> Not tricked, not screwed, not traitor.
> For I was not traitor to myself—
> I saw a dream
> and I reached it.
> *Another world*
>
> . . . .
> la raza.
> la raaaaa-zaaaaa.
>
> (199)

History is wrong to call her *chingada* because she decisively uses her power to create a new civilization. Rather than depicting Malinche as torn or crushed between two races, Tafolla places her on the threshold, beyond the clash between Spanish and Aztec. Tafolla's Malinche creates a new world through "my sweet mestizo new world child," bridging two cultures and producing a new, inclusive race. In this way, she values the "betweenness" of La Malinche and *mestizaje*.

65. Liliane describes the opposite of this image in a dream where she enters a restaurant full of white people in blackface but cannot get a table because she has no reservations (59–60). As Liliane often feels excluded from the African-American race, her dream suggests that she is also excluded from white appropriations or perceptions of her identity.

66. Pauline Hopkins's 1902–3 magazine novel, *Of One Blood*, reveals this same conflation of incest and miscegenation: the near-white heroine turns out to be the sister of both of her husbands. The taboo of interracial marriage, revealed with the knowledge of Dianthe's black heritage, is compounded by the discovery of familial relationship (and polygamy, since her first husband turns out not to be dead when she remarries). The husbands and wife are literally of one blood in terms of race and of kinship. Hopkins fuels her condemnation of the rape of black women by white men—"the accumulation of years of foulest wrongs heaped upon the innocent and defenceless women of a race"—by suggesting that the product of this foul crime is both miscegenation and incest (*Magazine Novels* 594). All three crimes come together in the person of the victimized Dianthe, the product of rape, incest, and miscegenation. Through the resultant crimes against nature and the "havoc wrought by evil deeds," the violation of the black woman emerges as a crime "worse than murder" and beyond the arm of the law (civic or biblical) (595, 607).

67. Traci Carroll invokes this play between sameness and difference, suggesting that racial passing (a product of racial mixture and ambiguity) is linked to incest. She compares the taboos surrounding the two: "It is no accident that narratives of incest and passing have often coincided in novels about race; both plots revolve around the uncanny and its play between sameness and difference, the familiar and the un-familiar" (188). Both taboos are a product of the feared sameness between races and the threatening mystery surrounding their mutual attraction.

2. Creoles and Color

1. Although the Caribbean and the United States have different histories of slavery, colonialism, mixture, and racial stratification, their differences revolve around the common factor of a color-based hierarchy. Despite the fact that the Caribbean has a larger percentage of "colored" or mulatto citizens, the United States is as completely biracial (or multiracial) as the Caribbean, with a broad spectrum of racial and cultural differences. While the United States' role as a colonizer makes it absurd to view most U.S. citizens through the lenses of postcolonial theory, the relationship between people of color and whites within the

U.S. is as postcolonial as Caribbean dynamics. Comparing U.S. and Caribbean histories reveals both their similarities and their differences.

2. Franklin Knight writes of the Europeans in the Caribbean, "It was not merely the climate of the tropics but also the process of Creolization within the peculiar socioeconomic structure of their own creation that surreptitiously undermined their original 'Europeanness'" (150). Europeans' whiteness was thus threatened by the tropical sun and the frequency of racial mixture that the plantation system facilitated.

3. Many racially mixed Afro-Caribbeans became wealthy, and some even owned slaves (Rogozinski x). Skin color, however, remained a factor in the social hierarchy. Initially, the dominant class was largely white, with a few mulattoes. Over time, increasing numbers of blacks entered this elite class, but the majority of the lower class was still black (Jácome 201).

4. Throughout the seventeenth and eighteenth centuries, Spain, France, Great Britain, and the Netherlands battled for control over the Caribbean. During this time, the European colonizers virtually destroyed the Carib and Arawak populations of the islands and imported millions of slaves. By the 1750s, the Caribbean had reached the highest proportion of black slaves in human history, up to 90 percent on some islands (Rogozinski 122). A disproportionately small number of white females led many men to seek partnerships with darker-skinned women. As in Mexico, racial mixture increased throughout the history of the Caribbean, and this mixture often led to social mobility. Racist hierarchies and pretenses to separatism were thus "far removed from the operational reality of day-to-day living," where boundaries of race, class, color, and condition were frequently crossed (Knight 128, 155).

5. See my readings of Puerto Rican literature later in this chapter for more on this tendency to blame the United States for importing racism to the Caribbean.

6. See T. Davis for an analysis of race dynamics in Faulkner's work.

7. Within the English and Spanish Caribbean, I limit my analysis to Barbados, Jamaica, Puerto Rico, and Cuba as representative of different caste and plantation dynamics. Barbados was the first major plantation society in the Caribbean, and Puerto Rico was the last. Jamaica is unique for its history of successful maroon colonies, and Cuban culture is significant for mulattoes' role in national identity. Limiting my historical survey to these four countries allows me to explore each in greater depth and provides the national background for the writers I discuss: Paule Marshall (Barbados); Michelle Cliff (Jamaica); Cirilo Villaverde (Cuba); and Rosario Ferré, Ana Lydia Vega, and Aurora Levins Morales (Puerto Rico).

8. C. L. R. James similarly claims that social position can be bought in the British Caribbean, where rich people of color are accepted into the margins of English society based on their "sacrifice of money, influence, and dignity" (55).

9. *Genus inconnu* is probably a play on *gens de couleurs*, people of color in the Caribbean who experience privilege based on their class standing.

10. Indeed, in his history of nineteenth-century Jamaica, Patrick Bryan suggests that with the demise of slavery, the planter class attempted to retain the plantation-based hierarchy by biologizing social differences, equating class status with color and thus fixing social status in the realm of essential identity (x). Such attempts reinforced some social hierarchies at the ideological level but failed to end the fluidity of categorization.

11. England officially abolished slavery in its colonies in 1834, but it required that the "freed" slaves serve a four-year term of unpaid labor, called an apprenticeship, before their full release (Rogozinski 178).

12. It has been said that Roman Catholic countries instituted a "milder or more humane form of slavery" than did the Netherlands or England (Rogozinski 138; Instituto 85). Yet the high death rates of African slaves in the French colonies suggests that Catholicism alone did not lead to "milder" slavery.

13. Before Puerto Rico was settled, Queen Isabella sent Nicolás de Ovando to Hispaniola (present-day Haiti and Dominican Republic) in 1502 to build a unified Catholic and Castilian nation, imitating Spanish culture and excluding non-Catholics (Knight 29). Obviously, this attempt at *insularismo* failed, as well.

14. In reality, the Caribs were already a mixed people. According to Franklin Knight, they frequently "recruited" Arawak women who had a large impact on the production of racial, cultural, and linguistic mixture (21).

15. Slavery was never as significant in Puerto Rico as on other Caribbean islands. Before the U.S. occupation of Puerto Rico in 1898, agriculture on the island operated on a small scale, dominated by independent peasant farmers (squatting on small plots of land) and few slaves. Property was not concentrated in the hands of a white minority. Most people of color in Puerto Rico were free, and whites formed a much higher percentage of the population than elsewhere in the Caribbean (Rogozinski 207–8). While most Caribbean islands profited from large, centralized sugar plantations, the sugar industry in Puerto Rico did not flourish until the twentieth century, long after the abolition of slavery. Although slavery had existed in Puerto Rico since the initial settlements, the slaves were not concentrated on large plantations. The absence of a plantation economy led to a different, less hierarchical race and class dynamic in Puerto Rico (207).

16. In contrast to Puerto Rico, Cuba developed an advanced plantation society as soon as Spain opened the island to international trade in the 1760s. The Cuban economy was dominated by sugar plantations throughout the nineteenth century, taking advantage of new technologies in production (planting, mechanized milling, railroad transportation). The black slave population increased rapidly, and the planters feared slave uprisings such as those that upset colonial authority in Haiti and Jamaica (Rogozinski 201–2).

17. William Luis regards *Cecilia Valdés* as "the most important novel written in nineteenth-century Cuba" (100). Similarly, Ineke Phaf calls *Cecilia Valdés* a "national epic" (176).

18. See Luis for the influence of Villaverde's U.S. exile.

19. Ana Lydia Vega claims that the emergence of a nationalist or native Puerto Rican consciousness was problematized by the fact that "everything is foreign" and "everyone is foreign" in Puerto Rico ("Women" 821). Each colonizer has left traces of its heritage in the "native" Puerto Rican culture, creating an international and multiracial syncretism within the one island. Puerto Rican identity includes multiple outsiders and foreigners, so it would be difficult to locate a single Puerto Rican center or standards for inclusion and exclusion. As each successive colonization further muddies the borders of Puerto Rican nationality, race, and culture, Puerto Rican identity becomes increasingly mixed.

20. See Moore and Pachon 32. In his 1940s memoirs, Bernardo Vega also emphasizes racial tolerance in Puerto Rico, and he claims that in the first Puerto Rican communities built in New York, "racial differences were of no concern" (Iglesias xiii, 12). As "El Barrio" was first consolidated in the 1920s, "whites and blacks lived together in harmony" (151). Racism came with the increasing Americanization of Puerto Rican communities. Judith Ortiz Cofer similarly suggests that hostility toward blacks is a U.S. phenomenon (*Silent Dancing* 146). However, Nicholasa Mohr attributes this belief in the absence of racial prejudice on the island to the idealized reminiscences of Puerto Rican migrants in the mainland. Mohr claims that this mythology has "little or nothing" to do with the reality of Puerto Rican culture (114).

21. This sense of whiteness as monstrous appears in several multiethnic U.S. texts. For example, in Maxine Hong Kingston's *The Woman Warrior*, the narrator's mother calls all non-Chinese people "ghosts," rendering them lifeless or immaterial. Referring to the dominant culture as ghosts devalues its racial identity and undermines its authority while invoking a fear of whites and their mysterious ways. The mother claims that "human beings do not need Mail Ghosts to send messages" and criticizes her daughter for listening to Teacher Ghosts and Scientist Ghosts because they challenge Chinese beliefs and traditions (116, 120). Likewise, in *The Temple of My Familiar*, Alice Walker assumes the perspective of Africans and suggests that to them whites would look like they had no skin, as if they were lacking or deformed: "It seemed to indicate a hideous personal deficiency" (361). In this way, Walker subverts the superiority of whiteness and valorizes blackness as the norm.

22. According to Margarita Fernández Olmos, "en contraste con el estilo de Ferré, Ana Lydia Vega despliega el habla de la calle. . . . Sus personajes son de la clase obrera y del lumpen proletario [in contrast to Ferré's controlled style, Ana Lydia Vega uses the talk of the street. . . . Her characters are of the working class and of the lumpen proletariat]" ("Desde" 309).

23. In *The House on the Lagoon*, Ferré stages many debates over the issue of Puerto Rican independence, and her different characters provide arguments for all sides. While the heroes of the novel ultimately come down on the side of independence

and the patriarchal Buenaventura argues for statehood, many of the characters remain ambivalent.

24. The rice is white (in a diminutive or endearing form) and "señoriteaba" (acted as a little lady). The "mulato" beans are flavorful (in a masculine way) and keen-witted. In this description, Vega genders racial differences, balancing two different identity categories at once. Significantly, in Cuba, beans and rice are called *moros y cristianos* (Moors and Christians), invoking racial allegory on the historical level.

25. Beyond their common racial ambiguity, Moraga and Cliff share an intermingling of genre in their work. Both use multiple literary forms to supplement their theoretical essays. In addition to theory, Moraga writes poetry, short stories, and plays, and Cliff writes poetry, short stories, and novels. Furthermore, while Moraga switches among Spanish, English, and Spanglish in her work, Cliff switches between English and patois.

26. See Raiskin, for example.

27. Perhaps Cliff turned to the African-American tradition for a model because the history of black women writers in the United States has gained more attention in mainstream anthologies and in American literary canons than the work of her Jamaican literary foremothers. In an interview, Cliff emphasizes the need to draw from the history of black feminism and cites Sojourner Truth and Frances Harper—U.S. women—as models that she wants to foreground ("Journey" 278).

28. According to Paula Rust's analysis of race and sexuality, "Because homosexuality represents assimilation, it is stigmatized as a 'white disease' or, at least, a 'white phenomenon.' Individuals who claim a bisexual, lesbian, or gay identity are accused of buying into white culture and thereby becoming traitors to their own racial or ethnic group" (65). Moraga addresses this dynamic in the context of Chicano culture, where Chicana lesbianism is construed as "being used by the white man" and being a traitor to Chicanos because "homosexuality is *his* disease with which he sinisterly infects Third World people" (*Loving* 114). See chapter 3 for a discussion of homosexuality in Cliff's work and Moraga's work.

29. In *Of Grammatology*, Derrida claims, "The outside bears with the inside a relationship that is, as usual, anything but simple exteriority. The meaning of the outside was always present within the inside, imprisoned outside the outside, and vice versa" (35). In "Structure, Sign, and Play," he describes the center as that which closes off the infinite play of signifiers, and decentering that center allows everything to become play (84). I would not claim that the inside equals the outside, because such a reductive paradigm misses the unequal power relations between inside and outside and the processes through which the two sides are involved. Yet decentering the center endows the system with greater flexibility.

30. Although Chesnutt does not deal with literal incest in this story, his protagonist, Mr. Ryder, initially looks for a wife within his elite society of the "Blue

Veins," a pseudofamily dedicated to the improvement of the light-skinned persons of the race (themselves).

31. For example, as I discuss later in this chapter, the relatively dark-skinned Zoe enjoys some of the same privileges as the light-skinned Clare by virtue of being her friend. Similarly, Kitty Savage and her darker daughter, Jennie, (often inadvertently) pass into privileged society as a result of Boy Savage's near-white skin and aristocratic manners. In one episode, they are allowed to stay in an all-white hotel when Boy claims descent from plantation owners (*No Telephone* 55–59).

32. Her name, light/pale savage, indicates this duality. Mordecai and Wilson suggest that Clare's name recalls *la négresse blanche* (an alienated, white woman of color) of an early francophone Caribbean novel by Mayotte Capécia (xvii).

33. Nada Elia emphasizes the ultimate breakup of Clare and Zoe's relationship as a critique of binary divisions that organize Jamaican society: "To illustrate the divisive binarism of the dominant discourse, Cliff presents us, in *Abeng* and *No Telephone to Heaven*, with a series of paired characters who are eventually pulled apart by the racial caste system that constitutes the social dynamics of Jamaica. In *Abeng* the young Clare and her friend Zoe play together but with an awareness, on Zoe's part, that their friendship cannot last" (361). In contrast, Clare, whose privilege enables her more mobile identity, wants to believe that hierarchies of the dominant society cannot split up her and Zoe's world.

34. While Clotel and her daughter both cross-dress, Brown never depicts possible erotic love without a definitely heterosexual pair. Siobhan Somerville elucidates the potential homoeroticism in Hopkins's *Contending Forces* and *Winona*, but any lesbian pairings in those novels are obscured by superficial heterosexuality. A relationship that comes close to Clare and Zoe's homosociality in Cliff's novel is the potentially homoerotic friendship between Clare and Irene in Nella Larsen's *Passing*, but these women are married and of the same class, and their contact ultimately results in Clare's destruction.

35. This friendship closely resembles that of the Creole Antoinette and the black servant's daughter, Tia, in Jean Rhys's *Wide Sargasso Sea* (1966), another marker of Cliff's literary inheritance, but Rhys's characters are unable to sustain the friendship because of race and class friction.

36. This image quite directly recalls Xarifa's story in Lydia Maria Child's "The Quadroons," Elizabeth Livermore's *Zoë*, Sappho's story in Hopkins's *Contending Forces*, and Cecilia Valdés. It also recalls the threat most feared by the mulatto women in *Clotel* and by Boucicault's *Zoe*, who kill themselves to avoid violation.

3. The Transitive Bi-

1. This effeminacy, too, is characteristic of racist stereotypes, which often emasculate black men to render them nonthreatening. Emasculation is the flip

side of the stereotypical hypermasculation of black men, and both racist stereotypes respond to the feared cross-racial attraction between white women and
black men. Judith Butler's reading of *Paris Is Burning* similarly questions the "status
of the desire to feminize black and Latino men" in performances that serve the
purpose of enacting "a visual pacification of subjects by whom white women are
imagined to be socially endangered" (*Bodies* 135). The emasculation of black men
is also often enacted in the service of white masculinity, reinforcing the supposed
superiority of white men. See also Wiegman 55.

2. I will be referring, often simultaneously, to sex, gender, sexuality, and sexual
identification/orientation, so I will clarify the distinctions I see between these
categories. I use *sex* to refer to anatomical sex, what one is born with: male, female, or hermaphroditic. *Gender* is the often fluid performance of masculinity or
femininity on the level of superficial, culturally specific cues. *Sexuality* describes
one's erotic life and sexual practices. *Sexual identification* and *orientation* describe an
individual's choices about how to manifest sexual identity and with whom to ally
oneself. Sexual identification, sexual orientation, sexual practices, gender, and
skin color are all public, fluid, nonbinary, culturally variable expressions. I would
suggest that our understanding of the biological race and sex that they signify is
also culturally variable, multiple, and fluid.

3. This multiplicity goes beyond the rare cases of hermaphrodites. Sigmund
Freud believed that all biological sex was multiple: "In every normal male or female individual, traces are found of the opposite sex" (*Three Essays* 28). He also
considered the possibility that this "bisexuality" might be particularly prevalent
in homosexuals, or "inverts," as he called them.

4. Eve Kosofsky Sedgwick suggests that biology or "nature"—sex—might be
more malleable than the culturally constructed terms of gender, given the au-
thoritative power of culture and the technological capacity to alter biological
conditions: "Increasingly it is the conjecture that a particular trait is genetically
or biologically based, *not* that it is 'only cultural,' that seems to trigger an estrus
of manipulative fantasy in the technological institutions of the culture" (43).

5. This anxiety about having misread a racial/sexual body is part of what leads
to the rape of Annie Christmas in Michelle Cliff's *Free Enterprise.* One could imagine that the immigration officer would react with vehemence if the truth of Anthony's body was revealed along with the homoeroticism beneath the officer's
misreading.

6. The adoption of a gay or lesbian identity also challenges sex and gender conventions but can potentially be interpreted as a singular or essentialist mode of
identification. Although bi- could perhaps be perceived as an alternative essence,
it cannot be mistaken for singularity.

7. Bisexuality certainly is not a new paradigm, nor is it necessarily a liberating one. One only has to turn to Freud to see that acknowledging the mobility of sexual desire and the foundation of sexuality in originary bisexuality does

not preclude teleological formulations of normative (hetero)sexual destiny. For Freud, bisexuality and the fluidity of desire are reserved for children and adults who are immature or stunted. He disregards the possibility that anything other than heterosexual identification might present alternative, mature sexualities. See Freud, *Three Essays;* and his Lecture 31, "Femininity."

8. For multiplicity in sex and gender theory, see the recent work of Bright, Butler, de Lauretis, Garber, and Irigaray, to name a few. For multiplicity in race and postcolonialism, see Anzaldúa, Davies, Mohanty, Trinh, and Young.

9. These four texts are certainly not the most frequently studied among contemporary Latina and Afro-Caribbean fiction. Perhaps their failure to achieve canonicity results in part from their overt defiance of sexual norms and the unclassifiable fluid identities they celebrate.

10. Historian Cheryl Foote suggests that Stevenson's insistence on regarding We'wha as a woman derives from Stevenson's personal deviation from prescribed gender roles as an aggressive ethnologist traveling alone in the Southwest in the 1880s and 1890s. Stevenson was sometimes called "la cacique mujer [the woman chief]"; *cacique* traditionally refers to men (Foote 127, 131). As a woman within the conservative, sometimes racist and elitist Bureau of American Ethnology, Stevenson's position was even more unusual. Curtis Hinsley notes her anomalous status within the bureau and her subversion of traditional femininity: "Merely being taken seriously as a scientist was a major accomplishment for a woman in the Bureau. Stevenson's 'pushiness' undoubtedly grew in part from intense pressures" (229n).

11. Stevenson claims that men in women's clothing were revered for their stature, their strength, and, interestingly, their great skill at doing laundry (380). Such individuals also served a spiritual function, and their duality was seen as empowering, sacred, and magical (MacKenzie 47). According to Evelyn Blackwood, Native Americans did not question an individual's decision to adopt a gender-transitive role and accepted such individuals according to the genders of their choice: "These tribes concurred in the social fiction of the cross-gender role despite the obvious physical differences, indicating the unimportance of biological sex to the gender role" (41).

12. In his historical study of Native American genders, Walter Williams rejects Blackwood's term, which is based on Euro-American gender binaries, claiming that there are really four Native American genders: masculine, feminine, *berdache,* and amazon (242). According to Williams, "Indians have options not in terms of either/or, opposite categories, but in terms of various degrees along a continuum between masculine and feminine" (88). The suggestion of a continuum positions masculine and feminine as different degrees of the same thing and indicates the existence of slippage between the two. Positioning terms on a continuum highlights their sameness over their difference and enables the possibility of erasing the difference (or the differentiation) between the two.

13. I question Blackwood's use of "opposite" here. If gender roles are as flexible as she suggests, there would be no true (binary) opposites.

14. The terms *homosexual* and *heterosexual* are an invention of the late nineteenth century. See Foucault 43; Sedgwick 2.

15. It is significant that Foucault targets the late nineteenth century as the originating moment for the separation of homosexuality and heterosexuality as discrete identities since social scientists were also theorizing a biological foundation for racial polarization at that time (43; see also chapter 1 for a description of nineteenth-century race studies). The second half of the nineteenth century was a time of intense social analysis and categorization during which both homosexuals and people of color were cordoned off into separate identities, fracturing communities into artificial homosexual-heterosexual and black-white binaries. In this way, contemporary homophobia and contemporary racism share a similar historical foundation.

16. Other historians, Blackwood included, claim that the cross-gendered tradition among Native Americans in the United States disappeared in the nineteenth century. However, Walter Williams and Paula Gunn Allen insist on a continuity between precolonial *berdache* and amazon traditions and contemporary gay and lesbian identities among Native Americans (Williams 250–51). See also Allen.

17. Chávez González uses a Darwinian approach to claim that American Indians were a weaker, less fertile, more feminine race that was saved from extinction only by contact with the stronger, more fertile, and more masculine Spaniards (99).

18. Or, as Butler argues in *Bodies that Matter,* sexual identity may be an illusion produced by those gender fables.

19. In contrast, Michael Warner claims that one cannot draw parallels or extrapolate between racial and sexual identities. He claims that the incommensurability between the reproductive logic of race and gender and the erotic logic of queerness "suggests that queerness, race, and gender can never be brought into parallel alignment" (xviii).

20. Garber discusses the popularity of bisexuality among the artistic avant-garde as part of a bohemian experimentation and rejection of convention (*Vice Versa* 19). Yet in this sense, bisexuality is once again cast as an aesthetic fad or an artistic movement rather than an expression of real sexual ambiguity. Moreover, in this text, Garber discusses white bohemians alongside African-American Harlem Renaissance writers and Mexican painter Frida Kahlo, with no self-consciousness about racial and cultural difference and their impact on sexual expression.

21. Maria Pramaggiore compares the bisexual and the mulatto as "figures of powerful and too often tragic ambiguity." She argues that because bisexual identity "stakes out a position between visibility and invisibility, a location 'between two worlds,' models of racial identity and passing are often adopted and elaborated on in order to examine bisexualities" (6). I would argue that the opposite

occurs in William Wells Brown's and William and Ellen Craft's narratives: they use gender crossing to articulate the more dangerous (at least in their context) ambiguities of racial mixture and passing.

22. The strong similarity between the two plots reinforces the notion that slave narratives adopt and revise stock formulas: passing, cross-dressing, and women throwing themselves into rivers to escape slavery. Harriet Jacobs also uses many of these stock formulas in *Incidents in the Life of a Slave Girl* (1861): while fleeing one hiding place in search of another, Linda Brent disguises herself in a sailor's uniform and blackens her face with charcoal to pass unnoticed through the town (111–13). Jacobs and the Crafts rewrite the conventional tragic mulatto scenario that ends in death. To imagine escape, they go beyond conventional notions of passing with the inclusion of cross-dressing, and Linda Brent's face blackening inverts the equation of passing with lightening. Similarly, in Harriet Beecher Stowe's *Uncle Tom's Cabin* (1852), Eliza escapes from slavery by cutting off her hair and "adapting to her slender and pretty form the articles of man's attire" (545). Despite the potential subversion of heterosexuality and (hetero)gender opposition that this cross-dressing poses for Eliza and George's marriage, the cross-dressing scene follows immediately after a passage in which George describes the ways that escape will allow him to assert his own masculinity: "the right of a man to be a man, and not a brute; the right to call the wife of his bosom his wife, and to protect her from lawless violence" (544). This juxtaposition suggests that Eliza's gender subversion is only temporary and that her subservient femininity will be restored with freedom. Finally, Pauline Hopkins's *Winona* (1902; *Magazine Novels*) describes the title character passing for a darker-skinned man, but Hopkins enacts a significant difference in her use of the stock convention. First, Winona passes for a mulatto man, not a white man. Also, she has already escaped from slavery at this point in the novel, and she dons her costume to gain admission to the prison where her white male rescuer (and future husband) is being held. This crossing thus inverts conventional power dynamics in that darker skin gains Winona greater mobility and male attire gains her access to prison, not to freedom. Although the costume paradoxically enables her first (apparently homoerotic) kiss with Maxwell, whiteness and maleness generally are not the keys to mobility in *Winona*. The fact that the white man is in prison while the racially mixed woman is free in John Brown's camp signals Hopkins's rejection of the race and gender power dynamics inherent in literary conventions. As I discuss in chapter 1, with reference to duplicated scenes in the works of Brown, Harper, and Hopkins, through intertextual repetition, these narratives are in dialogue with each other and with readers' recognition of conventional scenes. Such a dialogue enables writers to comment on tradition and to highlight that which is new in their work.

23. Both women pretend to be ill to mask their female faces (with poultices tied around their chins and green-tinted eyeglasses), to explain their small female

stature, and to excuse their inability to participate in conventional male activities (including writing, in the case of Ellen).

24. This is not the only instance of cross-gendered and cross-racial disguise in *Clotel.* Later in the novel, Clotel's daughter, Mary, helps her light-skinned lover escape from prison by lending him her clothes. In this disguise, George is allowed to leave the prison because the guards believe him to be Mary (226). It thus appears that cross-dressing is a logical, even common, method for escaping racial categories and slavery.

25. The narrative details several ironic double meanings in which people are duped by Ellen's disguise. When an officer at the customshouse in Charleston, South Carolina, asks William, "Boy, do you belong to that gentleman?" (the "gentleman" being Ellen in disguise), William responds, "'Yes sir' (which was quite correct)" (56). In another episode, a man sympathizes with the supposedly ill, supposedly white, and supposedly male Ellen and tells William to take care of his good master. William responds, "I promised that I would do so, and have ever since endeavoured to keep my pledge" (59). And when some white women fall in love with the weak "gentleman," William humorously suggests that "they fell in love with the wrong chap" (60).

26. In her reading of this narrative, Garber also interprets Ellen's cross-dressing as "a necessity, not a pleasure." Garber goes on to say that cross-dressing "was not in itself 'liberating' for the woman in disguise" (*Vested Interests* 284). However, Ellen's disguise is literally liberating, as she reaches freedom in Philadelphia in the guise of a man. And while she might not enjoy the crossover for its own sake, it does allow her many luxuries, such as first-class cars on trains, special treatment, and great respect.

27. This emphasis on the ways in which a body in motion communicates identity reflects Marshall's and Cliff's Caribbean racial definitions.

28. Marshall's association of sexual subversion with bohemian lifestyles supports Garber's point, discussed earlier, about the link between bisexuality and the artistic avant-garde (*Vice Versa* 19). This equation casts nonnormative sexuality as a temporary fad, an aesthetic experiment, rather than a viable, natural sexual alternative.

29. Merle's female lover could potentially be bisexual, since Merle says that she "collected" both men and women from all over the world, but the only relation that Marshall describes explicitly as sexual is the lesbian affair with Merle.

30. Neither Dorothy Hamer Denniston nor Joyce Pettis interrogates attitudes about homosexuality in their recent books on Marshall. In their descriptions of Merle's affair with the English woman, both eschew the sexual content (Denniston 110; Pettis 97). While Denniston acknowledges the "possible allegation that the author may be homophobic," she then skirts the issue by emphasizing the hierarchies of race, nationality, class, and age involved in the "apparent lesbian relationship" (112–13).

31. Marshall also provides an example of male-male desire in *The Chosen Place, the Timeless People* when the Anglo-American Allen discovers that he desires the Afro-Caribbean man, Vere. Allen sublimates his desire, and Vere is destroyed in a car wreck without Allen ever having an opportunity fully to express or to realize his desires. Since Allen helped Vere rebuild the car that kills him, the deadly vehicle potentially becomes an expression of Allen's (in this sense destructive) desire. Allen and Vere, like Merle and the English woman, represent both cross-racial and a same-sex pairings, but the real threat seems to lie in the subversion of heterosexual norms. Cross-racial erotics meet with much less fatal resistance. Merle and Saul's cross-racial heterosexual affair is opposed only by Saul's wife, Harriet, a financially privileged, racist Anglo-American who is ultimately defeated in her attempts to manipulate Saul. Although there is a sense of taboo surrounding mixed-race affairs, such as the adulterous affair between the white Dorothy Clough and the black Lyle Hutson, they are at least openly realized. In contrast, same-sex desire is denied, hidden, and devalued every time it surfaces.

32. Robert Corber analyzes homophobia in the Cold War period, and Katie King writes about the association of homosexuality with communism, which led to "whitelisting" people suspected of being gay during the 1950s McCarthyist panics (King 61–63). In her analysis of Lorde, King describes how race compounds both the supposed threat posed by gays in postwar America and the resultant fear instilled within gay and nonwhite communities. Marshall came of age as a writer during this time when many Americans of color feared association with homosexuality.

33. For Marshall's discussion of her emphasis on black heterosexual relations and the need for mutual support between black men and women, see her 1991 *Booklist* interview and 1992 interview with Dance.

34. This distinction between the Latina and Afro-Caribbean writers potentially supports the conventional opposition between fluid mestiza interracial dynamics and violent interracial conflict surrounding mulatta mixtures.

35. I use the term *bisexed* to signify duality in sexual identification, male and female, distinguished from *bisexual*, which signifies duality in sexual orientation, hetero- and homo-.

36. It is significant that both *Silent Dancing* and *Zami* are fictionalized autobiographies in which the authors explore the meanings of their own mixed identities with the greater flexibility of fictional personae.

37. AnaLouise Keating reaches the same conclusion in her analysis of *Sister Outsider,* claiming that Lorde "uses potentially essentializing self-definitions tactically" and demonstrates "the limitations of any fixed sociocultural inscription" (26).

38. I use *Audre* to refer to the semiautobiographical heroine in *Zami* and *Lorde* to refer to the author.

39. For example, when someone spits on Audre, Linda insists that it is just a low-class person spitting into the wind (18).

40. In contrast, Cliff, also of Afro-Caribbean descent, employs much more "postmodern" techniques in her definitions of race and sex identity. The difference between Lorde and Cliff is, at least in part, a result of the different moments in feminism in which they emerged as writers: Lorde in the 1960s and '70s, Cliff in the 1980s and '90s. It is significant that the more essentialist section of *Zami* was written and published earlier.

41. In her first description of Felicia, the first other black lesbian that Audre meets, she is described as "skinny and sharp-brown" (177). Later, meeting Afrekete, Audre wishes for a large woman with whom to share an identity, but still she does not find one: "I kept thinking she was bigger than she actually was, because there was a comfortable smell about her that I always associated with large women" (243). The large, black, Afro-Caribbean woman who most closely resembles Audre is her mother, Linda, who would rather die than identify as a dyke (15).

42. Behar claims that spiritism releases gender "from its fixity" and constructs identity as a mask that one assumes temporarily (316). As the medium adopts different personae, identity becomes transferable.

43. This acceptance mirrors some Native American communities' acceptance of cross-gendered identities and Paz's claim about the Mexican acceptance of same-sex heterogender relations.

44. Cliff also redefines the object of violation when Harry/Harriet is raped by a white man. This episode exposes white desire for rather than fear of black male bodies.

45. Nada Elia's recent reading of Harry/Harriet elides the assertion that "cyaan live split" and insists instead that "s/he ultimately represents the healthy coming together of diverse elements that would otherwise have led to fragmentation and paralysis. This is a truly subversive act, as it allows her/him to deconstruct dominant ideas of race, sex, and class without substituting new ones that would merely have the effect of creating additional divisive boundaries" (353). In contrast to this interpretation, I see Harry/Harriet's final choice as a strategic assertion of identity politics based on singular race, class, and sex affiliations, even though those affiliations contrast with his/her physical embodiment.

46. Cliff invokes the belief that the manipulation of racial genes produces a weak, sterile offspring, much like early-twentieth-century theories of racial mixing. The first time we see Clare, she is throwing up into a swimming pool. This illness is explained as a result of her British and American upbringings, which have made her ill-suited to Jamaican sun and food. At the same time, Cliff refers to Clare as "someone's overseas cousin pale from compulsive intermarriage" (*No Telephone* 21). These details imply that Clare's racial mixture, too, makes her diseased, literally pale.

4. *Millennial Mixtures*

1. Similarly, Butler's novel *Kindred* (1979) takes her heroine back and forth between the present and the antebellum South to experience firsthand the tragedies of slavery.

2. Interestingly, Haizlip also writes of dreaming about Frankenstein in her memoir about racial mixture (164).

3. This struggle is set in the late 1960s and early 1970s, during the burgeoning of postmodernism and the violent climax of the civil rights movement. Senna invokes both contexts—academic and activist—in *Caucasia*, but Birdie's struggle is firmly rooted in material conflict and racial specificity rather than in abstraction. Senna constantly reminds her readers of the street violence that forms the backdrop for this drama of identity.

4. See, for example, Jefferson.

5. Farai Chideya echoes this rhetoric in 1999, suggesting that "by the middle of the next century, race in America will be turned upside down," and "we could see a rising level of resentment among the nonwhite majority." Chideya interviews teenagers of the "Millennium Generation," who already reflect this "new" era and who have, according to a Los Angeles teen, "made America a different America" (54).

6. Jean-Luc Nancy similarly effaces history and codes mixture as a future horizon when he describes *mestizaje* as the "advent of the other," the "becoming" of something else (122–23).

7. See, for example, the chapter "Slave and Mistress" in Carby.

8. Another line of argument against multiracialists is that they are interested only in individual identity and personal self-esteem rather than in communal politics. Lisa Jones claims that multiracialists "are not calling for a biracial identity as a political movement. That identity they seek is to foster self-esteem" (quoted in Norment 110). Similarly, Ratnesar writes that multiracialists have no community but rather are adding fuel to identity politics (43).

9. Significantly, Blanca's throat was blown apart when her husband shot her. The unguarded throat is thus an illusion that masks the blown-apart beauty of prerevolutionary Cuban womanhood, again suggesting an anticommunist stance.

10. It is significant that Walker chooses Mexico as the home for the Mundo, which means "the world" in Spanish. Perhaps she is idealizing Mexico as a site where mixture and fluidity are valued, much like the historians I discuss in chapter 1.

11. The crucifix on her labia might indicate that this martyrdom is a reaction to her father's denial of her sexual pleasure.

Bibliography

Alarcón, Norma. "Conjugating Subjects: The Heteroglossia of Essence and Resistance." *An Other Tongue: Nation and Ethnicity in the Linguistic Borderlands*. Ed. Alfred Arteaga. Durham: Duke UP, 1994.

Alexander, Elizabeth. "'Coming Out Blackened and Whole': Fragmentation and Reintegration in Audre Lorde's *Zami* and *The Cancer Journals*." *American Literary History* 6 (1994): 695–715.

Alexander, M. Jacqui, and Chandra Talpade Mohanty, eds. *Feminist Genealogies: Colonial Legacies, Democratic Futures*. New York: Routledge, 1997.

Allen, Paula Gunn. *The Sacred Hoop: Recovering the Feminine in American Indian Traditions*. Boston: Beacon, 1986.

Allman, Karen Maeda. "(Un)Natural Boundaries: Mixed Race, Gender, and Sexuality." *The Multiracial Experience: Racial Borders as the New Frontier*. Ed. Maria P. P. Root. Thousand Oaks: Sage, 1996.

Andrews, William L. "Miscegenation in the Late Nineteenth-Century American Novel." *Southern Humanities Review* 13 (1979): 13–24.

Anzaldúa, Gloria. *Borderlands/La Frontera: The New Mestiza*. San Francisco: aunt lute, 1987.

———. "Coming into Play: An Interview with Gloria Anzaldúa." Interview with Ann E. Reuman. *MELUS* 25.2 (summer 2000): 3–45.

———. *Interviews/Entrevistas*. Ed. AnaLouise Keating. New York: Routledge, 2000.

———, ed. *Making Face, Making Soul = Haciendo Caras: Creative and Critical Perspectives by Feminists of Color*. San Francisco: aunt lute, 1990.

———. "Writing, Politics, and *las Lesberadas: Platicando con* Gloria Anzaldúa." Interview with AnaLouise Keating. *Frontiers* 14 (1993): 105–30.

Anzaldúa, Gloria, and Cherríe Moraga, eds. *This Bridge Called My Back: Writings by Radical Women of Color*. New York: Kitchen Table, 1981.

Aparicio, Frances R. "On Sub-versive Signifiers: U.S. Latina/o Writers Tropicalize English." *American Literature* 66 (1994): 795–801.

Appiah, Kwame Anthony. *In My Father's House.* New York: Oxford UP, 1992.

————. "Racism." *Anatomy of Racism.* Ed. David Theo Goldberg. Minneapolis: U of Minnesota P, 1990.

Applegate, Frank G. *Native Tales of New Mexico.* Philadelphia: Lippincott, 1932.

"Are the Children of Mixed Marriages Black or White?" *Jet* May 21, 1990: 52–54.

Arny, W. F. M. *Indian Agent in New Mexico: The Journal of Special Agent W. F. M. Arny, 1870.* Ed. Lawrence R. Murphy. Santa Fe: Stagecoach, 1967.

Arteaga, Alfred, ed. *An Other Tongue: Nation and Ethnicity in the Linguistic Borderlands.* Durham: Duke UP, 1994.

Ashcroft, Bill, Gareth Griffiths, and Helen Tiffin. *The Empire Writes Back: Theory and Practice in Post-Colonial Literatures.* New York: Routledge, 1989.

Avotcja. "What They See Is What They Get." *Compañeras: Latina Lesbians.* Ed. Juanita Ramos. New York: Routledge, 1994.

Baker, Houston, Jr. *Blues, Ideology, and Afro-American Literature.* Chicago: U of Chicago P, 1984.

————. *Workings of the Spirit: The Poetics of Afro-American Women's Writing.* Chicago: U of Chicago P, 1991.

Barnard, Ian. "Gloria Anzaldúa's Queer Mestisaje." *MELUS* 22.1 (spring 1997): 35–53.

Beckles, Hilary McD. "Black over White: The 'Poor-White' Problem in Barbados Slave Society." *After the Crossing: Immigrants and Minorities in Caribbean Creole Society.* Ed. Howard Johnson. London: Cass, 1988.

Begley, Sharon, and Esther Pan. "Jefferson's DNA Trail." *Newsweek* November 9, 1998: 66.

Behar, Ruth. *Translated Woman: Crossing the Border with Esperanza's Story.* Boston: Beacon, 1993.

————. "Writing in My Father's Name: A Diary of *Translated Woman's* First Year." *Women Writing Culture.* Ed. Ruth Behar and Deborah A. Gordon. Berkeley: U of California P, 1995.

Behar, Ruth, and Deborah A. Gordon, eds. *Women Writing Culture.* Berkeley: U of California P, 1995.

Benitez-Rojo, Antonio. "The Polyrhythm Paradigm: The Caribbean and the Postmodern Era." *Race, Discourse, and the Origin of the Americas.* Ed. Vera Lawrence Hyatt and Rex Nettleford. Washington: Smithsonian, 1995.

————. *The Repeating Island.* Trans. James Maraniss. Durham: Duke UP, 1992.

Bentley, Nancy. "White Slaves: The Mulatto Hero in Antebellum Fiction." *American Literature* 65.3 (1993): 501–21.

Berlant, Lauren. "The Face of America and the State of Emergency." *Disciplinarity and Dissent in Cultural Studies.* Ed. Cary Nelson and Dilip Parameshwar Gaonkar. New York: Routledge, 1996.

Berzon, Judith. *Neither White nor Black: The Mulatto Character in American Fiction.* New York: New York UP, 1978.

Bhabha, Homi. "Signs Taken for Wonders: Questions of Ambivalence and Authority under a Tree outside Delhi, May 1817." *Critical Inquiry* 12 (1985): 144–65.

"Bisexual Chic: Anyone Goes." *Newsweek* May 27, 1974: 90.

"Black America and Tiger's Dilemma." *Ebony* July 1997: 28–34.

Blackwood, Evelyn. "Sexuality and Gender in Certain Native American Tribes: The Case of Cross-Gender Females." *Signs* 10 (1984): 27–42.

Blom, Gerdien. "Divine Individuals, Cultural Identities: Post-Identitarian Representations and Two Chicana/o Texts." *Thamyris* 4.2 (autumn 1997): 295–324.

Borah, Woodrow. "Race and Class in Mexico." *Pacific Historical Review* 23 (1954): 331–42.

Boucicault, Dion. *Zoe, the Octoroon.* 1859. Upper Saddle River: Literature House, 1970.

Boulter, Amanda. "Polymorphous Futures: Octavia E. Butler's *Xenogenesis* Trilogy." *American Bodies: Cultural Histories of the Physique.* Ed. Tim Armstrong. Sheffield: Sheffield Academic, 1996.

Braxton, Joanne M., and Andrée Nicola McLaughlin, eds. *Wild Women in the Whirlwind: Afra-American Culture and the Contemporary Literary Renaissance.* New Brunswick: Rutgers UP, 1990.

Bright, Susie. *Susie Bright's Sexual Reality: A Virtual Sex World Reader.* Pittsburgh: Cleis, 1992.

Brooks, Kristina. "Mammies, Bucks, and Wenches: Minstrelsy, Racial Pornography, and Racial Politics in Pauline Hopkins's *Hagar's Daughter.*" *The Unruly Voice: Rediscovering Pauline Elizabeth Hopkins.* Ed. John Cullen Gruesser. Urbana: U of Illinois P, 1996.

Brown, Aggrey. *Color, Class, and Politics in Jamaica.* New Brunswick: Transaction, 1979.

Brown, Lois Lamphere. "'To Allow No Tragic End': Defensive Postures in Pauline Hopkins's *Contending Forces.*" *The Unruly Voice: Rediscovering Pauline Elizabeth Hopkins.* Ed. John Cullen Gruesser. Urbana: U of Illinois P, 1996.

Brown, William Wells. *Clotel; or, The President's Daughter.* 1853. New York: Arno, 1969.

Brundage, Karla. "Passing." *MultiAmerica: Essays on Cultural War and Cultural Peace.* New York: Penguin, 1997.

Bryan, Patrick. *The Jamaican People, 1880–1902: Race, Class, and Social Control.* London: Macmillan, 1991.

Bush, Barbara. *Slave Women in Caribbean Society, 1650–1838.* London: Currey, 1990.

Butler, Judith. *Bodies That Matter: On the Discursive Limits of "Sex."* New York: Routledge, 1993.

———. *Gender Trouble: Feminism and the Subversion of Identity.* New York: Routledge, 1990.

Butler, Octavia E. *Kindred.* 1979. Boston: Beacon, 1988.

———. *Wild Seed.* 1980. New York: Warner, 1988.

Byrd, William. *The Prose Works of William Byrd of Westover: Narratives of a Colonial Virginian.* Ed. Louis B. Wright. Cambridge: Belknap-Harvard UP, 1966.

Cabeza de Baca Gilbert, Fabiola. *We Fed Them Cactus.* Albuquerque: U of New Mexico P, 1954.

Cable, George Washington. *The Silent South; Together with the Freedman's Case in Equity and the Convict Lease System.* 1885. New York: Scribner's, 1907.

Calderón, Hector, and José David Saldívar, eds. *Criticism in the Borderlands: Studies in Chicano Literature, Culture, and Ideology.* Durham: Duke UP, 1991.

Campbell, John. "Negro-Mania." *DeBow's Review* 12 (1852): 507–24.

Carby, Hazel V. *Reconstructing Womanhood.* New York: Oxford UP, 1987.

Carroll, Traci. "Invisible Sissy: The Politics of Masculinity in African American Bisexual Narrative." *RePresenting Bisexualities: Subjects and Cultures of Fluid Desire.* Ed. Donald E. Hall and Maria Pramaggiore. New York: New York UP, 1996.

Castañeda, Antonia I. "Presidarias y Pobladoras: The Journey North and Life in Frontier California." *Chicana Critical Issues.* Ed. Norma Alarcón et al. Berkeley: Third Woman, 1993.

Castillo, Ana. *Massacre of the Dreamers: Essays on Xicanisma.* Albuquerque: U of New Mexico P, 1994.

———. *Sapogonia.* New York: Doubleday, 1990.

Chabram-Dernersesian, Angie. "'Chicana! Rican? No, Chicana-Riqueña!' Refashioning the Transnational Connection." *Multiculturalism: A Critical Reader.* Ed. David Theo Goldberg. Cambridge: Blackwell, 1994.

Chávez González, Rodrigo A. *El mestizaje y su influencia social en América.* Guayaquil: Imprenta i Talleres Municipales, 1937.

Chesnutt, Charles. *The House behind the Cedars.* 1900. Athens: U of Georgia P, 2000.

———. *The Wife of His Youth, and Other Stories of the Color Line.* 1899. Ridgewood: Gregg, 1967.

Chideya, Farai. "Shades of the Future: Will Race Provide the Midcentury Crisis?" *Time* February 1, 1999: 54.

Child, Lydia Maria. *The Oasis.* Boston: Bacon, 1834.

———. "The Quadroons." *Fact and Fiction: A Collection of Stories.* New York: Frances, 1846.

Christian, Barbara. *Black Feminist Criticism: Perspectives on Black Women Writers.* New York: Pergamon, 1985.

———. "The Race for Theory." *The Nature and Context of Minority Discourse.* Ed. Abdul JanMohamed and David Lloyd. New York: Oxford UP, 1991.

———. "A Rough Terrain: The Case of Shaping an Anthology of Caribbean Women Writers." *The Ethnic Canon: Histories, Institutions, and Interventions.* Ed. David Palumbo-Liu. Minneapolis: U of Minnesota P, 1995.

Cisneros, Sandra. *Woman Hollering Creek.* New York: Vintage, 1991.

Clayton, Jay. *The Pleasures of Babel: Contemporary American Literature and Theory.* New York: Oxford UP, 1993.

Cliff, Michelle. *Abeng*. 1984. New York: Plume, 1995.

———. *Bodies of Water*. New York: Dutton, 1990.

———. *Free Enterprise*. 1993. New York: Plume, 1994.

———. "Journey into Speech—A Writer between Two Worlds: An Interview with Michelle Cliff." Interview with Opal Palmer Adisa. *African American Review* 28 (1994): 273–81.

———. *The Land of Look Behind*. Ithaca: Firebrand, 1985.

———. *No Telephone to Heaven*. 1987. New York: Vintage, 1989.

———. *The Store of a Million Items*. New York: Mariner, 1998.

Clifford, James, and George Marcus, eds. *Writing Culture: The Poetics and Politics of Ethnography*. Berkeley: U of California P, 1986.

Combahee River Collective. "A Black Feminist Statement." *This Bridge Called My Back: Writings by Radical Women of Color*. Ed. Cherríe Moraga and Gloria Anzaldúa. New York: Kitchen Table, 1981.

Commager, Henry Steele. *The American Mind: An Interpretation of American Thought and Character since the 1880s*. New Haven: Yale UP, 1950.

Conniff, Michael L., and Thomas J. Davis. *Africans in the Americas: A History of the Black Diaspora*. New York: St. Martin's, 1994.

Cope, R. Douglas. *The Limits of Racial Domination: Plebeian Society in Colonial Mexico City, 1660–1720*. Madison: U of Wisconsin P, 1994.

Corber, Robert. *In the Name of National Security: Hitchcock, Homophobia, and the Political Construction of Gender in Postwar America*. Durham: Duke UP, 1993.

Corsello, Andrew. "Tyra without Hang-Ups." *GQ* February 1996: 126–29.

Cose, Ellis. "Census and the Complex Issue of Race." *Society* 34.6 (September–October 1997): 9–13.

Cotera, Martha P. *Diosa y Hembra: The History and Heritage of Chicanas in the United States*. Austin: Information Systems Development, 1976.

Craft, William, and Ellen Craft. *Running a Thousand Miles for Freedom*. 1860. New York: Arno, 1969.

Crèvecoeur, Hector St. Jean de. *Letters from an American Farmer*. 1782. New York: Dutton, 1957.

Croly, David Goodman. *Miscegenation*. New York: Dexter, 1864.

Crouch, Stanley. "Race Is Over." *New York Times Magazine* September 29, 1996: 170–71.

Cudjoe, Selwyn R., ed. *Caribbean Women Writers*. Wellesley: Calaloux, 1990.

Davies, Carole Boyce. *Black Women, Writing, and Identity: Migrations of the Subject*. New York: Routledge, 1994.

Davies, Carole Boyce, and Elaine Savory Fido, eds. *Out of the Kumbla: Caribbean Women and Literature*. Trenton: Africa World, 1990.

Davis, Thadious. *Faulkner's "Negro": Art and the Southern Context*. Baton Rouge: Louisiana State UP, 1983.

Davis, William W. H. *El Gringo; or, New Mexico and Her People.* 1857. New York: Arno, 1973.

De la Cruz, Sor Juana Inés. *Vida y obra de Sor Juana Inés de la Cruz, y carta a Sor Filotea.* Ed. F. García Chávez. Mexico City: Editores Mexicanos Unidos, 1975.

De Lauretis, Teresa. *The Practice of Love: Lesbian Sexuality and Perverse Desire.* Bloomington: Indiana UP, 1994.

———. "Sexual Indifference and Lesbian Representation." *Theatre Journal* 40 (1988): 155–77.

Denison, Mary A. *Old Hepsy.* New York: Burdick, 1858.

Denniston, Dorothy Hamer. *The Fiction of Paule Marshall: Reconstructions of History, Culture, and Gender.* Knoxville: U of Tennessee P, 1995.

Derrida, Jacques. *Of Grammatology.* Trans. Gayatri Chakravorty Spivak. Baltimore: Johns Hopkins UP, 1976.

———. "Structure, Sign, and Play in the Discourse of the Human Sciences." Trans. Alan Bass. *Critical Theory since 1965.* Ed. Hazard Adams and Leroy Searle. Tallahassee: Florida State UP, 1986.

Deutsch, Sarah. *No Separate Refuge: Culture, Class, and Gender in the American Southwest, 1880–1940.* New York: Oxford UP, 1987.

Dixon, Thomas. *The Clansman: An Historical Romance of the Ku Klux Klan.* 1905. Lexington: U of Kentucky P, 1970.

Dobie, J. Frank, ed. *Texas and Southwestern Lore.* Austin: Texas Folk-Lore Society, 1927.

DuBois, W. E .B. *The Souls of Black Folk.* 1903. New York: Signet, 1982.

Eagleton, Mary, ed. *Feminist Literary Theory: A Reader.* 2nd ed. Oxford: Blackwell, 1996.

Eddings, Jerelyn. "Counting a 'New' Type of American: The Dicey Politics of Creating a 'Multiracial' Category in the Census." *U.S. News and World Report* July 14, 1997: 22–23.

Edmondson, Belinda. "Race, Privilege, and the Politics of (Re)Writing History: An Analysis of the Novels of Michelle Cliff." *Callaloo* 16.1 (1993): 180–91.

Edwards, Tamala M. "Family Reunion." *Time* November 23, 1998: 85–86.

Elder, Arlene. *The "Hindered Hand": Cultural Implications of Early African-American Fiction.* Westport: Greenwood, 1978.

Elia, Nada. "'A Man Who Wants to Be a Woman': Queerness as/and Healing Practices in Michelle Cliff's *No Telephone to Heaven.*" *Callaloo* 23.1 (2000): 352–65.

Espacios de Mestizaje Cultural. III Anuario Conmemorativo del V Centenario de la Llegada de España a América. Mexico City: División de Ciencias Sociales y Humanidades y Departamento de Humanidades Area de Historia de México, Universidad Autónoma Metropolitana Unidad Azcapotzalco, 1991.

Esquivel, Laura. *The Law of Love.* New York: Crown, 1996.

Faulkner, William. *Absalom, Absalom!* New York: Vintage, 1990.

Fauset, Jessie Redmon. *Plum Bun: A Novel without a Moral.* 1929. London: Pandora, 1985.

Fehrenbach, T. R. *Fire and Blood: A History of Mexico.* New York: Da Capo, 1995.

Fergusson, Erna. *New Mexico: A Pageant of Three Peoples.* 2nd ed. Albuquerque: U of New Mexico P, 1973.

————. "Race Relations." 1949 lecture, from her collected papers. Center for Southwest Research, University of New Mexico Libraries.

————. "What Are New Mexicans?" 1948 lecture, from her collected papers. Center for Southwest Research, University of New Mexico Libraries.

Fernández, Carlos A. "Government Classification of Multiracial/Multiethnic People." *The Multiracial Experience: Racial Borders as the New Frontier.* Ed. Maria P. P. Root. Thousand Oaks: Sage, 1996.

Fernández Olmos, Margarita. "Desde una perspective femenina: La cuentística de Rosario Ferré y Ana Lydia Vega." *Homines* 8.2 (1984): 303–11.

————. "Sex, Color, and Class in Contemporary Puerto Rican Women Authors." *Heresies* 15 (1982): 46–47.

Ferré, Rosario. *Eccentric Neighborhoods.* New York: Farrar, 1998.

————. *The House on the Lagoon.* New York: Farrar, 1995.

————. *Papeles de Pandora: The Youngest Doll.* Trans. Rosario Ferré. Lincoln: U of Nebraska P, 1991.

Firestein, Beth A., ed. *Bisexuality: The Psychology and Politics of an Invisible Minority.* Thousand Oaks: Sage, 1996.

Foote, Cheryl J. *Women of the New Mexico Frontier, 1846–1912.* Niwot: UP of Colorado, 1990.

Forbes, Jack D. "Black Pioneers: The Spanish-Speaking Afroamericans of the Southwest." *Historical Themes and Identity: Mestizaje and Labels.* Ed. Antoinette Sedillo López. New York: Garland, 1995.

"Foreign Affairs." *Designing Women.* Episode 423. Lifetime Television.

Foucault, Michel. *The History of Sexuality, Volume I: An Introduction.* Trans. Robert Hurley. New York: Vintage, 1990.

Fox-Genovese, Elizabeth. "Slavery, Race, and the Figure of the Tragic Mulatta; or, The Ghost of Southern History in the Writing of African American Women." *Haunted Bodies: Gender and Southern Texts.* Ed. Anne Goodwyn Jones and Susan V. Donalson. Charlottesville: U of Virginia P, 1997.

Freedman, Diane P. "Writing in the Borderlands: The Poetic Prose of Gloria Anzaldúa and Susan Griffin." *Constructing and Reconstructing Gender: The Links among Communication, Language, and Gender.* Ed. Linda A. M. Perry et al. Albany: SUNY, 1992.

Freud, Sigmund. "Femininity." *New Introductory Lectures on Psychoanalysis.* Trans. and ed. James Strachey. New York: Norton, 1965.

————. *Three Essays on the Theory of Sexuality.* Trans. James Strachey. New York: Avon, 1962.

Fuchs, Lawrence H. "What We Should Count and Why." *Society* 34.6 (September–October 1997): 24–27.

Fusco, Coco. *English Is Broken Here: Notes on Cultural Fusion in the Americas.* New York: New Press, 1995.

Gaines, James R. "From the Managing Editor." *Time* December 2, 1993: 2.

Galán, Nely. "Latin Class." *Vogue* August 1997: 166–72.

Garber, Marjorie. *Vested Interests: Cross-Dressing and Cultural Anxiety.* New York: Harper Perennial, 1992.

———. *Vice Versa: Bisexuality and the Eroticism of Everyday Life.* New York: Simon, 1995.

García, Cristina. *The Agüero Sisters.* New York: Knopf, 1997.

———. *Dreaming in Cuban.* New York: Ballantine, 1992.

Gates, Henry Louis, Jr. "The Black Man's Burden." *Fear of a Queer Planet: Queer Politics and Social Theory.* Ed. Michael Warner. Minneapolis: U of Minnesota P, 1993.

———. *Race, Writing, and Difference.* Chicago: U of Chicago P, 1986.

———, ed. *Reading Black, Reading Feminist: A Critical Anthology.* New York: Meridian, 1990.

———. *The Signifying Monkey.* New York: Oxford UP, 1988.

Gillespie, Nick. "Blurred Vision: Seeing beyond Government Racial Categories." *Reason* 29 (July 1997): 7–8.

Gillman, Susan. "The Mulatto, Tragic or Triumphant? The Nineteenth-Century American Race Melodrama." *The Culture of Sentiment: Race, Gender, and Sentimentality in Nineteenth-Century America.* Ed. Shirley Samuels. New York: Oxford UP, 1992.

Glantz, Margo, ed. *La Malinche, sus padres y sus hijos.* Mexico City: Facultad de Filosofía y Letras, Universidad Nacional Autónoma de México, 1994.

Glissant, Edouard. *Caribbean Discourse: Selected Essays.* Trans. J. Michael Dash. Charlottesville: UP of Virginia, 1989.

———. "Creolization in the Making of the Americas." *Race, Discourse, and the Origin of the Americas.* Ed. Vera Lawrence Hyatt and Rex Nettleford. Washington: Smithsonian, 1995.

Goldberg, David Theo. *Racial Subjects: Writing on Race in America.* New York: Routledge, 1997.

Goldie, Terry. "Introduction: Queerly Postcolonial." *Ariel* 30.2 (April 1999): 8–26.

González, Aníbal. "Ana Lydia Pluravega: Unidad y multiplicidad caribeñas en la obra de Ana Lydia Vega." *Revista Iberoamericana* 59 (1993): 289–300.

González Mireles, Jovita. *Dew on the Thorn.* Ed. José Limón. Houston: Arte Público, 1997.

———. "Folk-Lore of the Texas-Mexican Vaquero." *Texas and Southwestern Lore.* Ed. J. Frank Dobie. Austin: Texas Folk-Lore Society, 1927.

———. *Jovita González Mireles Manuscripts,* ca. 1925–80. Benson Latin American Collection, General Libraries, University of Texas at Austin.

González, Patricia Elena, and Eliana Ortega, eds. *La sartén por el mango: Encuentro de escritores latinoamericanas*. Río Piedras: Ediciones Huracán, 1984.

Grant, Percy Stickney. "American Ideals and Race Mixture." *North American Review* 195 (1912): 513–25.

Grewal, Inderpal. "Autobiographic Subjects and Diasporic Locations: *Meatless Days* and *Borderlands*." *Scattered Hegemonies: Postmodernity and Transnational Feminist Practices*. Ed. Inderpal Grewal and Caren Kaplan. Minneapolis: U of Minnesota P, 1994.

Grewal, Inderpal, and Caren Kaplan, eds. *Scattered Hegemonies: Postmodernity and Transnational Feminist Practices*. Minneapolis: U of Minnesota P, 1994.

Griego y Maestas, José, and Rudolfo A. Anaya. *Cuentos: Tales from the Hispanic Southwest*. Santa Fe: Museum of New Mexico, 1980.

Grossman, Judith. "Constructing and Reconstructing: *The House on the Lagoon*, by Rosario Ferré." *Women's Review of Books* 13.5 (1996): 5.

Gruesser, John Cullen, ed. *The Unruly Voice: Rediscovering Pauline Elizabeth Hopkins*. Urbana: U of Illinois P, 1996.

Haizlip, Shirlee Taylor. "Passing." *American Heritage* 46 (February–March 1995): 46–54.

———. *The Sweeter the Juice: A Family Memoir in Black and White*. New York: Touchstone, 1994.

Hall, Carla. "You Gotta Be Cool, You Gotta Be Strong, You Gotta Be Wiser." *Glamour* June 1995: 149.

Hall, Christine C. Iijima. "2001: A Race Odyssey." *The Multiracial Experience: Racial Borders as the New Frontier*. Ed. Maria P. P. Root. Thousand Oaks: Sage, 1996.

Hall, Donald E., and Maria Pramaggiore, eds. *RePresenting Bisexualities: Subjects and Cultures of Fluid Desire*. New York: New York UP, 1996.

Hall, Lynda. "Writing Selves Home at the Crossroads: Anzaldúa and Chrystos (Re)Configure Lesbian Bodies." *Ariel* 30.2 (April 1999): 99–117.

Haraway, Donna. *Modest_Witness@Second_Millennium. Female Man©_Meets OncoMouse: Feminism and Technoscience*. New York: Routledge, 1997.

Harper, Frances. *Iola Leroy*. 1893. New York: Oxford UP, 1988.

Harris, Wilson. *The Womb of Space: The Cross-Cultural Imagination*. Westport: Greenwood, 1983.

Henderson, Mae Gwendolyn. "Speaking in Tongues: Dialogics, Dialectics, and the Black Women Writers' Literary Tradition." *Feminists Theorize the Political*. Ed. Judith Butler and Joan W. Scott. New York: Routledge, 1992.

Henry, William A., III. "Beyond the Melting Pot." *Time* April 9, 1990: 28–31.

———. "The Politics of Separation." *Time* December 2, 1993: 73–75.

Herndl, Diane Price. "Miscegen(r)ation or Mestiza Discourse? Feminist and Racial Politics in *Ramona* and *Iola Leroy*." *Beyond the Binary: Reconstructing Cultural Identity in a Multicultural Context*. New Brunswick: Rutgers UP, 1999.

Herrera-Sobek, María, ed. *Reconstructing a Chicano/a Literary Heritage: Hispanic Colonial Literature of the Southwest.* Tucson: U of Arizona P, 1993.

Herrera-Sobek, María, and Helena María Viramontes, eds. *Chicana Creativity and Criticism: New Frontiers in American Literature.* Albuquerque: U of New Mexico P, 1996.

Hinojosa, Rolando. *The Valley.* Ypsilanti: Bilingual, 1983.

Hinsley, Curtis M., Jr. *Savages and Scientists: The Smithsonian Institution and the Development of American Anthropology, 1846–1910.* Washington: Smithsonian, 1981.

Holloway, Karla F. C. *Moorings and Metaphors: Figures of Culture and Gender in Black Women's Literature.* New Brunswick: Rutgers UP, 1992.

hooks, bell. *Yearning: Race, Gender, and Cultural Politics.* Boston: South End, 1990.

Hopkins, Pauline E. *Contending Forces: A Romance Illustrative of Negro Life North and South.* 1900. New York: Oxford UP, 1988.

————. *The Magazine Novels of Pauline Hopkins.* New York: Oxford UP, 1988.

Horno-Delgado, Asunción, et al., eds. *Breaking Boundaries: Latina Writing and Cultural Readings.* Amherst: U of Massachusetts P, 1989.

Hughes, Langston. *Mulatto: A Tragedy of the Deep South. Five Plays by Langston Hughes.* Ed. Webster Smalley. 1931. Bloomington: Indiana UP, 1968.

Iglesias, César Andreu, ed. *Memoirs of Bernardo Vega.* Trans. Juan Flores. New York: Monthly Review, 1984.

Instituto Panamericano de Geografía e Historia. *El mestizaje en la historia de Ibero-America.* Mexico City: Editorial Cultural, 1961.

Irigaray, Luce. *Sexes and Genealogies.* Trans. Gillian C. Gill. New York: Columbia UP, 1993.

————. *This Sex Which Is Not One.* Trans. Catherine Porter. Ithaca: Cornell UP, 1985.

Jackson, Helen Hunt. *Ramona, a Story.* 1887. Boston: Little, 1932.

Jacobs, Harriet A. *Incidents in the Life of a Slave Girl, Written by Herself.* Cambridge: Harvard UP, 1987.

Jácome, Francine. "Las identidades étnicas y nacionales en el Caribe." *Diversidad cultural y construcción de identidades.* Ed. Daniel Mato, et al. Caracas: Fondo Editorial Tropykos, 1993.

James, C. L. R. *The C. L. R. James Reader.* Ed. Anna Grimshaw. Oxford: Blackwell, 1992.

Jefferson, Margo. "Seeing Race as a Costume That Everyone Wears." *New York Times* May 4, 1998: E2.

Jensen, Joan M., and Darlis A. Miller. *New Mexico Women: Intercultural Perspectives.* Albuquerque: U of New Mexico P, 1986.

Johnson, James Weldon. *The Autobiography of an Ex-Coloured Man.* 1912. New York: Knopf, 1979.

Jordan, June. "Naming Her Destiny! June Jordan Speaks on Bisexuality." Interview with Zélie Pollon. *Deneuve* 4 (1994): 27–28, 47.

—————. *Technical Difficulties: African-American Notes on the State of the Union.* New York: Pantheon, 1992.

Joyce, Joyce A. "The Black Canon: Reconstructing Black American Literary Criticism." *New Literary History* 18 (1987): 335–84.

Kader, Cheryl. "'The Very House of Difference': *Zami,* Audre Lorde's Lesbian-Centered Text." *Critical Essays: Gay and Lesbian Writers of Color.* Ed. Emmanuel S. Nelson. New York: Harrington Park, 1993.

Kassanoff, Jennie. "'Fate Has Linked Us Together': Blood, Gender, and the Politics of Representation in Pauline Hopkins's *Of One Blood.*" *The Unruly Voice: Rediscovering Pauline Elizabeth Hopkins.* Ed. John Cullen Gruesser. Urbana: U of Illinois P, 1996.

Keating, AnaLouise. "(De)Centering the Margins? Identity Politics and Tactical (Re)Naming." *Other Sisterhoods: Literary Theory and U.S. Women of Color.* Ed. Sandra Kumamoto Stanley. Urbana: U of Illinois P, 1998.

Kich, George Kitahara. "In the Margins of Sex and Race: Difference, Marginality, and Flexibility." *The Multiracial Experience: Racial Borders as the New Frontier.* Ed. Maria P. P. Root. Thousand Oaks: Sage, 1996.

King, Katie. "Audre Lorde's Lacquered Layerings: The Lesbian Bar as a Site of Literary Production." *New Lesbian Criticism: Literary and Cultural Readings.* Ed. Sally Munt. New York: Columbia UP, 1992.

Kingston, Maxine Hong. *The Woman Warrior.* New York: Vintage, 1977.

Knight, Franklin W. *The Caribbean.* 2nd ed. New York: Oxford UP, 1990.

Kurlansky, Mark. *A Continent of Islands: Searching for the Caribbean Destiny.* Reading: Addison, 1992.

Kutzinski, Vera. *Sugar's Secrets: Race and the Erotics of Cuban Nationalism.* Charlottesville: UP of Virginia, 1993.

Lamming, George. *The Pleasures of Exile.* 1960. Ann Arbor: U of Michigan P, 1992.

Larsen, Nella. *Quicksand and Passing.* New Brunswick: Rutgers UP, 1994.

Lawrence, Leota S. "Women in Caribbean Literature: The African Presence." *Phylon* 44 (1983): 1–11.

Leland, John, and Gregory Beals. "In Living Colors." *Newsweek* May 5, 1997: 58–60.

Levins Morales, Aurora, and Rosario Morales. *Getting Home Alive.* Ithaca: Firebrand, 1986.

Lewis, R. W. B. *The American Adam: Innocence, Tragedy, and Tradition in the Nineteenth Century.* Chicago: U of Chicago P, 1955.

Light, Ivan, and Cathie Lee. "And Just Who Do You Think You Aren't?" *Society* 34.6 (September–October 1997): 28–30.

Limón, José E. "*Agringado* Joking in Texas Mexican Society." *Perspectives in Mexican American Studies* 1 (1988): 109–30.

—————. *Dancing with the Devil: Society and Cultural Poetics in Mexican-American South Texas.* Madison: U of Wisconsin P, 1994.

Lionnet, Françoise. "Of Mangoes and Maroons: Language, History, and the Multicultural Subject of Michelle Cliff's *Abeng*." *De/Colonizing the Subject: The Politics of Gender in Women's Autobiography*. Eds. Sidonie Smith and Julia Watson. Minneapolis: U of Minnesota P, 1992.

Lipschutz, Alejandro. *El problema racial en la conquista de America, y el mestizaje*. Santiago de Chile: Editorial Andres Bello, 1967.

Livermore, Elizabeth. *Zoë; or, The Quadroon's Triumph: A Tale for the Times*. 2 vols. Cincinnati: Truman, 1855.

Liz. "The Difference between Black and Blanco." *Compañeras: Latina Lesbians*. Ed. Juanita Ramos. New York: Routledge, 1994.

López, Antoinette Sedillo. *Historical Themes and Identity: Mestizaje and Labels*. New York: Garland, 1995.

López-Medina, Sylvia. *Cantora*. Albuquerque: U of New Mexico P, 1992.

Lorde, Audre. *The Black Unicorn*. New York: Norton, 1978.

———. "Tar Beach." *Conditions* 5 (1979): 34–47.

———. *Zami: A New Spelling of My Name*. Freedom: Crossing, 1982.

Luckhurst, Roger. "'Horror and Beauty in Rare Combination': The Miscegenate Fictions of Octavia Butler." *Women: A Cultural Review* 7.1 (1996): 28–38.

Luis, William. *Literary Bondage: Slavery in Cuban Narrative*. Austin: U of Texas P, 1990.

MacKenzie, Gordene Olga. *Transgender Nation*. Bowling Green: Bowling Green State U Popular P, 1994.

Magoffin, Susan. *Down the Santa Fe Trail and into Mexico: The Diary of Susan Shelby Magoffin, 1846–1847*. Ed. Stella M. Drumm. New Haven: Yale UP, 1926.

Maingot, Anthony P. "Race, Color, and Class in the Caribbean." *Americas: New Interpretive Essays*. Ed. Alfred Stepan. New York: Oxford UP, 1992.

Marcus, Lisa. "'Of One Blood': Reimagining Genealogy in Pauline Hopkins's *Contending Forces*." *Speaking the Other Self: American Women Writers*. Ed. Jeanne Campbell Reesman. Athens: U of Georgia P, 1997.

Marriott, Michel. "Multiracial Americans Ready to Claim Their Own Identity." *New York Times* July 20, 1996: 1, 7.

Marshall, C. E. "The Birth of the Mestizo in New Spain." *Hispanic American Historical Review* 19 (1939): 161–84.

Marshall, Paule. "The Booklist Interview." *Booklist* October 15, 1991: 410–11.

———. *Brown Girl, Brownstones*. 1959. New York: Feminist, 1981.

———. *The Chosen Place, the Timeless People*. 1969. New York: Vintage, 1992.

———. *Daughters*. New York: Plume, 1992.

———. *The Fisher King*. New York: Scribner, 2000.

———. Interview with Daryl Cumber Dance. *Southern Review* 28 (1992): 1–20.

———. *Praisesong for the Widow*. New York: Plume, 1983.

Martí, José. *Nuestra América*. Havana: Editorial Trópico, 1939.

Martínez-Fernández, Luis. *Torn between Empires: Economy, Society, and Patterns of Political Thought in the Hispanic Caribbean, 1840–1878*. Athens: U of Georgia P, 1994.

Martínez, Rubén. "Technicolor." *Half and Half: Writers on Growing up Biracial and Bi-cultural*. Ed. Claudine Chiawei O'Hearn. New York: Pantheon, 1998.

Matthiessen, F. O. *American Renaissance: Art and Expression in the Age of Emerson and Whitman*. New York: Oxford UP, 1941.

Mato, Daniel, et al. *Diversidad cultural y construcción de identidades: Estudios sobre Venezuela, América Latina y el Caribe*. Caracas: Fondo Editorial Tropykos, 1993.

McCullough, Kate. "Slavery, Sexuality, and Genre: Pauline Hopkins and the Representation of Female Desire." *The Unruly Voice: Rediscovering Pauline Elizabeth Hopkins*. Ed. John Cullen Gruesser. Urbana: U of Illinois P, 1996.

McDowell, Deborah E. *"The Changing Same": Black Women's Literature, Criticism, and Theory*. Bloomington: Indiana UP, 1995.

McWilliams, Carey. *North from Mexico: The Spanish-Speaking People of the United States*. New York: Greenwood, 1990.

Meléndez, Edwin, and Edgardo Meléndez, eds. *Colonial Dilemma: Critical Perspectives on Contemporary Puerto Rico*. Boston: South End, 1993.

Mena, María Cristina. *The Collected Stories of María Cristina Mena*. Ed. Amy Doherty. Houston: Arte Público, 1997.

Mencke, John G. *Mulattoes and Race Mixture: American Attitudes and Images, 1865–1918*. Ann Arbor: UMI Research, 1976.

Meyer, Michael C., and William L. Sherman. *The Course of Mexican History*. New York: Oxford UP, 1995.

Michaels, Walter Benn. *Our America*. Durham: Duke UP, 1995.

Mohanty, Chandra Talpade, Ann Russo, and Lourdes Torres, eds. *Third World Women and the Politics of Feminism*. Bloomington: Indiana UP, 1991.

Mohr, Nicholasa. "Puerto Rican Writers in the U.S.; Puerto Rican Writers in Puerto Rico: A Separation beyond Language." *Breaking Boundaries: Latina Writing and Critical Readings*. Eds. Asunción Horno-Delgado et al. Amherst: U of Massachusetts P, 1989.

Moore, Joan, and Harry Pachon. *Hispanics in the United States*. Englewood Cliffs: Prentice, 1985.

Mora, Magdalena, and Adelaida R. Del Castillo, eds. *Mexican Women in the United States: Struggles Past and Present*. Los Angeles: Chicano Studies Research Center, U of California, 1980.

Moraga, Cherríe. "Algo secretamento amado." *The Sexuality of Latinas*. Eds. Norma Alarcón, et al. Berkeley: Third Woman, 1993.

———. *The Last Generation*. Boston: South End, 1993.

———. *Loving in the War Years: Lo que nunca pasó por sus labios*. Boston: South End, 1983.

Morales-Carrión, Arturo. *Puerto Rico and the Non-Hispanic Caribbean: A Study in the Decline of Spanish Exclusivism*. Río Piedras: U of Puerto Rico P, 1971.

Mordecai, Pamela, and Betty Wilson, eds. *Her True-True Name: An Anthology of Women's Writing from the Caribbean*. Oxford: Heinemann International, 1989.

Morganthau, Tom. "What Color Is Black?" *Newsweek* February 13, 1995: 63–65.

Morrison, Toni. *Beloved*. 1987. New York: Signet, 1991.

––––––. *Playing in the Dark*. New York: Vintage, 1992.

Morton, Carlos. "Celebrating 500 Years of *Mestizaje*." *MELUS* 16.3 (1989–90): 20–22.

Mossell, N. F. *The Work of the Afro-American Woman*. 1908. New York: Oxford UP, 1988.

Moya, Paula M. L. "Postmodernism, 'Realism,' and the Politics of Identity: Cherríe Moraga and Chicana Feminism." *Feminist Genealogies, Colonial Legacies, Democratic Futures*. Ed. M. Jacqui Alexander and Chandra Talpade Mohanty. New York: Routledge, 1997.

Nakashima, Cynthia L. "Voices from the Movement: Approaches to Multiraciality." *The Multiracial Experience: Racial Borders as the New Frontier*. Ed. Maria P. P. Root. Thousand Oaks: Sage, 1996.

Nancy, Jean-Luc. "Cut Throat Sun." Trans. Lydie Moudileno. *An Other Tongue: Nation and Ethnicity in the Linguistic Borderlands*. Ed. Alfred Arteaga. Durham: Duke UP, 1994.

Niesen de Abruna, Laura. "Twentieth-Century Women Writers from the English-Speaking Caribbean." *Caribbean Women Writers*. Ed. Selwyn Cudjoe. Wellesley: Calaloux, 1990.

Niggli, Josephina. *Mexican Village*. Chapel Hill: U of North Carolina P, 1945.

Norment, Lynn. "Am I Black, White, or in Between?" *Ebony* August 1995: 108–12.

Nowatzki, Robert. "Miscegenation and the Rhetoric of 'Blood' in Three Turn-of-the-Century African American Novels." *Journal of Contemporary Thought* 6 (1996): 41–50.

O'Hearn, Claudine Chiawei, ed. *Half and Half: Writers on Growing up Biracial and Bicultural*. New York: Pantheon, 1998.

Ortiz Cofer, Judith. *The Line of the Sun*. Athens: U of Georgia P, 1989.

––––––. *Silent Dancing: A Partial Remembrance of a Puerto Rican Childhood*. Houston: Arte Público, 1990.

Paredes, Américo. *Uncle Remus con chile*. Houston: Arte Público, 1993.

Parker, Lonnae O'Neal. "Halle Berry, in Character." *Washington Post* August 20, 1999: C1, C8.

Paz, Octavio. *El laberinto de la soledad*. Mexico City: Fondo de Cultura Económica, 1950.

Pérez, Louis A., Jr., ed. *Slaves, Sugar, and Colonial Society: Travel Accounts of Cuba, 1801–1899*. Wilmington: Scholarly Resources, 1992.

Perlmann, Joel. "Multiracials, Intermarriage, Ethnicity." *Society* 34.6 (September–October 1997): 20–23.

Pettis, Joyce. *Toward Wholeness in Paule Marshall's Fiction*. Charlottesville: UP of Virginia, 1995.

Phaf, Ineke. "Women and Literature in the Caribbean." *Unheard Words: Women and*

Literature in Africa, the Arab World, Asia, the Caribbean, and Latin America. Ed. Mineke Schipper. Trans. Barbara Potter Fasting. London: Allison, 1985.

Piedra, José. "His and Her Panics." *Dispositio* 16 (1991): 71–93.

Pramaggiore, Maria. "Bi-introduction I: Epistemologies of the Fence." *RePresenting Bisexualities: Subjects and Cultures of Fluid Desire.* Ed. Donald E. Hall and Maria Pramaggiore. New York: New York UP, 1996.

Pryse, Marjorie, and Hortense Spillers, eds. *Conjuring: Black Women, Fiction, and Literary Tradition.* Bloomington: Indiana UP, 1985.

Raiskin, Judith. "Inverts and Hybrids: Lesbian Rewritings of Sexual and Racial Identities." *The Lesbian Postmodern.* Ed. Laura Doan. New York: Columbia UP, 1994.

Ramírez, Arturo. "El feminismo y la frontera: Gloria Anzaldúa." *A Ricardo Gullón: Sus discípulos/a cargo de Adelaida López de Martínez.* Erie: ALDEEU, 1995.

Ramos, Juanita, ed. *Compañeras: Latina Lesbians.* New York: Routledge, 1994.

Ratnesar, Romesh. "Washington Diarist: Beating the Wrap." *New Republic* June 30, 1997: 43.

Raynaud, Claudine. "'A Nutmeg Nestled inside Its Covering of Mace': Audre Lorde's *Zami.*" *Life/Lines: Theorizing Women's Autobiography.* Ed. Bella Brodzki and Celeste Schenck. Ithaca: Cornell UP, 1988.

Reade, John. "The Intermingling of Races." *Popular Science Monthly* 30 (1886): 336–51.

"Rebirth of a Nation, Computer-Style." *Time* December 2, 1993: 66–67.

Rebolledo, Tey Diana. *Women Singing in the Snow: A Cultural Analysis of Chicana Literature.* Tucson: U of Arizona P, 1995.

Rebolledo, Tey Diana, and Eliana S. Rivero, eds. *Infinite Divisions: An Anthology of Chicana Literature.* Tucson: U of Arizona P, 1993.

Reed, Ishmael. *MultiAmerica.* New York: Penguin, 1997.

Reuter, Edward Byron. *The Mulatto in the United States.* Boston: Gorham, 1918.

Rhys, Jean. *Wide Sargasso Sea.* London: Deutsch, 1966.

Richard, Nelly. "The Cultural Periphery and Postmodern Decentring: Latin America's Reconversion of Borders." *Rethinking Borders.* Ed. John C. Welchman. Minneapolis: U of Minnesota P, 1996.

Rodriguez, Richard. "Mixed Blood: Columbus's Legacy: A World Made *Mestizo.*" *Harper's* November 1991: 47–56.

Rogozinski, Jan. *A Brief History of the Caribbean: From the Arawak and the Carib to the Present.* New York: Meridian, 1994.

Rojas, Lourdes. "Latinas at the Crossroads: An Affirmation of Life and Rosario Morales and Aurora Levins Morales' *Getting Home Alive.*" *Breaking Boundaries: Latina Writings and Critical Readings.* Ed. Asunción Horno-Delgado et al. Amherst: U of Massachusetts P, 1989.

Root, Maria P. P., ed. *The Multiracial Experience: Racial Borders as the New Frontier.* Thousand Oaks: Sage, 1996.

Rosell, Sara. "*Cecilia Valdés* de Villaverde a Arenas: La (re)creación de la mulata." *Afro-Hispanic Review* 18.2 (fall 1999): 15–21.

Rosenblat, Angel. *La población indígena y el mestizaje en América.* Buenos Aires: Editorial Nova, 1954.

Ruiz de Burton, María Amparo. *The Squatter and the Don.* Eds. Rosaura Sánchez and Beatrice Pita. 1885. Houston: Arte Público, 1992.

————. *Who Would Have Thought It?* Eds. Rosaura Sánchez and Beatrice Pita. 1872. Houston: Arte Público, 1995.

Russel y Rodríguez, Mónica. "Mexicanas and Mongrels: Policies of Hybridity, Gender, and Nation in the U.S.-Mexican War." *Latino Studies Journal* 11.3 (fall 2000): 49–73.

Rust, Paula C. "Managing Multiple Identities: Diversity among Bisexual Women and Men." *Bisexuality: The Psychology and Politics of an Invisible Minority.* Ed. Beth A. Firestein. Thousand Oaks: Sage, 1996.

Ryan, James. "Tyra Banks Is the Real Thing." *GQ* June 1995: 176–77.

Sánchez, Rosaura. "Postmodernism and Chicano Literature." *Aztlán* 18.2 (1987): 1–14.

Sandoval, Chéla. "*Mestizaje* as Method: Feminists-of-Color Challenge the Canon." *Living Chicana Theory.* Ed. Carla Trujillo. Berkeley: Third Woman, 1998.

Schaefer, Claudia. *Danger Zones: Homosexuality, National Identity, and Mexican Culture.* Tucson: U of Arizona P, 1996.

Sedgwick, Eve Kosofsky. *Epistemology of the Closet.* Berkeley: U of California P, 1990.

Senna, Danzy. "A Black Spy in White America." *Glamour* May 1998: 102.

————. *Caucasia.* New York: Riverhead, 1998.

————. "The Mulatto Millennium." *Half and Half: Writers on Growing up Biracial and Bicultural.* Ed. Claudine Chiawei O'Hearn. New York: Pantheon, 1998.

Shange, Ntozake. *Liliane.* New York: Picador, 1994.

Silko, Leslie Marmon. *Ceremony.* New York: Penguin, 1977.

Sirias, Silvio, and Richard McGarry. "Rebellion and Tradition in Ana Castillo's *So Far from God* and Sylvia López-Medina's *Cantora.*" *MELUS* 25.2 (summer 2000): 83–100.

Smith, Barbara. "The Truth That Never Hurts: Black Lesbians in Fiction in the 1980s." *Feminisms: An Anthology of Literary Theory and Criticism.* Ed. Robyn R. Warhol and Diane Price Herndl. New Brunswick: Rutgers UP, 1991.

Smith, Henry Nash. *Virgin Land: The American West as Symbol and Myth.* Cambridge: Harvard UP, 1950.

Smith, Shawn Michelle. *American Archives: Gender, Race, and Class in Visual Culture.* Princeton: Princeton UP, 1999.

Smith, Sidonie. "The Autobiographical Manifesto: Identities, Temporalities, Politics." *Autobiography and Questions of Gender.* Ed. Shirley Neuman. London: Cass, 1991.

Smolowe, Jill. "Intermarried . . . with Children." *Time* December 2, 1993: 63–65.

Sollors, Werner. "'Never Was Born': The Mulatto, an American Tragedy?" *Massachusetts Review* 27 (1986): 293–316.

Somerville, Siobhan. *Queering the Color Line: Race and the Invention of Homosexuality in American Culture.* Durham: Duke UP, 2000.

Spickard, Paul R. *Mixed Blood: Intermarriage and Ethnic Identity in Twentieth-Century America.* Madison: U of Wisconsin P, 1989.

Spivak, Gayatri. *Outside in the Teaching Machine.* New York: Routledge, 1993.

Springfield, Consuelo López. "*Mestizaje* in the Mother-Daughter Autobiography of Rosario Morales and Aurora Levins Morales." *Auto/biography Studies* 8 (1993): 303–15.

Stevenson, Matilda Coxe. "The Zuñi Indians." *Twenty-Third Annual Report of the Bureau of American Ethnology to the Secretary of the Smithsonian Institution, 1901–1902.* Washington: Government Printing Office, 1904.

Stone, Alfred Holt. *Studies in the American Race Problem.* New York: Negro Universities P, 1908.

Stowe, Harriet Beecher. *Uncle Tom's Cabin.* 1852. New York: Penguin, 1986.

Streeter, Caroline A. "Ambiguous Bodies: Locating Black/White Women in Cultural Representations." *The Multiracial Experience: Racial Borders as the New Frontier.* Ed. Maria P. P. Root. Thousand Oaks: Sage, 1996.

Tate, Claudia. "Allegories of Black Female Desire; or, Rereading Nineteenth-Century Narratives of Black Female Authority." *Changing Our Own Words.* Ed. Cheryl Wall. New Brunswick: Rutgers UP, 1991.

Thomas, Piri. *Down These Mean Streets.* 1967. New York: Vintage, 1991.

Tichi, Cecelia. "American Literary Studies to the Civil War." *Redrawing the Boundaries: The Transformation of English and American Literary Studies.* Ed. Stephen Greenblatt and Giles Gunn. New York: MLA, 1992.

Todorov, Tzvetan. "Dialogism and Schizophrenia." Trans. Michael B. Smith. *An Other Tongue: Nation and Ethnicity in the Linguistic Borderlands.* Ed. Alfred Arteaga. Durham: Duke UP, 1994.

Trinh T. Minh-Ha. *When the Moon Waxes Red: Representation, Gender, and Cultural Politics.* New York: Routledge, 1991.

———. *Woman, Native, Other.* Bloomington: Indiana UP, 1989.

Trujillo, Carla, ed. *Chicana Lesbians: The Girls Our Mothers Warned Us About.* Berkeley: Third Woman, 1991.

———, ed. *Living Chicana Theory.* Berkeley: Third Woman, 1998.

Turner, Frederick Jackson. *The Frontier in American History.* Huntington: Krieger, 1976.

Valle, Victor, and Rodolfo Torres. "Mestizaje and the 'Race' Problematic." *Culture and Difference.* Ed. Antonia Darder. Westport: Bergin, 1995.

Vasconcelos, José. *The Cosmic Race/La raza cósmica.* Ed. Didier T. Jaén. Baltimore: Johns Hopkins UP, 1997.

Vega, Ana Lydia. *Encancaranublado y otros cuentos de naufragio.* Río Piedras: Editorial Antillana, 1983.

———. "En puertorriqueño: Una entrevista a Ana Lydia Vega." Interview with Frances Negron Muntaner. *Dactylus* 11 (1991): 15–24.

———. "Women and Writing in Puerto Rico: An Interview with Ana Lydia Vega." Interview with Elizabeth Hernández and Consuelo López Springfield. *Callaloo* 17 (1994): 816–25.

Velásquez Treviño, Gloria. "Cultural Ambivalence in Early Chicana Prose Fiction." Diss. Stanford U, 1985.

Vélez, Diana. "*Pollito Chicken:* Split Subjectivity, National Identity, and the Articulation of Female Sexuality in a Narrative by Ana Lydia Vega." *Americas Review* 14 (1986): 68–76.

———. "We Are (Not) in This Together: The Caribbean Imaginary in *Encancaranublado* by Ana Lydia Vega." *Callaloo* 17.3 (1994): 826–33.

Vigil, James Diego. *From Indians to Chicanos.* St. Louis: Mosby, 1980.

Villaverde, Cirilo. *Cecilia Valdés: Novela de Costumbres Cubanas.* 1882. Mexico City: Editorial Porrúa, 1986.

Villegas de Magnón, Leonor. *The Rebel.* Ed. Clara Lomas. Houston: Arte Público, 1994.

Walker, Alice. *By the Light of My Father's Smile.* New York: Random House, 1998.

———. *The Temple of My Familiar.* New York: Pocket, 1990.

Wall, Cheryl, ed. *Changing Our Own Words: Essays on Criticism, Theory, and Writing by Black Women.* New Brunswick: Rutgers UP, 1989.

Wallace, Michele. *Invisibility Blues.* London: Verso, 1990.

Wallace, Susan E. *The Land of the Pueblos.* New York: Alden, 1888.

Warner, Michael, ed. *Fear of a Queer Planet: Queer Politics and Social Theory.* Minneapolis: U of Minnesota P, 1993.

Washington, Mary Helen. *Invented Lives: Narratives of Black Women, 1860–1960.* Garden City: Doubleday, 1987.

Weisman, Jan. "An 'Other' Way of Life: The Empowerment of Alterity in the Interracial Individual." *The Multiracial Experience: Racial Borders as the New Frontier.* Ed. Maria P. P. Root. Thousand Oaks: Sage, 1996.

West, Dorothy. *The Living Is Easy.* 1948. New York: Feminist, 1982.

Wharton, Vernon Lane. "Jim Crow Laws and Miscegenation." *The Origins of Segregation.* Ed. Joel Williamson. Lexington: Raytheon, 1968.

Wiegman, Robyn. *American Anatomies.* Durham: Duke UP, 1995.

Williams, Claudette. *Charcoal and Cinnamon: The Politics of Color in Spanish Caribbean Literature.* Gainesville: U of Florida P, 2000.

Williams, Patricia. "Big Words, Small Divisions." *Nation* August 25–September 1, 1997: 9.

Williams, Walter L. *The Spirit and the Flesh: Sexual Diversity in American Indian Culture.* Boston: Beacon, 1986.

Williamson, Joel. *New People: Miscegenation and Mulattoes in the United States*. New York: Free, 1980.

————, ed. *The Origins of Segregation*. Lexington: Raytheon, 1968.

Wilson, Kimberly A. C. "The Function of the 'Fair' Mulatto: Complexion, Audience, and Mediation in Frances Harper's *Iola Leroy*." *Cimarron Review* 106 (1994): 104–14.

Woodward, C. Vann. "The Genesis of Segregation." *The Origins of Segregation*. Ed. Joel Williamson. Lexington: Raytheon, 1968.

Wooten, Mattie Lloyd, ed. *Women Tell the Story of the Southwest*. San Antonio: Naylor, 1940.

Wright, Lawrence. "One Drop of Blood." *New Yorker* July 25, 1994: 46–55.

Wright, Luther. "Who's Black, Who's White, and Who Cares: Reconceptualizing the United States's Definition of Race and Racial Classifications." *Vanderbilt Law Review* 48 (1995): 513–69.

Yarbro-Bejarano, Yvonne. "Gloria Anzaldúa's *Borderlands/La Frontera*: Cultural Studies, 'Difference,' and the Non-Unitary Subject." *Contemporary American Women Writers: Gender, Class, Ethnicity*. Ed. Lois Parkinson Zamora. New York: Longman, 1998.

————. "The Multiple Subject in the Writing of Ana Castillo." *Americas Review* 20.1 (1992): 65–72.

Young, Iris Marion. "The Ideal of Community and the Politics of Difference." *Feminism/Postmodernism*. Ed. Linda J. Nicholson. New York: Routledge, 1990.

$\mathcal{I}ndex$